Job Stress
and
Blue Collar Work

WILEY SERIES ON
STUDIES IN OCCUPATIONAL STRESS

Series Editors

Professor Cary L. Cooper
Department of Management Sciences,
University of Manchester
Institute of Science and Technology

Professor S. V. Kasl
Department of Epidemiology,
School of Medicine,
Yale University

Stress at Work
Edited by Cary L. Cooper and Roy Payne

White Collar and Professional Stress
Edited by Cary L. Cooper and Judi Marshall

Stress, Work Design and Productivity
Edited by E. N. Corlett and J. Richardson

A Behavioural Approach to the Management of Stress
H. R. Beech, L. E. Burns and B. F. Sheffield

**Living Abroad: Personal Adjustment and Personnel Policy in the
Overseas Setting**
Ingemar Torbiorn

The Mechanisms of Job Stress and Strain
John R. P. French, Jr., Robert D. Caplan and R. Van Harrison

Noise and Society
Edited by Dylan M. Jones and Antony J. Chapman

Job Stress and Blue Collar Work
Edited by Cary L. Cooper and Michael Smith

Further titles in preparation

Job Stress
and
Blue Collar Work

Edited by

Cary L. Cooper
University of Manchester
Institute of Science and Technology
England

and

Michael J. Smith
University of Wisconsin
USA

JOHN WILEY & SONS
Chichester · New York · Brisbane · Toronto · Singapore

Library of Congress Cataloging in Publication Data:

Job stress and blue collar work.
  (Wiley series on studies in occupational stress)
  Includes index.
  1. Job stress—Addressses, essays, lectures.
2. labor and laboring classes—Addresses, essays, lectures. I. Cooper, Gary L. II. Smith, Michael
J. (Michael James), 1945– . III. Series.
HF5548.85.J64 1985   158.7   85-12022

ISBN 0 471 90811 8

British Library Cataloguing in Publication Data:

Cooper, Cary L.
  Job stress and blue collar work.—(Wiley series on studies in occupational stress)
  1. Job stress   2. Labor and laboring classes—Psychology
  I. Title   II. Smith, M. J. (Michael James)
  158.7   HF5548.85

ISBN 0 471 90811 8

Printed and bound in Great Britain.

Contributors

Editors

CARY L. COOPER
Professor of Organizational Psychology and Head of Psychosocial Factors and Occupational Health Research Group, University of Manchester Institute of Science and Technology, Manchester, England

MICHAEL J. SMITH
Professor of Industrial Engineering, University of Wisconsin, Madison, Wisconsin, U.S.A., formerly Chief of Motivation and Stress Research, National Institute for Occupational Safety and Health, U.S. Department of Health and Human Services, Cincinnati, Ohio, USA

MICHAEL J. COLLIGAN
Research Psychologist, Applied Psychology and Ergonomics Branch, National Institute for Occupational Safety and Health, U.S. Department of Health and Human Services, Cincinnati, Ohio, USA

TOM COX
Head of Stress Research Group, Department of Psychology, University of Nottingham, Nottingham, England

COLIN G. DRURY
Professor of Industrial Engineering, Department of Industrial Engineering, State University of New York at Buffalo, Amherst, New York, USA

SHIRLEY FISHER

Director of the Stress Research Unit, Department of Psychology, University of Dundee, Dundee, Scotland

JAMES S. HOUSE

Program Director of Survey Research Center and Professor of Sociology, University of Michigan, Ann Arbor, Michigan, USA

JOSEPH J. HURRELL, JR.

Research Psychologist, Applied Psychology and Ergonomics Branch, National Institute for Occupational Safety and Health, U.S. Department of Health and Human Services, Cincinnati, Ohio, USA

ANGUS G. S. MACLEOD

Assistant Director, Institute of Industrial Relations, University of California, Los Angeles, USA

TIMOTHY H. MONK

Professor of Psychology in Psychiatry, Department of Psychiatry, Cornell University Medical College, Ithaca, New York, USA

LAWRENCE R. MURPHY

Research Psychologist, Applied Psychology and Ergonomics Branch, National Institute for Occupational Safety and Health, U.S. Department of Health and Human Services, Cincinnati, Ohio, USA

CARINA NILSSON

Senior Staff Officer, Swedish Confederation of Trade Unions, Stockholm, Sweden

OLOV ÖSTBERG

Director of Human Factors Research, Swedish Telecommunications Administration, Farsta, Sweden

ARTHUR B. SHOSTAK

Professor of Sociology, Department of Psychology, and Sociology, Drexel University, Philadelphia, Pennsylvania, USA

DONALD I. TEPAS

Professor of Psychology, Department of Psychology, University of Connecticut at Storrs, Connecticut, USA

DAVID R. WILLIAMS

Survey Research Center, University of Michigan, Ann Arbor, Michigan, USA

Contents

Editorial Forword ix

1. Introduction: Blue Collar Workers Are 'At Risk' 1
   Cary L. Cooper and Michael J. Smith

PART ONE: OVERVIEW

2. Blue Collar Worker Alienation 7
   Arthur B. Shostak

3. Control and Blue Collar Work 19
   Shirley Fisher

PART TWO: STRESSFUL WORKING CONDITIONS AND SITUATIONS

4. Machine-paced Work and Stress 51
   Michael J. Smith

5. Shift Work 65
   Timothy H. Monk and Donald I. Tepas

6. Repetitive Work: Occupational Stress and Health 85
   Tom Cox

7. Stress and Quality Control Inspection 113
   Colin G. Drury

8. Alternative Work Schedules: Flextime and the Compressed
   Work Week 131
   Joseph J. Hurrell, Jr. and Michael J. Colligan

9. **Emerging Technology and Stress** 149
    Olov Östberg and Carina Nilsson

10. **An Apparent Case of Mass Psychogenic Illness in an
    Aluminium Furniture Assembly Plant** 167
    Michael J. Colligan

PART THREE: CONTROLLING THE BLUE COLLAR STRESS

11. **EAPs and Blue Collar Stress** 185
    Angus G. S. MacLeod

12. **Union Efforts to Relieve Blue Collar Stress** 195
    Arthur B. Shostak

13. **Social Support and Stress Reduction** 207
    David R. Williams and James S. House

14. **Individual Coping Strategies** 225
    Lawrence R. Murphy

Index 241

Editorial Foreword to the Series

This book, *Job Stress and Blue Collar Work*, is the ninth book in the series of *Studies in Occupational Stress*. The main objective of this series of books is to bring together the leading international psychologists and occupational health researchers to report on their work on various aspects of occupational stress and health. The series will include a number of books on original research and theory in each of the areas described in the initial volume, such as Blue Collar Stressors, The Interface Between the Work Environment and the Family, Individual Differences in Stress Reactions, The Person-Environment Fit Model, Behavioural Modification and Stress Reduction, Stress and the Socio-technical Environment, The Stressful Effects of Retirement and Unemployment and many other topics of interest in understanding stress in the workplace.

We hope these books will appeal to a broad spectrum of readers—to academic researchers and postgraduate students in applied and occupational psychology and sociology, occupational medicine, management, personnel, etc.—and to practitioners working in industry, the occupational medical field, mental health specialists, social workers, personnel officers, and others interested in the health of the individual worker.

Cary L. Cooper,
University of Manchester Institute of
  Science and Technology (UK)
Stanislav V. Kasl,
Yale University

Job Stress and Blue Collar Work
Edited by C. L. Cooper and M. J. Smith
© 1985 John Wiley & Sons Ltd

Chapter 1

Introduction:
Blue Collar Workers are 'At Risk'

Cary L. Cooper and Michael J. Smith

Work is by its very nature, about violence—to the spirit as well as to the body. It is about ulcers as well as accidents, about shouting matches as well as fistfights, about nervous breakdowns as well as kicking the dog around. It is, above all (or beneath all), about daily humiliations. To survive the day is triumph enough for the walking wounded among the great many of us.

Studs Terkel in his acclaimed book *Working* reflects the attitudes and concerns of many groups of blue collar workers. The commonly held belief about the pressures of work, coronary heart disease, and many other stress-related illnesses is that they are found predominantly among white collar and professional groups, i.e. that they are the 'bosses' diseases. But is this true?

If we examine Table 1.1, we can see that frequencies of deaths in the United Kingdom due to major causes in the working population increase as we move from professional and white collar jobs down to the unskilled. This applies both to stress-related illnesses such as ischaemic heart disease and to other illnesses such as pneumonia and prostate cancer. These statistics are very similar to mortality data from the United States and other developed countries. In terms of almost all the major and many of the minor causes of death among persons in the working population age groups, the blue collar and unskilled are at greater risk than the white collar and professionals. This extends not only to mortality statistics, but also to morbidity data as well. It can be seen in Table 1.2 that many blue collar workers show a greater number of 'restricted activity days' and consultations with medical practioners than do white collar workers in the United Kingdom.

Blue collar workers, therefore, seem to be a vulnerable group to occupational stressors and their manifestations. It was to focus attention on the unique problems of blue collar workers that this book was originally conceived. Our underlying objective was twofold: (1) to provide the reader with some insight into the potential stressful working conditions and situations of workers in blue collar jobs and (2) to make a small beginning in suggesting some alternative strategies or courses of action to help alleviate, minimize, or cope with them. We will attempt to bring together as much of the recent research

1

Table 1.1. Deaths by major causes and types of occupations, 1970–1972 (standardized mortality rates = 100)

Causes of deaths, persons aged 15–64 (males)	Professional and similar	Intermediate	Skilled, non-manual	Skilled, manual	Partly skilled	Unskilled
Trachea, bronchus, and lung cancer	53	68	84	118	123	143
Prostate cancer	91	89	99	115	106	115
Ischaemic heart disease	88	91	114	107	108	111
Other forms of heart disease	69	75	94	100	121	157
Cerebrovascular disease	80	86	98	106	111	136
Pneumonia	41	53	78	92	115	195
Bronchitis, emphysema, and asthma	36	51	82	113	128	188
Accidents other than motor vehicle	58	64	53	97	128	225
All causes	77	81	99	106	114	137

Source: U.K. Office of Population Censuses and Surveys.

Table 1.2. Acute sickness and consultations with general medical practitioners, 1974–1975

	Average number of restricted activity days per person per year (males)			Average number of consultations per person per year (males)		
	15–44	45–64	All ages	15–44	45–64	All ages
Professional	9	16	12	2.1	2.7	2.7
Employers and managers	11	13	14	1.8	2.4	2.7
Intermediate and junior non-manual	10	21	15	2.0	4.3	3.1
Skilled manual and own account non-professional	15	24	17	2.8	4.0	3.2
Semiskilled manual and personal service	16	23	18	2.7	4.5	3.7
Unskilled, manual	21	28	20	3.5	4.8	3.6
All persons	13	21	16	2.4	3.8	3.1

Source: General Household Survey, 1974 and 1975 (by U.K. Government).

literature as possible in both identification of problem areas and methods of stress management.

The book is divided into three primary parts. In Part One, we explore the trends in blue collar worker attitudes and worker alienation. Chapter 2 in this section will review changes in blue collar worker attitudes, feelings, and perceptions about their work from the early 1970s up to the present. It will provide a perspective on the sociological background of blue collar workers, over which specific job stress factors can be superimposed. It will also highlight the reasons for blue collar alienation and dissatisfaction with their work. Chapter 3 will discuss in detail one of the underlying reasons that blue collar work is so stressful, *lack of control*. Research on control and blue collar work is thoroughly reviewed, together with a brief number of suggestions about ameliorating job stress (which will be more comprehensively covered in Part Three).

Part Two of the book will examine a variety of stressful working conditions and situations. This part of the volume will review the research evidence on machine-paced work generally, and in greater detail the impact of stress on repetitive work, quality control inspection tasks, the impact on worker health and satisfaction of work overload and underload, and the health consequences of shift work. In addition to these more obvious blue collar stressors, there will also be chapters on some newly emerging working conditions. There will be a chapter on alternative working schedules, which explores 'extended workdays', 'shortened work weeks', and other forms of alternate work schedules in industry, with their potential implications for stress and health fully highlighted. This part concludes with two very topical issues: the potential impact of new technology (such as robotics) and the outbreak of acute psychogenic reactions in blue collar factory settings.

Part Three will explore the various methods of dealing with blue collar stress. We will start with an overview of various approaches and techniques for controlling worker stress, including Employee Assistance Programmes (EAPs), union efforts to relieve stress, social support, and individual coping. With a growing number of EAPs in industry, a chapter is devoted to the use of EAPs for stress reduction. This will highlight some notable examples of successful EAPs in a variety of organizations. This will be followed by a chapter on union efforts at relieving stress. The various roles of unions, such as 'advocates', 'buffers', 'critics', 'initiators', and 'providers' will be thoroughly explored.

Perhaps the fastest growing research area in the stress field is the link between social support and stress reduction. It has been used in numerous research projects as an intervening variable and its role as a stress mediator discussed *ad nauseum*. What is its real importance in stress inoculation and reduction, and how has it been applied?

Finally, we will explore what the individual can do to help him/herself. The application of individual coping strategies, their usefulness in symptom reduction, and examples of successful use will be covered.

Stress in the workplace is currently a topical issue among the ordinary public, educationalists, the 'helping professions', occupational health medics, and others responsible for the well-being of people. As Cooper and Payne (1980) indicate, 'We have been shocked by *Future Shock* (Toffler), hurried by *A Types* (Friedman and Rosenman), transported by *Transcendental Meditation*, bemused by Biorhythms, amused (yet horrified) by Joseph Heller's comment that *Something Happened*. But has anything happened?' Have governments, health authorities, work organizations, or, indeed, individuals themselves, really committed themselves to systematic and continuous action plans designed to minimize unnecessary and debilitating work stress, to substantially enhance the well-being of themselves or the people they are responsible for, or to confront the problems generated by the old and new technologies in the workplace? Unfortunately, the answer is only a qualified 'some have'. It is to encourage an unqualified 'yes' that this book is dedicated. The time has long passed to simply hold another stress conference, symposium, or workshop; what we need now are well-designed diagnostic and preventive programmes of stress management, whose primary objective is to provide more liveable environments for all employees, and particularly for those most vulnerable, the blue collar workers.

Reference

Cooper, C. L., and Payne, R. (1980). *Current Concerns in Occupational Stress*, John Wiley & Sons, New York.

PART ONE
Overview

Job Stress and Blue Collar Work
Edited by C. L. Cooper and M. J. Smith
© 1985 John Wiley & Sons Ltd

Chapter 2

Blue Collar Worker Alienation

Arthur B. Shostak
Department of Psychology and Sociology,
Drexel University, Philadelphia, Pa., USA

... the essential problems of men at work are the same whether they do their work in some famous laboratory or in the messiest vat room of a pickle factory (Hughes, 1971, p. 342).

Before the middle of the 1800s, Thomas Arnold, the headmaster of Rugby, urged his countrymen to note sources of blue collar alienation in the still-young factory system:

A man sets up a factory and *wanted hands*; I beseech you, sir, to observe the very expressions that are used, for they are all significant. What he wants of his fellow creatures is the loan of their hands; of their heads and hearts he thinks nothing (Hammond and Hammond, 1934, p. 45).

Now, nearly 150 years later, much blue collar work remains similarly deprived of well-rounded involvement and wholesome challenge, a weakness Marx labelled the 'alienation' that attends labour in an industrial system.

Decades of workplace research since the early 1900s have identified several clear-cut sources of modern blue collar alienation, all of which can usefully be grouped in two broad categories of excess. Manual workers complain of *too little* autonomy, challenge, compensation, control over the task, health protection, promotion opportunity, safety protection, security in job retention, and status at and from the job (Pfeffer, 1979). Blue collarites are also offended by *too much* arbitrary supervision, insistence on petty rules and regulation, rejection of worker input into workplace decision-making, repetitive or rigid work duties, and shortages of indispensable tools or supplies (Berg *et al.*, 1978). Both of these lists, of course, are incomplete and could be considerably extended; they suffice, however, to make the point of the alienating significance of imbalance at work (Hersey, 1932; Spencer, 1977; Pfeffer, 1979, Pascarella, 1984).

ALIENATION AND SHORTFALL

To draw a considerable amount of complex and diverse material into a cogent and manageable framework, three 'too little' matters are singled out below for special attention: inadequate health and safety protection, inadequate compensation levels, and inadequate job security.

Health and safety anxieties

Why blue collar alienation at work? In part, because a deep-set suspicion persists among certain workers that profit mania, bureaucratic ineptitude, callousness on the part of supervisors, timidity on the part of company medical personnel, and ineffectiveness on the part of the local union leave workers pawns to an unnecessarily hazardous fate at work (White, 1983).

Those who subscribe to this alienating point of view draw support from 'insider' anecdotes about the origins of serious industrial accidents; e.g.

> ... objects had been falling from the top of this construction project so often that the secretary-treasurer of the building trades council himself had asked the company to construct safety nets five or six times to no avail ... on the day of the accident, a Friday, no one should have been working directly under a work crew on top of the tall building, but the contractor was anxious to finish the job and didn't want to pay double time for Saturday work (White, 1983, p. 14).

Over 12,000 workers are annually killed in shop, dock, mine, and warehouse accidents, and 100,000 or more are permanently disabled in the nation's annual toll of 5 million occupational injuries (Engler, 1984). About one-fourth of the 21.3 milion displaced people in the United States are disabled because of job-related injuries (Lambrinos and Johnson, 1984, p. 24).

Many present on the job fear new workplace dangers that are often silent, colourless, odourless, and invisible—but no less toxic and deadly for all of that. Over 14 million workers are thought to be exposed daily to chemicals and other work materials suspected of being injurious to human health. Such blue collarites worry with reason about becoming a statistic among 100,000 or so workers who die prematurely every year from industry-related diseases, or 300,000 others who contract a disabling industry-related disease over the same time period (O'Toole, 1974, p. 26; Kagis and Grossman, 1982; White, 1983).

Why deep-seated alienation? Because many blue collarites resent avoidable and preventable safety and health risks they feel they commonly run at work. Routine injuries that happen year in and year out are thought to 'demonstrate clearly that industrial injuries and occupational disease are not just accidents. They are a built-in feature of the system of production in many workplaces' (White, 1983, p. 19).

Compensation grief

A second major source of alienation involves dissatisfaction with take-home pay and the standard of living it actually makes possible.

Shortfall here can be traced to the historic toll taken by inflation. Throughout the post-war period, and especially in the 1970s, inflation undercut earnings so severely that few blue collar families even stayed abreast of the rising cost of living (Gappert, 1978, p. 47). More recently, 60 per cent. of those workers who regained jobs after a layoff (1979 to 1983) reported having to accept pay cuts of 20 per cent. or more (Hartson, 1984, p. 10). Since the late 1960s some 67 per cent. of all new jobs have been in industries that paid average annual wages and salaries of less than $13,600 (in 1980 dollars), In 1969, only 45 per cent. of all jobs were in that low category. By contrast, 'smokestack' industries that paid average wages of more than $20,250—nearly all of them in manufacturing—grew the least after 1970 (Harrison and Bluestone, 1984).

Along with a sense of losing ground on an income treadmill, many blue collarites harbour considerable envy of the salaries, stock options, bonuses, and perks they think the good fortune of many in the front office and executive suite. Anecdotes and rumours abound in the factory about the disparity in earnings between 'us' and 'them'. Tabloids and television point out that while the average worker in the United States earned $12,621 annually in 1981, and the average UAW assembly-line worker, $24,273, the CEO of 400 large manufacturing firms took an average of $325,700 in salary and bonus. Similarly, the CEOs of companies with over $5 billion in sales earned $528,000 in salary and bonus (Green, 1982). Workers respond by wondering aloud: 'Is it reasonable for an executive to earn as much in a day as blue collarites do all year?'

Bitterness and envy also mix in blue collar interest in management's use of clever tax avoidance moves, corporate tax shelters, lush corporate health spas, hunting lodges, vacation resorts, company cars, credit cards, and other such frills of the executive life—the 'good life' never to be earned and enjoyed by 'hard-hats' at the bottom of the corporate pyramid. Unable in a consumption-oriented, materialistic culture to avoid making dissonant comparisons, blue collar envy edges along here very close to shame and anger, all three comingling on dramatic occasions.

As if to rub salt into the wound, another alienating stressor derives from the many rollback agreements forced on blue collarites during the 1980–1983 recession. Between those manual workers who gave up hard-won gains in wages and fringe benefits, and those many others whose earnings were frozen, blue collarites felt they lost considerable ground.

As telling as was the blow to the worker's standard of living was a related blow to faith in their ability to bargain wage gains from an appreciative and dependent employer. The rollback campaign undermined any illusions workers may have held about their negotiating clout and work-role indis-pensability. Warned to take their pocket-book losses bravely, they were bluntly advised that plant closings, technological displacement, or the shipment of their jobs overseas hovered as very real possibilities—should their rollback losses provoke anything more than conventional grumbling from them in response.

Job loss jitters

Why alienation? In part because blue collar work appears less secure to more workers than possibly ever before in American history.

Haunted by the knowledge that each of the recessions since 1947 has left a higher level of intractable joblessness than the preceding one, millions of blue collarites worry that they will be next. As many reluctantly concede, 'There's only one thing worse than the stress of holding down an unpleasant job. And that's the stress of holding down no job' (Smith, 1983, p. 126).

Examples of displacement are well known to rank-and-filers, thanks to the labour press, occasional television specials, the nightly local television news, and stressful first-hand knowledge; e.g.:

> In 1982, Hormel, the nation's third largest pork processor, built the most efficient plant in the industry: 'Making heavy use of robots, computerized inventory controls, and sophisticated processing machines—many of them invented and patented by Hormel engineers—the company has slashed its work force by 33%' (Anon., 1984, p. 136).
>
> Since 1979, the auto workers union has lost 27 per cent. of those members who build cars, although auto production rates have bounded back to 1979 levels. *Business Week* explains that 'job losses persist because Detroit has stepped up its use of such labor-reducing technology as robots' (Anon., 1984b, p. 105).
>
> In 1984 GE began a new $52 million 'factory of the future' to produce aircraft engine parts. Relying on robot carts to move engine parts between 30 computer-controlled machining centres, the automated factory in Lynn, Massachuetts, will require half of the jobs in a conventional plant (Anon., 1984a, p. 43).

Blue collarites alert to these developments turn some of their anxiety into anger and much of the rest into workplace alienation (Schwartz and Neikirk, 1983).

Manufacturing, the leading blue collar stronghold, continues to decline as an employer, and while the labour force grew by 24 per cent. between 1964 and 1978, manufacturing employment grew by less than 4 per cent. (Appelbaum, 1984). Workers link these numbers to media-featured pronouncements from influential management consultants, people of consequence who emphatically warn that '... in the current competitive environment, companies will either reduce their employment by 25 per cent. or 100 per cent.' (Salisbury, 1984). A combination of job-loss trends and threats is a powerful one, and few blue collarites escape its unnerving impact.

Indeed, there is much reason to believe uneasiness about job-holding is reaching farther into the ranks than ever before. Low-skilled or low-seniority types often threatened before are joined now by previously secure members of the 'labour aristocracy', the upper stratum of blue collar America. Craftsmen and high-seniority types now live, many for the first time, in an alienating limbo: '... a place of in-between, where everyone is suddenly confronted with the frightening, totally unexpected prospect of being pushed down into povery, and where, for some, that fear will become reality' (Harrington, 1984, p. 40).

ALIENATION AND EXCESS

Along with the toll taken by shortfall in too little health and safety protection, earned income, and job security, much of the alienation of blue collarites is also fed by the very opposite problem, or an *excess* of negative workplace experiences that demoralize and 'distance' employees as do few others. Specifically, manual workers are put down and put off by two particular types of excess—workplace authoritarianism and 'technomania'—neither of which suggest that contemporary employers appreciate the head and heart of workers as much as some have long valued their hands.

Workplace authoritarianism

While the details will vary widely, the typical worksite is entangled in 'do and don't' regulations that blue collarites resent as insulting, infantilizing expressions of company mistrust in their adulthood and maturity. Manual workers can feel intimidated by rigid rules about their dress, demeanour, and comings, and goings at work. Prohibitions against chatting with coworkers to relieve boredom, the resort to horseplay to enliven routine, or the use of chewing gum or cigarettes are aggravating parts of workplace lore in this exasperating and nerve-touching matter.

Sporadic and provocative crackdowns on petty-ante card-playing at lunch, voluntary sales of (legal) pornography during coffee breaks, and other 'grey area' activities unrelated to production output remind irate blue collarites that no other segment of the business world has its workplace behaviour so closely regulated and policed; no other segment is under such pressure to leave personality and idiosyncracies outside the plant gate, and merge passively instead into the bland and colourless machinery of the place.

A flurry of research in the early 1970s spotlighted the toll exacted by this sort of supervisory authoritarianism and the retreat-from-work attitude it provokes. Researchers concluded that 'the message is clear: the Blue Collar Blues are predominantly associated with those working conditions that discourage good work performance, impede personal growth, and stiff autonomy and creativity' (Seashore and Barnowe, 1974, p. 549).

Authoritarian styles of management persist in the 1980s, despite widespread espousement by business statesmen of more enlightened ways. Typical is this 1984 characterization by *Business Week* of shopfloor realities in the steel industry:

> Although there hasn't been a major steel strike since 1959, the good relations between the negotiators have not been mirrored in the plants. Daily fights over grievances and work practices, aggravated by the traditional 'do as I say, don't talk back' style of mill managers, have kept workers and supervisors in enemy camps.

While encouraged by anti-authoritarian steps now being taken by U.S. Steel, in particular, the magazine warns that 'it may take years to turn the company's decades-old adversary system into cooperation at the plant level' (Hoerr, 1984,, p. 52).

'Technomania'

At issue here is a widely overlooked source of alienation, or the insult blue collarites feel when their talent with things is starkly ignored and down-graded by knowledgeable supervisors.

Enamoured of technology, many supervisors go overboard in their reliance on automation, computer-assisted manufacture techniques, and other advanced electronic aids. Instead of including their blue collar workforce in every step of the way and drawing on experienced employees as (pre-purchase) advisers, product testers, and product comparers, the supervisors buy new tools and equipment in an arbitrary way, and expect only passive and rapid accommodation from their underlings.

All too many supervisors find it easier to switch to new 'toys' rather than meet worker requests for equipment alterations or overhaul. A recent study by Westinghouse Electric of its own mistakes in robot installation found the demoralizing message the company had given its employees was clear: 'We have not listened to your pleas to repair your equipment—we have spent our money on a robot instead' (Foulkes and Hirsch, 1984, p. 96).

A common viewpoint on this overreliance on new gadgets and under-reliance on worker capabilities concerns an unseemly interest in the use of cybernetic technology. Enthusiasts hold out the promise of the plant as a perfect machine, empowered by complete backup and fail-safe systems. Colourful talk escalates about worker-less factories, unmanned workplaces, and people-less worksites—or, at the very least, factories whose blue collarites do only the simplest and least-significant tasks. Magazine advertisements, television specials, and tabloid feature stores echo and enlarge on the theme, and remind already apprehensive blue collarites of the eagerness certain supervisors have to be done with them, once and for all (Noble, 1984).

A contrary argument exists, of course, though blue collarites hear far too little of it. Few learn from management what their shopfloor experience teaches—that the fantasy of eliminating the need for human skill and judgement is profoundly mistaken. Indeed:

> ... the new cybernetic machines create new sources of error and failure with which only skilled workers, ready to learn and adapt to new production conditions, can content. ... Paradoxically, just as we are developing technologies characterized by the utmost mathematical abstraction,we must increasingly rely on informal learning and the ability to deal with the unpredictable (Hirschhorn, 1984, pp. 1, 3).

Why alienation? In part, because blue collarites resent both being confused with machine parts and being undervalued as masters of work processes. Proud of their experience-derived insights into work, they claim ideas well worth attention from a respectful and rewarding management. Generally ignored, however, as a storehouse of productivity-boosting advice, many blue collarites seethe at the thought that certain key supervisors desire more de-skillinization of manual work and further dilution of dependence on (human) manual workers. Insulted, hurt, and threatened, the targets of this 'worker-less factory' fantasy retreat from job commitment and contribution to the (false) comfort of indifference, alienation, and anxiety.

Case Study: Non-traditional Blue Collar Women

To fully understand the 'too little/too much' approach to blue collar alienation sketched above, it is helpful to single out a cohort of manual workers whose distinctive quality of work life illuminates the complex nature of alienation in modern work.

Although commonly overlooked in academic discussions of manual work, about 28 per cent. of the nation's 32 million blue collarites are women (a block equal to about 15 per cent. of the nation's 43 million women workers) (O'Farrell, 1982). While most are concentrated in low-paying, dead-end operative jobs, a small but rapidly growing number of females have sought blue collar jobs seldom, if ever, previously held by women. These pioneers are changing the culture of the 'male-only' workplace, challenging their male peers as never before and illuminating aspects of blue collar alienation well worth pondering (Fox and Hesse-Biber, 1984).

Women in non-traditional fields like welding, carpentry, truck hauling, mechanics, or crane operation remain social oddities regarded with skepticism. To succeed they must have unusually strong reasons for their job choice, and either compelling needs or a great deal of self-confidence to back up their decision. Many find it necessary to 'go it alone' on occasion, and must fight an often negative tide of family, public, and coworker doubts and rebuffs.

Their profile where job satisfaction is concerned appears distinctive and positive:

> Rather than being tangential, work is central to these women's identities; rather than lacking ambition and concern about pay, skilled women workers appear to be highly motivated; rather than seeking comfortable sociable work environments, women workers appear to value physicality and solitary tasks; rather than wanting direction and supervision, these women want autonomy and control over the work process; rather than experiencing boredom and unhappiness in the workplace, these women see blue-collar employment as a satisfying alternative to domestic and clerical roles (Walshok, 1981, pp. xvii–xviii).

Jobs that generations of male workers have come to view as alienating, tiresome, and routine strike many among new generations of female workers as challenging, interesting, and financially rewarding—a clear advance over traditional women's work.

What then, if anything, explains alienation in this situation? First and foremost is the initial hostility of traditional 'macho' blue collar men, skeptical types who have never or seldom interacted with women as work peers. In a normal and rational way many question the sincerity of a women's interest and commitment to a 'man's job'. Many question whether she has the technical or mechanical competence, or the physical strength and agility to do the job. In addition, many resent her for taking a job away from one of their own, especially in times of high unemployment (McIlwee, 1982, p. 299).

Unfortunately, the situation can and does get out of hand; a small number of men go beyond doubting, crude 'put-downs', and initially cool treatment. Women in non-traditional settings confront persistent sexual innuendos, or harassment, actual acts of hostility or sabotage, withholding of opportunities for training or information, and supervisory indifference to all of the aforegoing. With no common basis for sharing, communicating, and understanding, the sexes at work can retreat into extreme suspicion of one another, and that can translate into behaviour that intimidates or isolates the blue collar female.

Isolation, in turn, can become a major source of alienation. Few blue collar women in non-traditional jobs are tied into the feminist movement (Ferree, 1980). Few have families rooting for them. Many feel frozen out of tightly knit friendship groups at work, and their capacity to be an 'outsider' is therefore a critical factor in their factory perseverance.

Overall, they appear stark victims of a remarkable managerial oversight:

> Currently there is virtually nothing being done to prepare men or women to work together in the blue collar workplace. They are just thrown together ... hired in the rush to satisfy government guidelines, [blue collar women] are simply left at the mercy of a work environment that at best is uninterested and simply resigned to their presence (Walshok, 1981, pp. 232, 244).

Women in traditional blue collar jobs confront these hazards and more (Rosen, 1981). Research continues to confirm an important distinction between the path-breaking blue collar 'pioneers', or skilled women integrating the crafts, and many other women in far less-skilled work (bench assembly, packers, assembly-line workers).

Those in traditional jobs have extremely low levels of job satisfaction. Many feel their work lives spoiled by the costly effects of sexual harassment, the 'one occupational hazard all women are vulnerable to, whether they are working in traditional or non-traditional jobs' (Frank, 1984, p. 12). Many resent the pressure they experience over workplace risks to their child-bearing capacity. They ask if protective restrictions based on female fertility are actually a convenient device to mask discrimination against women securing high-paying industrial jobs: 'The basic policy dispute,' a concerned feminist argues, 'centers on whether to clear out the workers or clean up the workplace' (Scott, in Chavkin, 1984, p. 132).

Above all, blue collar women in traditional jobs come to resent the vapidness of their jobs, the banality of years at the same task, the absence of job challenge and promotion opportunities, the low and inadequate level of compensation, and the patronizing sexism of company and union alike. Unlike better-off 'pioneers' in craft ranks, many of the less-skilled blue collar females dream of nothing so much as walking out on it all some day soon, and alleviating their considerable workplace alienation in this clear-cut way (Rosen, 1982, pp. 23–24).

Research Limitations

Diversity in blue collar ranks, as made clear by the example above of traditional versus non-traditional female job-holders, underlines serious drawbacks in contemporary academic analysis of blue collar alienation. Despite decades of concerted field research and classic theorizing, many biases, contradictions, and gaps remain in the record (Pfeffer, 1979, pp. 231–261).

Far too little is known, for example, about blue collar jobs in fast-growing continuous-process technology and craft technology, both areas where alienation may be significantly less serious than in older, declining assembly-line and machine technologies (Blauner, 1964; Tulin, 1984).

Similarly, far too little is known about the less-than-obvious sources of satisfaction possible at work:

> All too often, we patronizingly assume that only well-educated people have complex feelings about their work and that they require more challenge and gratification from their work than do blue-collar workers ... [we fail] to give sufficient attention to the process whereby interests and commitments to jobs develop in non-professional fields (Walshok, 1981, p. 272).

Research on blue collar alienation must expand to include important types conspicuous by their absence thus far from the literature, types like young workers, 'downward' occupational skidders, aging workers, non-white workers, illegal workers, handicapped workers, and the diverse type (Levitan, 1981).

Labour's part in the entire tale warrants far more attention than it has thus far earned. At the local level many blue collarites experience considerable frustration with limits on the union's greivance-winning abilities, while disgruntlement with contract terms negotiated at the regional or industry-wide level remains a far-too-common aspect of negotiation scenarios. Dissatisfaction with labour's political clout appears widespread, and dues-payers may therefore trace a considerable amount of their workplace dissatisfaction to their disillusionment with their prime mechanism for collective gain (Aronowitz, 1973; Reynolds, 1984; Freeman and Medoff, 1984).

Finally, research must soon expand to include veiled stressors and their possible contribution to worker alienation (Simmons and Mares, 1983). Typical here is the sub rosa matter of corporate devaluation of the manufacturing function per se and, thereby, of everyone connected with it, blue collarites included. To typical U.S. business executives, manufacturing is 'beat to fit, paint to match. If you never hear from them, you must be doing something right.' Workers may be sensitive to the location of manufacturing at the bottom of the corporate totem pole, and some of their ambivalence about the company, their skepticism about supervisory adequacy, and their misgivings about the plant's future could be linked to this self-abnegating insight.

Summary

When reasons for blue collar worker alienation are explored, the twin challenge of both *deficiency* and *surplus* becomes clear. Manual workers commonly feel they have too little of what most average adults hope for in and from work. They also resent their inordinate share of what everyone's work is better off without. Many criticize persistent and serious deficiencies in 'life and limb' safeguards, standard of living aids, and lifetime job security. They are embittered by a persistent and serious surplus of petty, tyrannical rules and an insulting indifference to their work process insights. All of this, in combination, offends their collective sensibilities about their lifelong investment and equity in the workplace status quo.

Blue collar alienation, in sum, draws profoundly on an insistence by manual workers that they are more adult, more creative, more caring, and far more capable of contributing than the modern work setting seems to respect or facilitate. Hurt by this far-reaching denial, many blue collarites withdraw into a classic mode of alienation, a style of quiet desperation that tempts them to make the least best of life's chances. Their style of life, one neither entirely to their liking nor entirely of their conscious making, costs *all* of us dearly. For alienation from the job, from their output potential, from their union and employer, and from the world of work in general remains for us, as Marx indicated, the weak link in a chain of productive well-being vital to us all.

REFERENCES

Anon. (1984a). Swapping work rules for jobs at GE's 'factory of the future', *Business Week*, 10 September 1984, p. 43.

Anon. (1984b). Showdown in Detroit, *Business Week*, 10 September 10, 1984, p. 105.

Anon. (1984c). Hormel: trying to trim the industry's fattest wages to keep making money in meat, *Business Week*, 10 September 1984, p. 136.

Applebaum, E (1984). 'High Tech' and the structural employment problems of the eighties. In *American Jobs and the Changing Industrial Base* (Ed. E. Collins), Ballinger, New York.

Aronowitz, S. (1973). *False Promises: The Shaping of American Working Class Consciousness*, McGraw-Hill, New York.

Berg, I. *et al.* (1978). *Managers and Work Reform: A Limited Engagement*, Free Press, New York.

Blauner, R. (1964). *Alienation and Freedom*, University of Chicago Press, Chicago, Ill.

Engler, R. (1984). *A Job Safety and Health Bill of Rights*, Philadelphia Area Project on Occupational Safety and Health, Philadelphia, Pa.

Ferree, M. M. (1980). Working class feminism: a consideration of the consequences of employment, *The Sociological Quarterly*, **21**, 173–184.

Foulkes, F. K., and Hirsch, J. L. (1984). People make robotics work, *Harvard Business Review*, January–February 1984, pp. 94–102.

Fox, M. F., and Hesse-Biber, S. (1984). *Women at Work*, Mayfield, New York.

Frank, M. (1984). Caution, women: work is hazardous to health, *In These Times*, 12–18 September 1984, p. 12.

Freeman, R. B., and Medoff, J. L. (1984). *What Do Unions Do?* Basic Books, New York.

Gappert, G. (1978). *Post-Affluent America: The Social Economy of the Future*, Franklin Watts, New York.

Green, M. (1982). Richer than all their tribe, *New Republic*, 6 and 13 January 1982, pp. 21, 24–26.

Hammond, J. L., and Hammond, B. (1934). *The Bleak Age*, Oxford, London.

Harrington, M. (1984). *The New American Poverty*, Holt, Rinehart and Winston, New York.

Harrison, B., and Bluestone, B. (1984). More jobs, lower wages, *N.Y. Times*, 19 June 1984, p. A-27.

Hartson, M. (1984). Recessions took 5.1 million jobs over five years, *Philadelphia Inquirer*, 1 December 1984, pp. 1, 10.

Hersey, R. B. (1932). *Workers' Emotions in Shop and Home*, University of Pennsulvania Press, Philadelphia, Pa.

Hirschhorn, L. (1984). *Beyond Mechanization*, MIT Press, Cambridge, Mass.

Hoerr, J. (1984). Why steel is tempering labor relations on the shop- floor, *Business Week*, 3 September 1984, p. 52.

Hughes, E. C. (1971). *The Sociological Eye*.

Kagis, R., and Grossman, R. L. (1982). *Fear at Work: Job Blackmail, Labor and Environment*, Pilgrim Press, New York.

Lambrinos, J., and Johnson, W. J. (1984). Robots to reduce the high cost of illness and injury, *Harvard Business Review*, May–June 1984, pp. 24–28.

Levitan, S. (Ed.) (1981). *Blue-Collar Workers: A Symposium on Middle America*, McGraw-Hill, New York.

McIlwee, J. S. (1982). Work satisfaction among women in nontraditional occupations, *Work and Occupation*, **9**, 3 August 1982, 299–335.

Noble, D. (1984). *Forces of Production*, MIT Press, Cambridge, Mass.

O'Farrell, B. (1982). Women and nontraditional blue collar jobs in the 1980s: an overview. In *Women in the Workplace* (Ed. P. A. Wallace), Auburn, Boston, Mass., pp. 135–165.

O'Toole, J. (Ed.) (1974). *Work in America*, MIT Press, Cambridge, Mass.

Pascarella, P. (1984). *The New Achievers: Creating a Modern Work Ethic*, Free Press, New York.

Pfeffer, R. M. (1979). *Working for Capitalism*, Columbia University Press, New York.

Reynolds, M. O. (1984). *Power and Privilege: Labor Unions in America*, Universe Books, New York.

Rosen, E. (1981). Hobson's choice: employment and unemployment among factory workers in New England, Social Welfare Research Institute, Boston, Mass.

Rosen, E. (1982). The changing jobs of american women factory workers, Social Welfare Research Institute, Boston, Mass.

Salisbury, D. F. (1984). The coming industrial revolution, *The Christian Science Monitor*, 20 November 1984, pp. 37, 44.

Schwartz, G. G., and Neikirk, W. (1983). *The Work Revolution: The Future of Work in the Post-Industrial Society*, Rawson Associates, New York.

Scott, J., as quoted in Chavkin, W. (1984). *Double Exposure: Women's Health Hazards on the Job and at Home*, Monthly Review Press, New York.

Seashore, S., and Barnowe, J. T. (1974). Demographic and job factors associated with the 'Blue Collar Blues'. In *The 1972–73 Quality of Employment Survey* (Eds. R. P. Quinn and L. J. Shepard). University of Michigan Soc. Res.

Simmons, J., and Mares, W. (1983). *Working Together*, Alfred A. Knopf, New York.

Smith, R. E. (1983). *Workrights*, E. P. Dutton, Inc., New York.

Spencer, C. (1977). *Blue Collar: An Internal Examination of the Workplace*, Lakeside Charter, Chicago, Ill.

Tulin, R. (1984). *A Machinist's Semi-Automated Life*, Singlejack Books, San Pedro, Calif.

Walshok, M. L. (1981). *Blue-Collar Women: Pioneers on the Male Frontier*, Anchor Books, New York.

White, L. (1983). *Human Debris: The Injured Worker in America*, Seaview/Putnam, New York.

Job Stress and Blue Collar Work
Edited by C. L. Cooper and M. J. Smith
© 1985 John Wiley & Sons Ltd

Chapter 3

Control and Blue Collar Work

Shirley Fisher

Stress Research Unit,
Department of Psychology,
University of Dundee, Dundee, Scotland

INTRODUCTION

Within the last few years there has been increasing interest in the concept of control and its influence in initiating or moderating the behavioural and psychological responses of human beings to stressful conditions. The term 'control' is generally defined as 'power' or 'mastery' over the environment and is closely bound with the concept of competence. Philosophically, the concept of control is linked with the view that organisms seek to establish themselves as masters of their environment. It has been argued that the exercise of power or control over all aspects of the environment is a powerful motivating force (see White, 1959).

Stressful conditions, whether physical, as in the case of bodily assault, harsh environments, and conditions of deprivation, or psychological, as in the case of failure, loss of prestige, and social pressure, are generally thought of as conditions which the individual would like to avoid. If the individual has control there is the potential for reversing, attenuating, or terminating conditions which are less than desirable. An important point is that the individual who operates effective control may not only suffer less of the unpleasant conditions, but at the same time gains information about his/her own competence because he/she is able to perceive that he/she has coped successfully. The latter aspect of control may explain possible gains from reversing potentially hazardous environments. The motivational gains acquired from potential challenges may explain the attraction of 'risk sports' such as ski jumping, free-fall parachute jumping, high-speed driving, etc. Carruthers (1974) identifies the noradrenaline-linked 'arousal jag' as an attractive aspect of fast driving in racing car drivers.

Although the concept of control and its associations with reaction to stress has been explored in some detail in an experimental and largely 'laboratory' context, (e.g. see Fisher, 1984), the application to the reactions to life events and to the daily living conditions experienced by people is really only just

19

beginning to be explored. At least one of the problems is that both 'stress' and 'control' are complex 'umbrella' terms with a variety of descriptive forms. This encourages the temptation to explain away attitudes or behaviour in terms of intuitive links with control.

This chapter is concerned with stress and control as factors in blue collar work. Blue collar workers are the skilled and unskilled groups in service or production industries, who carry out the essential manual and monitoring operations required by the production process. In general, they have less jurisdiction over their working duties in that, unless they have power because of union or managerial position on the shopfloor, they carry out those work activities specified by the employers. One of the results of automation and the introduction of capital-intensive systems has been to distance the worker from direct contact with the product itself and to shift the balance of activities towards monitoring and 'machine minding' (Welford, 1960). As a result, the stresses are changed: direct contact with the product or industrial process involves exposure to adverse conditions (machine noise, dirt, high event rates, danger, vibration, etc.), whereas automation and remote contact resulting in the need for fault detection and the need for sustained monitoring involves boredom. Additionally, capital-intensive systems result in the introduction of shift work which creates conditions of work at times which are against the dictates of circadian rhythm.

Generalizing, those who carry out skilled and unskilled jobs could be expected to incur different stresses than those who are in clerical, managerial, or professional posts. Additionally, the levels of control experienced by blue collar workers are likely to be lower than those in managerial, office, or professional jobs. Firstly, there is likely to be less control over how time is spent at work; work is dictated by the state of the industrial process. Secondly, there is less chance to influence the conditions of the task itself; specified operations must be carried out, usually in an organized way, because the overall coordination of the product is the result of all the processes involved. Thirdly, there is less chance to attenuate, terminate, or avoid unpleasant conditions; the only option may be to put up with the conditions or leave the job. Finally, by virtue of the fact that blue collar positions tend to be in the lower wage levels, there may be less total jurisdiction over whether to leave the job or not and less control over daily existence because many material advantages cannot be obtained. This set of assumptions provides the basis for the development of ideas in this chapter.

One of the problems with the analysis of stress and control as factors in the working lives of blue collar workers is that both the pattern of stresses which occur *and* the level of jurisdiction of control may vary independently. Therefore, the implications for the worker may be dependent on the interaction of unique combinations of variables. General statements about blue collar and white collar differences may turn out to be less informative than more specific between-job comparisons. Before these and other issues can be discussed, it is necessary to consider some of the salient aspects of the concepts of 'stress' and 'control'.

The nature of stress

Stress is best described as an umbrella term for a wide variety of circumstances and reactions. The first definition of importance is of stress as the *independent variable*. By this definition it is conceived of as 'out there' in the environment: the individual does not create the stressful condition but is confronted with it. A sudden accident or encounter with a traumatic event or the exposure to adverse environments conform to this paradigm. Many authors and researchers concerned with stress depict it in these terms. However, stress may also be defined in terms of the *dependent variable*; stress is the response a person produces. Thus neurotic fears are eligible for inclusion because the source of a person's reaction is unimportant; a person who fears birds may suffer stress if exposed to them. The reaction produced may be physiological or psychological and measured in terms of the mental or physical health of the individual.

The second distinction, which is not entirely independent of the first, is the involvement of the person in creating stressful conditions. Failing an examination is only stressful if there is high personal cost attached to success. Fisher (1984) defined 'internally derived' stresses as those which depend on the values held by the individual. These values dictate the aims or ambitions which translate into the detail of the planning of daily tasks. Work on achievement motivation (McClelland *et al.*, 1953; Atkinson 1957) has identified two fundamentally different motives in the performance of tasks. The first is achievement oriented; the individual seeks success and generally is reluctant to undertake very simple tasks in which success is deemed trivial, or very complex, demanding tasks in which success is impossible. By contrast, the second motive is described as 'fear of failure'. The individual who is thus characterized will undertake either a very simple task where success is inevitable or a very difficult task where failure would be expected, thereby gaining credit for trying but suffering no prestige loss due to failure. Laboratory studies in which individuals select aspects of task-difficulty levels provide support for this distinction (e.g. see Moulton, 1965; Atkinson and Feather, 1966). It could be argued that those whose daily tasks are largely dictated for them could be subjected to pressures if the nature of the task does not match with personal perception of likely success levels, whereas those who do have jurisdiction are free to be selective unless other dictates (such as the need for promotion, increased salary, etc.) create higher level constraints.

The 'work ethic' derived from the influence of Protestantism has been argued to be an important factor in the lives of Western civilization. McClelland (1961) examined the content of children's stores in various cultures. The number of times achievement was emphasized in each story examined was found to be specifically related to economic development of the country of origin. In particular, the protestant ethic and the capitalist motive encourage work and concern with success.

Mills (1973) has examined incidence data on stress-related phenomena such as suicide rates, depression, and anorexia nervosa. He reports substantial increases in the incidence of all three, especially in young people. For example, his figures on anorexia nervosa suggest incidence rates which were about 10 times as high as they were 10 years before. Mills argues that the pressures of a competitive capitalist society operate to raise the aims and ambitions of the individual.

As early as 1937, Horney drew attention to the conflict produced by two fundamental motives in society. The stated ideal of kindness and humanity is espoused but society continues to reward success. The material possessions of the capitalist system go to those who are successful.

In the context of the current chapter it is useful to speculate in this respect on the pressures on the blue collar worker. The position at work may not be mobile and the 'rewards' for increased effort may not be forthcoming. Thus, whilst it might be possible to argue that there is protection against the pressures for success, there may be other pressures operating in that the possession of material goods is made less easy. Work could be argued to set the parameters which define a number of conditions experienced in life.

The nature of control

As described earlier, the concept of control implies power or mastery and implies that there is the potential for instrumentality or reversibility. The latter aspect is the important feature as far as stress is concerned because having control means that a disliked (stressful) feature of the psychosocial environment can be changed. Miller (1979) developed the 'minimax hypothesis' in accordance with which control involves the ability to minimize maximum future danger. Fisher (1984) defined control in cognitive terms; control involves the knowledge that there is a response available that can bring about a desired state of affairs (this could include making changes in the exercise of personal competence or reversing an undesirable state of affairs).

The preference for predictability and control

A number of laboratory studies have been concerned with the human preference for predictability and control as features of unpleasant stimulation; while most people express a preference for both, the effect on physiological responses has not been convincing.

One of the earliest studies by Haggard (1943) showed that, for human subjects, self-administered shock resulted in smaller skin conductance changes than shock administered by the experimenter and was perceived as less unpleasant. A difficulty with the interpretation of this finding is the confounding of control and predictability, but at least amelioration of the physiological response to shock was demonstrated.

Pervin (1963) carried out a detailed study of the role of prediction and control in conditions of threat, in order to try to partition the effects of control and predictability. Control was manipulated by allowing the subject to self-administer shocks (S control) or by allowing the experimenter to do so (E control). There were three conditions of predictability (signal; no signal; inconsistent signal) provided by means of three different lights indicating when and whether shock would occur. The data included subjective preferences, pain ratings, anxiety ratings, subjective reports of experiences, reaction times for decisions. In terms of personal assessment there was a preference for control. A number of reasons were provided: (1) subjects imagined that shock duration might be shortened; (2) greater correspondence between switch and shock reduced surprise; (3) mastery, freedom, and choice were equated with control. For the small proportion of subjects who did not like having control, reasons given included: (1) it produced concentration on signals, creating anxiety; (2) it resulted in conflict about whether to press the switch or not; (3) it represented unnecessary punishment of the self.

There was also preference expressed for predictable occurrence of shock. Subjects reported that they could prepare for shock by developing an attitude of acceptance towards it or by bracing the limb to be shocked. They could also rest in the intervals between shock. The absence of predictability led to conflicting expectations and experience of surprise, frustration, anger, and depression. Predicting no-shock and receiving shock was reported as most painful.

Overall, Pervin's study showed the difference between S control and E control to be small. Most of the effects were in terms of self-reported experience. Pervin emphasizes the importance of psychological meaning and suggests that the feeling of mastery is preferable and less arousing than no instrumentality. With regard to the preference for predictability, Pervin reported that it was less influential with increasing trials. He took this to mean that complete predictability is more important in threatening situations and less important in repetitive, less-threatening situations.

Extrapolating, it appears that in situations where there is danger and threat most individuals will prefer predictability and control, although there may be little underlying physiological or performance change. Poulton (1978), in an extensive discussion on stresses at work for blue collar workers, underlines the possibility that subjective judgements may not always predict objective outcomes. Conditions such as noise or vertical vibration at 5 Hz can help maintain alterness, although people complain of it. Recently, Fisher (1983, 1984) has shown that people expect deterioration in performance in stressful conditions and has argued that the characteristics of actual performance in these conditions may represent attempted compensation.

A study by Ball and Vogler (1971) illustrated the importance of idiosyncratic factors in decisions about control. Subjects were given an initial choice of being self-shocked or machine-shocked. In addition, once a subject had developed a pattern of preference, the choice was given of continuing with it but at the cost of receiving double shocks. Out of 36 subjects, 25 chose self-shock and 21 claimed this was to reduce uncertainty. In spite of the penalty of incurring double shocks if the change to machine-shock was not made, 7 subjects preferred to continue with their original self-shock choice. However, out of the 11 subjects who choose machine-shock originally, 4 subjects were prepared to accept double machine-shock rather than change, giving as reasons that shock was enjoyable, that random delivery increased excitement, or that the aim had to foil the experimenter.

This study draws attention to the importance of idiosyncracies in attitudes to control, even in case of painful stimulation. Not everyone perceives the situation in the same way and it may be that it is the perception of demand characteristics which is important. Thus, the acceptance of adverse working conditions and task characteristics may be possible if the worker perceives the job in a wider context, such as a source of an increased standard of living at home, a means of payment for a leisure pursuit, etc.

Work by Glass and colleagues (Glass, Singer, and Friedman, 1969; Glass and Singer, 1972) investigated performance on a variety of tasks in the presence of loud aversive noise delivered in 9-second bursts. Subjects showed some adaptation to the noise, but later when two subsequent tasks were presented, there were differences in performance as a function of the experience of the noise condition. Those subjects who received a random schedule of noise bursts made fewer attempts at problem-solving on an unsolvable problem task, as compared with controls and the subjects who had experienced predictable noise.

Perhaps more importantly, if subjects were provided with a switch for controlling the noise, there was a marked beneficial effect on performance. For example, on the unsolvable problem task, those subjects who had been provided with a switch to control the noise attempted five times the number of puzzles. On a proof-reading task fewer errors were reported. It seems that the mere presence of a *potential* source of control is sufficient to prevent the occurrence of negative carryover effects. The effect is true even when subjects were only able to operate the switch by asking another person to operate it for them (Glass, Rheim, and Singer, 1971).

This has implications for certain forms of blue collar work. Those who work on assembly lines may, for example, have relatively little control over factors such as noise levels, the rate at which the product moves on, the timing of the process, or the position or posture which has to be assumed to maintain the operations necessary.

Studies conducted in a sawmill by Frankenhaeuser and Gardell (1976) showed that conditions such as restricted work posture are associated with self-reported feelings of irritation and high noradrenaline. Repetition and short duration of work cycle reduce feelings of well-being and are associated with increased adrenaline. Moreover, control of work pace is important; workers report greater irritation and show higher noradrenaline levels when the work pace is controlled by machine.

These studies fit rather neatly with the laboratory studies which suggest that control over administration is a critical moderator variable likely to affect tolerance of unpleasant conditions. Lack of tolerance could itself result in the irritation and discomfort necessary for changes in stress hormone levels; mood-inducing experiences have been found in the laboratory to produce changes in physiological response (see Ax, 1953; Averill, 1969).

'Control by avoidance'

Work with animals exposed to treatments of electric shock has provided a major contribution to the understanding of the importance of the availability of instrumental response which facilitates avoidance or escape of noxious stimulation, as a major factor in determining a number of reactions indicative of stress. The research literature contains an interesting contradiction. While the weight of evidence suggests that absence of an appropriate instrumental response (helplessness) results in more stressful symptoms than conditions where a response is available, studies with 'executive' monkeys suggest that the reverse might be the case; responsibility may sometimes be more stressful.

Early studies with rats by Mowrer and Viek (1948) showed that when hungry rats could turn off the electrification of the grid on the floor of the cage by leaping into the air, they were more likely to approach and eat food 10 seconds before each shock than were rats who were yoked to the executive animals so that they received the shock the executive animals failed to avoid. The yoked (helpless) group showed much more disruption of the previously learned positive responses to food. Thus, it seemed that having instrumentality available decreased the fear of anticipated shock.

Against the view that instrumentality provides a basis for the reduction of stressful effects of shock, studies on primates by Brady et al. (1958) suggested that it might increase stress. 'Executive' monkeys were restrained in chairs but were able to avoid shock by pressing a lever every 20 seconds. Control monkeys who were yoked to the executive group and were effectively helpless, received the same shock as the executive monkeys. The results of Brady's studies showed that the executive group were vulnerable to ulcers; some monkeys died in the middle of the experiment. Weiss (1968) criticized the design used by Brady because the monkeys were not assigned at random to the two groups; those monkeys who had learned avoidance-responding well were assigned to the executive group.

Moreover, work by Weiss (1968) with albino rats showed that those who could avoid shock delivered to the floor of the cage by leaping up to a platform were *less* vulnerable to the effects of stress than those who were helpless. The design was such that, having escaped, the animal would then be pushed gently back on to the floor of the case again (a situation over which there was no control). The yoked animals with control over shock showed a greater decrease in body weight, largely because of failure to gain weight after the stress sessions. The difference in comparison with the group with control was after only one exposure to the stress situation. In the second experiment the stress levels were increased because animals were restrained in small tubular cages and control was exercised by touching a small copper contact disc with front paws or nose. The duration of the stress session was 20 hours. The principal variable under study this time was the severity of stomach lesions. Avoidance-responding by the avoidance group occurred on an average of 35 per cent. of the trials. Both avoidance and yoked animals lost more weight than non-shock animals. The yoked, helpless animals, however, developed more extensive lesions than avoidance and non-shock animals. Again the increased vulnerability of the helpless animal was confirmed.

There are some important points of difference with the studies by Brady and colleagues. Firstly, Brady used primates and there was some degree of pre-selection. Secondly, the sessions used by Brady were conducted for different work schedules over a period of days, whereas the Weiss study involved durations of up to but no greater than 20 hours. In spite of the obvious difficulties in generalizing from animal laboratory studies to real-life conditions of human beings, there are some interesting implications for comparison of different occupational settings. Blue collar workers who operate directly on the process or product are more likely to be helpless in that at work they are less able to avoid unpleasant conditions. Those in managerial positions may have the jurisdiction which enables them to avoid circumstances they do not like, but there may be penalties. Firstly, the exercise of responsibility may produce its own pressures. Deadlines may have to be met. In a group of American tax accountants studied by Friedman, Rosenman, and Carroll (1958), pressures of time stress increased levels of serum cholesterol and accelerated blood clotting time. This could be argued to represent loss of control or to involve 'control by avoidance', since meeting the tax deadline with work avoids the penalties imposed by the State on clients and indirectly on accountants.

Secondly, as argued by Fisher (1984), the exercise of 'control by avoidance' incurs the penalty of lack of feedback which informs a person that control is possible. An individual who changes his/her behaviour to avoid unpleasant consequences (meeting a deadline, avoiding an encounter with an angry colleague, trying not to notice an attitude taken by a colleague, avoiding involvement in an office problem), incurs the penalty that he/she never knows that the behaviour was effective, precisely because it *is* effective. The unpleasant event is avoided successfully but the individual remains uncertain about this. These conditions might be less likely to be experienced by a person in a structured defined job situation. In this sense low control on a regular basis could be argued to be less stressful!

Fisher (1985) has furthered the notion of 'control by avoidance' as a concept which aids the understanding of the escalation of anxiety and elaboration of behavioural repertoires for avoidance in phobic conditions. The phobic patient never receives the information which gives assurance that phobic-avoidance behaviour is effective. The patient may be operating control but perceiving possible loss of control. It remains plausible that a distressed executive or manager has aspects of behaviour which may have features in common with phobic avoidance. The situation is less likely to develop for a blue collar worker.

These animal studies have been reviewed in some detail because, taken collectively, they suggest both that being helpless and being responsible create stressful conditions in some circumstances. There are the often-stated difficulties of applying animal research to the investigation of the reaction of human beings, but it is at least useful to consider the implications of what has been contributed to the understanding of the conditions of the blue collar worker and the white collar groups.

Returning to the original dichotomy, the blue collar worker is argued to incur more unpleasant working environments (noise, heat, cold, vibration, glare, externally paced event rates, restricted posture, etc.) with low control over them. The blue collar worker also has less jurisdiction over how time is spent at work and therefore cannot rest when he/she feels tired, relieve postural discomfort when limbs ache, etc. There is a direct point of comparison with the animal studies of helplessness in that the worker cannot avoid adverse working conditions or perhaps more importantly take avoidance action for sudden intolerable changes (e.g. blast furnace becomes too hot, rate of events in the production line becomes too fast because of re-scheduling or human error). There is in theory an ultimate set of control procedures; the worker could complain to the management, or the union, or leave the job. In reality there may be pressures which prevent the worker taking those courses of action (e.g. need to retain a weekly income; fear of creating bad feeling at work; fear of job loss, etc.). As will be discussed later in this chapter, there may be a hierarchy of control decisions and loss of control may arise because of the implications at a higher level in the hierarchy.

In the case of those in managerial and professional positions, the links with the exercise of responsibility defined by the executive monkey experiments are less apparent because the paradigm involves activity instrumental in avoiding punishment. It would seem unrealistic to assume that most working situations adhere to this paradigm. There are, however, cases where a person in a managerial position may need to meet deadlines, keep another person employed, 'prove' his/her competence, or incur the risk of loss of prestige, etc. In these situations there may be some parallels with the plight of the executive monkey; action to avoid unpleasant consequences has to take place regularly. The lower grades of managerial professional staff may be more likely to be in this position in that there are those in authority higher in the chain of command who may operate such sanctions. It might be hypothesized that the more hierarchically structured the company or institution, the more likely it is that 'executive monkey' conditions for those in less influential positions will occur.

'Control by irrelevant means'

An aspect of control hardly explored is that individuals might be able to gain some advantage in an unpleasant situation by operating what Fisher (1984) terms 'control by irrelevant means'. The notion is best illustrated by means of an example from an autobiographical account by Dolgun (1965) of his survival of depreviation and interrogation procedures in a prison in Moscow during the period of Stalin's regime. Extreme sleep deprivation, constant beatings and interrogation, isolation and food deprivation, and low temperature conditions combined to produce a set of stresses which most individuals were thought not to survive for long. Dolgun's account of his own survival includes reference to 'conditioning the guards'; he could determine whether the guards came in to shake him awake or not. Additionally, Dolgun reported in some detail how he walked around his cell imagining himself to be walking through France and making decisions about which way to turn at crossroads and villages. Procedures such as these, Dolgun believes, accounted for his survival.

The phrase 'control by irrelevant means' was used by Fisher because Dolgun had achieved little control over the *relevant* sources of his distress in that the conditions of deprivation remained virtually unchanged; he had, however, achieved a degree of personal control over aspects of his daily life in prison. The question of interest is whether achieving control over *some* aspect of life, however trivial or seemingly irrelevant, could counter the effects of adverse experiences elsewhere. The concept of 'control by irrelevant means' may be of importance for the understanding of some of the recent findings concerning factors which appear to influence the ability of workers to remain unaffected by stress at work. The possibility will be reconsidered in the section on blue collar work.

'Locus of control'

The phrase 'locus of control' evolved with work on the ideology of attitudes to control and is generally taken to mean the stable disposition of the individual with regard to whether or not control is possible in life. The scale introduced by Rotter and his colleagues (Rotter, 1966) evolved from Rotter's work on social learning theory (Rotter, 1954), and was based on the notion of a unitary dimension from 'externality', the belief that outcomes in life are decided by fate, chance, or other people, to 'internality', the belief that outcomes are personally determined.

There is now a substantial research literature on locus of control (see Lefcourt, 1966, 1972, 1981) and a number of research developments have led to: (1) the general belief that the original concept of a unidimensional scale is simplistic; (2) the belief that there may be different domains of control from *personal* (control over objects in the environment) through to higher *socio-political* levels (control over major decisions concerning political issues and social change); (3) the belief that internality–externality distinctions are circumscribed and more likely to be manifest in situations where outcomes are likely to be negative.

Decisions about control ideology could be considered to be of primary importance in determining whether a person sees him/herself as helpless or able to take effective action in a particular situation. Fisher (1984) argued that 'control ideology' decisions could determine the type of stress experienced in a particular situation. The profile of attitudes and responses by those who were strong in internality was found by relatively early research to be different in many respects from those who were high in externality. For example, when confronted with personal illness, those high on internality were found to acquire more knowledge about the disease than those who were high on externality (Seeman and Evans, 1962). Equally, reformatory inmates who were internalizers showed enhanced recall of information relevant to parole but not of information which was irrelevant (Seeman, 1963). The mode of information processing may therefore be quite different for internalizers and externalizers faced with unpleasant situations. The difference is in the expected direction on the hypothesis that internalizers will engage the problem and externalizers are more likely to react with helplessness. This is further confirmed by laboratory evidence showing that, in general internalizers take longer to make decisions on a task when skill, as compared with chance, is involved in the outcome (Rotter and Mulry, 1965). Moreover, decision time for internalizers is more likely to reflect task-difficulty levels, than it is for externalizers (Julian and Katz, 1968).

The origins of control ideology have never been made clear, although Rotter evolved the concept from social learning theory, suggesting that it was a learned attitude. Fisher (1984) argued that successive life experiences might be hypothesized to alter the memory for control so that a person who experienced uncontrollable, bad outcome conditions would gradually shift the decision criteria from a specific (I cannot control x, y, z) to the general (I cannot control anything). This would support the findings that under-privilege and poverty tend to be associated with high externality scores (see Griffin, 1962; Lefcourt and Ludwig, 1965).

One of the interesting developments from animal research in the 1970s was the concept of learned helplessness (Seligman, 1975). Dogs pretreated with inescapable (uncontrollable) shock subsequently failed to learn avoidance responses in a task where escape was possible. The pretreated dogs were characterized by passivity and failed to learn the escape procedure even when helped to cross the barrier to safety. Helplessness is closely identified with depression by Seligman. It was assumed that as a result of an uncontrollable pretreatment, the dogs had learned to expect lack of contingency between action and outcome. The question of interest raised by Seligman is why all who experience uncontrollability are not helpless. On a one-exposure hypothesis, every animal and human being should be helpless because low or zero control situations are common.

Studies with human subjects by Hiroto (1974), using a finger shuttlebox where a specified avoidance response could terminate loud noise, showed that a pretreatment of uncontrollable exposure to the noise slowed down the learning of the avoidance response. Hiroto and Seligman (1975) further demonstrated that the presence of adverse stimulation alone is not a pre-condition for helplessness; unsolvable discrimination-learning tasks were shown to produce subsequent impairment on an anagram task.

There have been a number of major difficulties in the attempts to generalize from the learned helplessness model to the understanding of the origin of inappropriate helplessness. For example, the phenomenon has been reported as circumscribed; passivity and slow learning are not always consequences, sometimes human beings persist in producing responses (see Peterson, 1982; Fisher, 1985). It was considerations such as these which led to the revised helpless model (Abramson, Seligman, and Teasdale, 1978) in accordance with which depression is not equated with helplessness but with blame constantly directed at the self for negative outcomes. The authors propose that low self-esteem is a central feature of depression and arises from attributions for negative outcomes which are internal (self-directed), global (generalized), and stable (reliable over time).

This has helped to resolve the problem of the paradox that the depresed appear to accept blame for situations which are universally uncontrollable. In

the studies by Brown and Harris (1978), working class women were interviewed in a door-to-door survey in Camberwell, London. For those who were
found to be depressed, there was a 'soup' of factors which seemed to be
critical: there were environmental conditions of poverty, lack of prospect for
employment, more than three children at home, lack of a confiding relationship with another person, plus a life history profile characterized by loss of a
parent before the age of 11. The prevailing personality characteristic was low
self-esteem. Given the 'soup' of circumstantial factors identified by the
investigators as being prevalent for the depressed women, low self-esteem
would seem to be an inappropriate reaction in that it involves self-blame for
objectively uncontrollable conditions.

On the revised helplessness hypothesis it should be possible to encounter
negative outcome situations and yet not become depressed. In fact, the
emphasis has created a more refined definition of depression as being
associated with personal but not universally apparent helplessness (see
Garber and Hollen, 1980).

The implication for the shift of emphasis as far as the plight of the blue
collar worker is concerned is that low control may not itself be a sufficient
condition for depression. The way it operates may be to leave the worker
exposed to conditions which may be disliked, such as noise, extreme tem-
peratures, glare, high event rates, restricted posture; but if the worker
perceives others as experiencing the same conditions and accepts no personal
responsibility for negative experiences he/she may not become depressed.
The worker may, however, be rendered vulnerable to the direct effects of
those situations which are disliked and cannot be controlled; these may
create secondary effects.

Domains of control

Because human 'everyday' life is complex, many potential spheres of control
may coexist. An individual may experience high control in some domains and
relatively low control in another. This is of importance to the understanding
of the concept of 'locus of control' because the issue of interest is: control
over what (see Fisher, 1985). There are many occasions where control is
readily relinquished. For example, people do not normally expect to care for
their own teeth; they consult a dentist and in a sense relinquish all control
over what is done to their teeth by way of treatment. It would seem strange to
decribe this relinquishing of control to an expert as a form of helplessness, yet
strictly speaking this is the case. What is retained, however, is control over
the decision to consult the expert and presumably some control throughout
over whether the expert can continue. Before discussing this issue in the
context of exercise of control by the blue collar worker, some more detailed
evidence from recent 'locus of control' research should be considered.

In addition to the research suggesting that the locus of control dimension is not unitary, a finding which seemed paradoxical was the reported positive correlation between machiavellianism and externality (Prociuk and Breen, 1976). The latter finding, that those who attempt to manipulate others perceive themselves as more external, seems to run contrary to intuitive expectations. The difficulty is overcome if a person is thought of as occupying several positions simultaneously with respect to domains of control. Paulhus and Christie (1981) provide the basis of a partitioning of control into three behaviour domains or theatres. The first is seen as central and is concerned with the self and personal achievement in a non-social context. Solving puzzles, building bookcases, climbing mountains are all aspects of personal skill and achievement. Perceived control is defined in terms of *personal efficacy* in this domain. Secondly, the individual acts in a social context and may or may not acquire *interpersonal control*. Thirdly, the individual acts within a sociopolitical context; he/she may organize demonstrations or strikes or run campaigns to achieve social or political aims. If successful, *sociopolitical control* is acquired.

On the basis of this conceptualization three scales were introduced by Paulhus and Christie with the assumption that there may be different expectancies of control in each of the three domains, although the three expectancies should show a moderate correlation. This approach provides the basis for a *control profile* measured by means of the 'spheres of control' (SOC) battery. The authors point to three advantages obtained by the tripartite divisions: (1) it entails partitioning in terms of spheres of activity; (2) it provides a basis for separating and assessing interpersonal control; (3) it subdivides the internal core to provide a meaningful set of attributes. The machiavellian individual is likely to score low on sociopolitical control because of cynicism but in interpersonal situations is likely to try to manipulate others. Intercorrelation data provided by Paulhus and Christie support this hypothesis. Thus a person may 'specialize' in operating in one domain, relinquishing control in another.

A comparison was made of the control profiles of college athletes divided further into footballers and tennis players, and non-athletes. Paulhus and Christie predicted that athletic groups should have higher personal and interpersonal control scores than non-athletes. Football players were hypothesized as likely to have higher interpersonal control scores than tennis players because football is a game which depends on teamwork. Tennis players were hypothesized to have high control in the personal efficiency domain because tennis is individualistic and competitive. This analysis seems to be an oversimplification because it could be equally plausible to argue that football players have high personal skills as well. Also, the mere fact of the importance of teamwork could provide a basis for hypothesizing that interpersonal skill should be reduced in favour of accepting directions from key personnel (team captain, trainers, and managers). However, the profile of control scores was found to support the predictions.

The partitioning provided by Paulhaus and Christie is more than just a specification of spheres of influence. They present a 'fact analysis' based on four critical parameters or facets: source, target, valence, and sphere of control. They describe a fundamental statement capable of generating a $3 \times 2 \times 2 \times 3 = 36$ kernal sentence:

$$\begin{bmatrix} \text{Chance, skill} \\ \text{and/or} \\ \text{hard work} \end{bmatrix} \text{determines} \begin{bmatrix} \text{success} \\ \text{failure} \end{bmatrix} \text{that} \begin{bmatrix} \text{I} \\ \text{people} \end{bmatrix} \text{have in} \begin{bmatrix} \text{personal achievement} \\ \text{interpersonal life} \\ \text{sociopolitical activity} \end{bmatrix}$$

The authors speculate that the entire domain of perceived control may derive from a linguistic or attributional structure centred round a generator sentence such as [X controls Y in situation Z] or [X causes Y under circumstance Z]. The model not only incorporates the major aspects of perceived control defined by other researchers but provides a basis for understanding control in terms of causal schema and linguistic structures.

The hierarchical decision model of the perception of control

Fisher (1984) provided a descriptive analysis of the decisions involved in the perception of control for any situation. A hierarchical model was proposed in that some decisions were argued to occupy a superordinate position, whereas others were more situational in character and at a lower level of the hierarchy. As shown in figure 1, any situation confronting a person could be analysed in terms of what is objectively true and what is subjectively possible. Only a positive selection of the matrix of objective and subjective elements is represented in the figure. For example, in Figure 1(a) a situation where control is objectvely possible is depicted. This implies that there must be a means of instrumentality (facility available) and the skills needed must be objectively possible for the individual (skill available). The individual assesses these factors and may make realistic (objectively valid) or pessimistic (objectively not valid) decisions. The individual may perceive that there is no facility available when there is (perhaps the means for control may not be noticed; perhaps the facility is not regarded as being reliable). Equally, the individual may doubt his/her own skills when objectvely he/she does have the skills to cope. Figure 1(b) depicts the reverse situation when control is objectively impossible but the individual assumes that it is. As already emphasized, at each level of decision a subordinate set of possibilities exists.

Figure 2 illustrates the basis of Fisher's hierarchical decision model. Locus of control ideology occupies a superordinate position in the hierarchy. If a person is strongly polarized in the belief that events are externally controlled

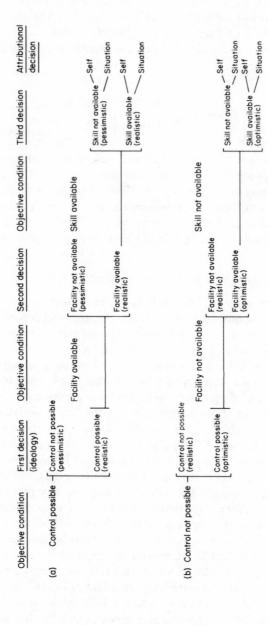

Figure 1   Selection of some possible sequences of decisions from a matrix of decisions that must logically be involved in determining the outcome of a stressful scenario

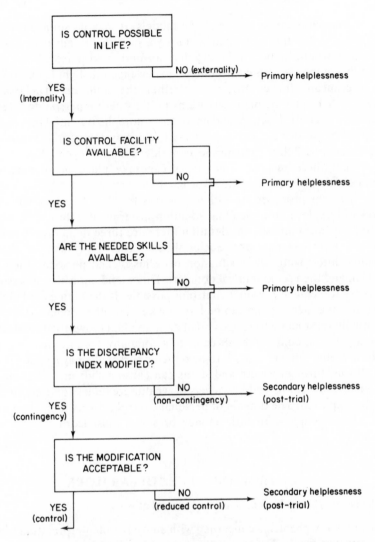

Figure 2   Hierarchy of decisions in determining effort, struggle, and persistence compared with different types of perceived helplessness in a stressful scenario

in life, there is no need to make any further decisions. If a person is not strongly polarized in this respect, or is polarized in favour of the belief that personal control is possible (internality), then subordinate decisions are required concerning the control facility or the availability of necessary skills. It is assumed that at each stage in the hierarchy the individual may be rendered effectively helpless.

It may not be necessary for the individual to explore the situation in the ideal procedure mapped by the above models. It may be sufficient in some circumstances for the individual to make a decision in advance based on more general information in knowledge; an untrained person *knows* he/she cannot fly Concorde without needing to experience the flight deck, to decide what the means for control are, whether the skills are available, etc. However, there may be many situations in life where a person does feel the possibility for control is there and needs to explore the potential for control; a person who can drive a car and ride a cycle may feel it is appropriate to explore the possibility that he/she can ride a motor cycle. Fisher (1984) argued that these mental explorations can take place in advance of an encounter and provide a functional aspect of worrying.

A refinement proposed by Fisher (1985) is to allow the possibility that a person will explore an impending situation in terms of different domains of control. On the simplest consideration there are three domains represented: personal, interpersonal, and sociopolitical. One possibility is that the individual interrogates each situation in terms of first personal, then inter-personal, and then sociopolitical domains. This would imply that a person will always try to achieve personal control if possible. If the anticipated outcome is negative the memory file can be interrogated for other domains. However, it is equally reasonable to suppose that an individual grows used to success in some domains of control; the director of a company need not tackle the task of wiring a plug but can order it to be done or personally pay someone else to do it. Power through wealth and status can cause a shift in control domain. Conversely, low status and low levels of wealth create less options about the domains explored. The domain of personal control is likely to be dominant in these cases; people with little money or status must learn to wire a plug themselves.

CONTROL AND BLUE COLLAR WORK

Problems with the analysis of stress and control at work

There are many problems concerned with analysis and interpretation of stress and control at work. The first is that studies are largely correlational; some aspect of the working environment (hypothesized stress feature or control condition) is linked to a mental state such as anxiety or depression. Correlations do not imply causation; if it is the case that more car drivers involved in car accidents are wearing seat belts this does not imply that wearing seat belts causes car accidents. This is an important point to make because it could be argued that, to some extent, workers represent a self-selected group in different working conditions. Thus, it may be, for example, that depressed people are likely, by virtue of reduced competence or choice, to be more likely to be involved in certain kinds of employment. Those with low self-esteem might be more prepared to accept demeaning work or adverse conditions.

The second problem is that there is a natural tendency on the part of the investigators to select some aspects of a total working environment. Thus, there may be a particular hypothesized level of control. The effect of control level should interact with the objective and perceived level of stress; therefore low control in one job may not have the same overall result as low control in another. Also, the result of not having control is that the individual is exposed to the effects of the adverse conditions which prevail. Therefore in one environment the individual may have to tolerate, for example, restricted work posture; in another, high noise; in another, boredom; in another, unacceptably high event rates. In each case the level of control could be the same. It would be a mistake to attribute the differences to differences solely caused by control loss. Equally, from what has been argued previously, the level of control is a perception made by the individual which may take into account a number of domains of control. A worker may accept low control because it is part of a wider plan to work hard in adverse conditions and earn a high income so that he can retire early.

A third problem is that of a comparison group. If a comparison is to be made between blue and white collar work, which groups are selected as representative? The range of job activities may be so great within these two major groups that the within-group variation is at least as great as the between-group variation.

The influence of work on life and leisure

There are two arguments concerning the wider significance of experiences at work on the rest of the life of an individual. Firstly, it could be argued that the 'personal meaning' a person gives to the job is the important determinant of how pervasive an influence stress at work has. Those who perceive their jobs as nothing more than a means of earning money might be expected to be less affected than those who accept responsibility, perceive achievement at work as important, and are strongly committed to the job as part of their ambition for a successful life. It might be expected that blue and white collar workers differ in this respect. Rapoport and Rapoport (1965) argue that maximum involvement and commitment is likely for the professions, where occupational role is highly individualized, whereas in the low status occupations, there is little source of gratification and work has less salience or may be conceived as largely negative.

However, the result of national surveys of the hopes and fears of US citizens suggested that rather low importance was attached to 'good job' and 'congenial work', since these were mentioned by no more than 6 to 9 per cent. of respondents. Even unemployment was only mentioned by 10 to 14 per cent. of respondents. By contrast, good health and better living standards are two most frequent sources of hopes and fears for up to 40 per cent. of respondents (Cantril and Roll, 1971). Although Campbell, Converse, and Rodgers (1976) found higher levels of concern about job characteristics in that 38 per cent. of a national sample indicated that an interesting job was important, the result is in contrast with a much higher level for 'good health' (70 per cent.), a happy marriage (74 per cent.), good family life (67 per cent.), and a good country to live in (62 per cent.).

A second argument is that the conditions experienced at work have an importance in the lives of individuals, not because of wider personal significance but because the state of mind produced at work will carry over into home life. A person who experiences helplessness all day and feels depressed is spending a great proportion of his total life in an unpleasant mental or physical state. The point is that the daily experiences of white and blue collar workers may differ in accordance with control or jurisdication afforded. Therefore, there are differential effects on life.

Broadbent (1982) has developed the idea that conditions at work are likely to have a pervasive effect on life after work. He cites correlations of between 0.2 and 0.4 for job dissatisfaction with anxiety and depression respectively. Although the causal relationship remains unclear because there are groups of workers who differ in satisfaction levels and have the same mental health, and vice versa, the point of importance is that the job experience may have a profound influence on a person's life.

Moreover, work may not just influence psychological well-being through satisfaction; factors intrinsic to the physical design of the job may be influential. In a study of nurses, Parkes (1980) examined the effects of moving to a new hospital ward. Nurses who were assigned to stressful medical wards where there was low control over outcome and less sense of team involvement showed a rise in symptom level on the Middlesex Hospital Questionnaire.

A study by Arias-Galicia (1982) investigated the difference between those of 'managerial' status and operatives classified as 'technicians' or 'clerks'. The question of interest was whether managers are more anxious than operatives because of the increased decision-making demand. Two samples of employees were involved. The first sample of 92 males was taken from a government organization in Mexico City; 40 per cent. were managers, 35 per cent. were technicians, and 25 per cent. were clerks. The second sample of 83 males contained 52 per cent. blue collar workers and 48 per cent. managers. In both samples, managers were significantly less anxious than operatives, were more satisfied with their jobs, and experienced less conflict, although they took more work home. The finding is compatible with the results of Karasek (1981) from a sample taken at random from the Swedish male work force in that jobs with a low decision latitude (associated with low status occupations) provide an independent risk factor in coronary disease.

The Otmoor studies conducted by Jenner, Reynolds, and Harrison (1980) involved the sampling of populations in a group of villages north of Oxford in Britain. The results of analysis of levels of catecholamines in urine suggested that while in general executive, managerial, and professional occupations have high adrenaline levels relative to population norms, those groups engaged in repetitive manual work have the highest level of all groups. However, a finding in the Otmoor studies was that the difference between the white collar and blue collar groups is less evident on leisure days. This would argue against the proposal that work conditions have a pervasive influence on the rest of life after work.

One of the problems with differential comparisons of the effects of a job on the period immediately after work is that the groups involved with different jobs differ. For example, Frankenhaeuser and Johansson (1982) found evidence of raised adrenaline levels in computer programmers who spent 50 to 90 per cent. of their time at the keyboard as compared with a group who only spend about 10 per cent. of the time so employed. The effect was apparent not only during work but also after work. However, the groups differ in job status. Those spending less time were secretaries and typists; those spending more time were programmers.

The effort and distress model

The possibility that some situations require raised effort and result in high adrenaline levels and other situations involve distress with raised adrenaline and raised cortisol levels, provides the basis of a model proposed by Frankenhaeuser and colleagues. In a laboratory experiment quoted by Frankenhaeuser and Johansson (1982), subjects performed a choice reaction time task where there was a high degree of personal control. Subjects first established a preferred work pace and then were given an opportunity to make modifications during the task. Self-reports showed that the task was seen to induce 'effort' but no 'distresss'; the work conditions were thus perceived as pleasant. Hormone balance appeared to reflect these perceptions; adrenaline levels were increased but cortisol levels were reduced relative to a low control situation. Frankenhaeuser compared this result directly with an industrial situation involving control-room operators in which telephone, radio, and computer-based coordination of a steel plant was involved (Johansson and Sanden, 1982). The operators faced high demand, had high motivation and job satisfaction, and their physiological pattern was characterized by raised adrenaline and decreased cortisol levels.

A laboratory study of an externally paced, 1-hour, low control, light intensity detection task (Lundberg and Foresman, 1979; Frankenhaeuser, Lundberg, and Foresman, 1980; Lundberg and Frankenhaeuser, 1980) produced self-report data to suggest raised effort and distress, relative to a condition where there was control over the work pace. In an industrial setting, Johansson and Sanden investigated the effect of being presented with a monotonous process control task over which there was little jurisdiction. There were reported feelings of boredom and slight uneasiness accompanied by increased levels of adrenaline and cortisol.

It would be quite inappropriate to assume that all white collar jobs are characterized by high control and involve only increased effort whereas blue collar jobs are characterized by low control and distress. However, it is at least plausible that some features of the work environment encountered by blue collar workers may conform to the effect and distress paradigm because of the prevalence of low control as a feature of the job. The increasing use of computers in the working environment may reconcile the difference because of the demands made by the creation of a data base or by programming. The concept of a 'mental assembly-line task' may be increasingly applicable as a description of the job of some groups of white collar workers.

Loss of control as a factor in job stress

Recent industrial studies have emphasized the complexity of the relationship between job characteristics, job satisfaction, and mental health. For example, Broadbent and Gath (1979, 1981) report the results of studies of the effects of repetition and pacing in the car industry in Britain. Results listed by Broadbent and Gath (1981) show that repetition is associated with dislike of the job. However, in spite of Jenner's findings (Jenner, Reynolds, and Harrison, 1980) that repetitious environments are associated with high adrenaline levels, Broadbent and Gath's study showed no strong effect on anxiety; although the trend was towards increased anxiety, the result was only of borderline significance on a one-tailed test. By contrast, paced work is not necessarily disliked but is associated with anxiety and the effect is exacerbated for meticulous workers.

These findings are not easily handled by a control hypothesis. Loss of control over unpleasant conditions should be associated with the perception of helplessness and exposure to the effect of the adverse circumstance. The jobs associated with repetition should be associated with depression and anxiety as well as being disliked. The position with paced work is even more difficult because, according to the Broadbent and Gath results, workers are not dissatisfied in spite of the fact that anxiety is increased.

One possibility is that the total meaning a job has for the individual has to be considered. The notion of 'domains of control' discussed previously may need developing in the context of mental health and work. The results of surveys of different job characteristics and worker response led Broadbent and Gath (1979, p. 121) to point out that the objective nature of the job is less successful than prediction from the subjective perception of the job as departing from the ideal of the individual worker.

The impact of a job on health, whilst affected by a number of environmental factors, may be mediated by variables in a much wider context such as social relationships and financial rewards and leisure activities. These may give a person a sense of increased control in other domains and may provide a source of cognitive input which counteracts other negative inputs.

A model of the fit between the worker and his job was developed by Van Harrison (1978). The social environment and mental health research programme in Michigan has elaborated a model which makes provision for two kinds of fit between worker and job. The first is the match between the skills and abilities of the individual and the demands of the job. The second is the extent to which the work environment meets the individual's needs. A basic distinction is between the environment surrounding the person and cognitive representations. A good fit of person–environment (P–E fit) occurs if the job features are within the capabilities of the individual and when the total job environment meets the needs of the invididual in terms of money, social facilities, and opportunity for achievement.

Van Harrison further distinguishes the P–E fit between the *objective person* and the *objective environment* as compared with the *subjective person* and the *subjective environment*. An example provided by Van Harrison, which illustrates the four types of P–E fit is in terms of the typing speed of a secretary. A secretary who thinks she is able to type 55 words per minute (subjective person) may actually type 40 words per minute (objective person). The employer may expect 70 words per minute (objective environment) and the secretary may think she is expected to produce 60 words per minute (subjective environment). These P–E measures are all represented on the same dimension. Good P–E fit is associated with low discrepancy on each of the four comparisons and is assumed to be associated with good health. Discrepancies are associated with dissatisfaction, anxiety, complaints of insomnia, restlessness, and physiological symptoms of raised blood pressure, raised serum cholesterol, increased smoking, and overeating.

The complex relationship between job features, satisfaction, and mental health is not easily explained on the P–E fit model. In particular, it does not account for the cases where there is dissatisfaction but no change in mental health or change in mental health but no job dissatisfaction.

Warr and Wall (1975) emphasize that situations may occur where there are negative associations between job satisfaction, well-being, and mental health. Able trained immigrants or people unemployed in their own profession may find themselves restricted to menial work below their capabilities, or business employees keen to succeed may be held in check by their boss. In such cases, the need to achieve and express ability is thwarted so that job satisfaction and well-being may be low. Warr and Wall point out that such a reaction is not a sign of ill health. However, what they do not point out is it could eventually result in poor mental health since one of the inputs to knowledge on which the perception of control is based is ambition. Ambition dictates intentions and if these are thwarted by circumstance, perceived loss of control should result.

The analysis of job descriptions provided by Swedish and American workers by Karasek (1979, 1980) indicated two independent dimensions, one of which reflects work demand and one of which reflects control or discretion. Broadbent (1982) confirmed the findings of Karasek, but emphasized that for a sample of electricity workers, 'demand' was perceived in terms of the amount of 'slack' time spent alone or talking with people. Interestingly, the pacing of work was perceived of as related to 'demand' rather than control. This may help to explain why anxiety rather than depression is more likely as a response to paced work.

The two-dimensional view of job stress provides a basis for understanding some of the major differences between blue and white collar occupations. In the former, demand may be high but discretion is low, whereas for responsible white collar groups, demand and discretion are raised.

In the groups of electricity workers studied by Broadbent, there was a significant correlation between inability to talk to others at work and depression. It is also correlated with working much of the time alone. From the previously stated synthesis preesented by Broadbent, this could indirectly tie depression in with 'demand' since slack time creates opportunities for talking with others. Depression may, therefore, relate as much to demand as to jurisdiction and control.

AMELIORATING FACTORS IN JOB STRESS

Research which has been concerned with factors which appear to ameliorate job stress has emphasized the importance of the total meaning of 'job plus life' variables for the individual and raises the issue of 'domains of control' or 'control over what?'.

Social support

The finding that social interaction is a factor which helps to ward off depression in workers faced with tedious tasks is generally in keeping with the finding of Brown and Harris (1978) in the Camberwell studies, which showed that the working class women who were depressed were distinguished not only in terms of a set of circumstances such as poverty, isolation, and young children at home but by the lack of a confiding relationship with another person. However, the influence of social factors may have a different influence on depression at work. Observations with car workers and electricity workers suggest that general social interaction ameliorates depression. Fisher (1984) speculated that social interaction might provide alternative sources of information to offset an unpleasant job, might reduce the time a person had available to think about personal problems, may prevent a person becoming preoccupied with him/herself, and may provide a basis for sampling the opinions of others concerning personal difficulties. Generally, social interaction may help to create a feeling of control in the domain of interpersonal relationships. A person who is popular with work-mates may gain a feeling of control or well-being which could offset the unpleasant experiences associated with the job.

The Brown and Harris studies of women at home suggested a more profound influence of social support; depression was ameliorated by the presence of a confiding relationship. This may indicate that the exchange of personal ideas has a more important influence in cases where there are genuine life problems. Fisher (1984) has speculated that the person may be encouraged by a confidant to have a more realistic attitude about control in life, or to ward off self-blaming attributions in cases where experiences result in negative outcomes.

Leisure activities

Broadbent (1982) also reported evidence to suggest that commitment to a leisure activity may ameliorate depression at work. Satisfaction with leisure activity shows a main effect on anxiety and depression. However, there was no evidence of a simple interaction with either demand or control. In electricity workers, depression is a likely result if a person is unhappy with leisure and dissatisfied with work.

Fisher (1984) argued that a straightforward distraction hypothesis is less applicable because leisure occurs after work. A plausible explanation is that leisure pursuits create a means of 'control by irrelevant means' as described earlier. A person with low control over features of the job may gain from success and commitment to a leisure pursuit. The leisure pursuit thus provides a cognitive input which counteracts other situations of loss of control. Equally, success with a leisure activity may ward off the development of generalized tendencies towards internal attributions. Finally, there remains the possibility of reversed causal associations; ability to take up a satisfying leisure activity may reflect attitude to work or may be a manifestation of personality factors.

Rewards

Studies with paced work in the car industry has provided some information to suggest that monetary rewards can have an ameliorating effect. Broadbent

(1982) reported that monetary rewards for paced 'high demand' work is associated with reduction in anxiety. Broadbent argues that there is protection afforded by motives. It remains possible, as argued by Fisher (1984), that the effect may be one of tolerance; high arousal is interpreted in terms of anxiety in cases where monetary reward is low but in terms of being excited or aroused if monetary reward is high. The control model proposed in this chapter assumes that gains in one domain of control can ameliorate unpleasant experiences associated with loss of control in others. Thus a person may accept an unpleasant working condition if paid a high wage because the high wage enables better control over other domains of life to be obtained.

SUMMARY AND CONCLUSIONS

Differential pressures between blue and white collar workers

It could be argued that comparison between white collar and blue collar groups does not provide a sensitive enough analysis of the role of stress and control at work. In spite of this a few general comparisons might be made. The blue collar worker faces a greater range of industrial hazards and uncomfortable physical working conditions than do white collar groups and, by virtue of his/her status, has reduced possibility for control. He/she also has less jurisdiction over whether or not he/she leaves the job because he/she has less income and reduced options. On this analysis the blue collar worker should incur more distress at work.

The white collar worker may pay a price for more jurisdiction over his/her working environment. This may be particularly evident when he occupies a superordinate position in an organizational structure. Raised effort needed may not be offset by increased control; the managerial employee may need to accept decisions made by those in higher level positions. Therefore, effort and distress may be characteristic.

In addition, the white collar worker may incur the pressures of avoiding conflicts and confrontations in social relations at work. Since part of his/her job may involve dealing with colleagues, he may become an 'executive monkey' in certain cases avoiding difficult situations by pre-empting the decisions of others or meeting deadlines. The blue collar worker may be protected from these pressures.

Domains of control

The simple distinctions between effort and discretion as main factors in determining job strain (Karasek, 1979), now needs further development to take account of the domain of control in which a worker operates and the possible way in which social and leisure activities may off-set unpleasant working conditions. The white collar worker continues to have the advantage over the blue collar worker in that the opportunities for social activity at work are greater if there is more discretion. Equally, greater income and educational opportunity should increase the range and interest of leisure and holiday pursuits. the blue collar worker has less means of off-setting adverse work environments by control in other domains.

ACKNOWLEDGEMENT

I would like to acknowledge the help given by George McPherson, who read and commented on the early drafts of the article.

REFERENCES

Abramson, L. Y., Seligman, M. E. P., and Teasdale, J. D. (1978). Learned helplessness in humans: critique and reformulation, *Journal of Abnormal Psychology*, **87**, 49–74.

Arias-Galicia, F. (1982). Job level and anxiety, Presented at the 20th International Congress of Applied Psychology, Edinburgh, 25–31 July.

Atkinson, J. W. (1957). Motivational determinants of risk taking behaviour, *Psychological Review*, **64**, 359–327.

Atkinson, J. W., and Feather, N. (Eds.) (1966). *A Theory of Achievement Motivation*, John Wiley, New York.

Averill, J. R. (1969). Autonomic response patterns during sadness and mirth, *Psychophysiology*, **5**, 399–414.

Ax, A. F. (1953). The physiological differentiation between fear and anger in humans, *Psychological Medicine*, **15**, 433–442.

Ball, T. S., and Vogler, R. E. (1971). Uncertain pain and the pain of uncertainty, *Perceptual Motor Skills*, **33**, 1195–1203.

Brady, J. V., Porter, R. W., Conrad, D. G., and Mason, J. W. (1958). Avoidance behaviour and the development of gastroduodenal ulcers, *Journal of the Experimental Analysis of Behaviour*, **1**, 69–72.

Broadbent, D. E. (1982). Some relations between clinical and occupational psychology, Paper delivered at the 20th International Congress of Applied Psychology, Edinburgh, 25–31 July.

Broadbent, D. E., and Gath, D. (1979)

Broadbent, D. E., and Gath, D. (1981). Ill-health on the line: sorting out myth from fact, *Employment Gazette*, March, 157–160.

Brown, G. W., and Harris, T. H. (1978). *The Social Origins of Depression: A Study of Psychiatric Disorders in Women*, Tavistock, U.K.

Campbell, A., Converse, P. E., and Rodgers, W. L. (1976). *The Quality of American Life*, Russell Foundation, New York.

Cantril, A. H., and Roll, C. W. (1971). *Hopes and Fears of American People*, Universe Books, New York.

Carruthers, M. (1974). *The Western Way of Death*, Davis-Paynter, London.

Dolgun, A. (1965). *Alexander Dolgun's Story: An American in the Gulag*, Knopf, New York.

Fisher, S. (1983). Pessimistic noise effects: the perception of reaction time in noise, *Canadian Journal of Psychology*, **37** (2), 258–271.

Fisher, S. (1984). *Stress and the Perception of Control*, Lawrence Erlbaum Associates, London.

Fisher, S. (1985). *Stress and Strategy*, Lawrence Erlbaum Associates, London.

Frankenhaeuser, M., and Johansson, J. (1982). Stress at work: psychobiological and psychosocial aspects, Paper presented at the 20th International Congress of Applied Psychology, Edinburgh, 25–31 July.

Frankenhaeuser, M., Lundberg, U., and Foresman, L. (1980). Dissociation between sympathetic-adrenal and pituitary-adrenal response to an achievement situation characterized by high controllability: comparison between type A and type B males and females, *Biological Psychology*, **10**, 79–91.

Friedman, M., Rosenman, R., and Carroll, V. (1958). Changes in the serum cholesterol and blood clotting time in men subjected to cyclic variation of occupational stress, *Circulation*, **XVII**, 852–861.

Garber, J., and Hollen, S. D. (1980). Universal versus personal helplessness in depression: belief in uncontrollability or incompetence, *Journal of Abnormal Psychology*, **89** (1), 56–66.

Glass, D. C., Rheim, B., and Singer, J. E. (1971). Behaviour consequences of adaptation to controllable and uncontrollable noise, *Journal of Experimental Social Psychology*, **7**, 244–257.

Glass, D. C., and Singer, J. E. (1972). *Urban Stress: Experiments on Noise and Social Stressors*, Academic Press, New York.

Glass, D. C., Singer, J. E., and Friedman, L. N. (1969). Psychic cost of adaptation to an environmental stressor, *Journal of Personality and Social Psychology*, **12**, 200–210.

Griffin, J. H. (1962). *Black Like Me*, Houghton-Mifflin, Boston, Mass.

Haggard, E. A. (1943). Experimental studies in affective processes. I. Some effects of cognitive structure and active participation on certain autonomic reactions during and following experimentally induced stress, *Journal of Experimental Psychology*, **33**, 257–284.

Hiroto, D. S. (1974). Locus of control and learned helplessness, *Journal of Experimental Psychology*, **102**, 187–193.

Hiroto, D. S., and Seligman, M. E. P. (1975). Generality of learned helplessness in man, *Journal of Personality and Social Psychology*, **14**, 263–270.

Horney, K. (1937). *Neurotic Personality of Our Times*, Norton, New York.

Jenner, D. A., Reynolds, V., and Harrison, G. A. (1980). Catecholamine excretion rates and occupation, *Ergonomics*, **23**, 237–246.

Johansson, G., and Sanden, P. (1982). Mental load and job satisfaction of control room operators, Rapporter (Department of Psychology, University of Stockholm) No. 40.

Julian, J. W., and Katz, S. B. (1968). Internal versus external control and the value of reinforcement, *Journal of Personality and Social Psychology*, **76**, 43–48.

Karasek, R. A. (1979). Job demands, job decision latitude, and mental strain: implication for job re-design, *Administrative Science Quarterly*, **24**, 285–309.

Karasek, R. (1980). Job socialization and job strain, the implications of two related mechanisms for job design. In *Man and Working Life* (Eds. B. Gardell and G. Johansson), John Wiley and Sons, London.

Karasek, R. (1981). Job decision latitude, job demands and cardiovascular disease: a prospective study of Swedish men, *American Journal of Public Health*, **71** (7), 694–705.

Lefcourt, H. M. (1966). *Locus of Control*, Lawrence Erlbaum Associates, Hillsdale, N.J.

Lefcourt, H. M. (1972). Recent developments in the study of the locus of control. In

Progress in Experimental Personality Research (Ed. B. A. Maher), Academic Press, New York.

Lefcourt, H. M. (Ed.) (1981). *Research with the Locus of Control Construct*, Vol. I, *Assessment Methods*, Academic Press, New York.

Lefcourt, H. M., and Ludwig, G. W. (1965). The American Negro: a problem in expectancies, *Journal of Personality and Social Psychology*, 1, 377–380.

Lundberg, U., and Foresman, L. (1979). Adrenal-medullary and adrenal-corticol responses to under-stimulation and over-stimulation, *Biological Psychology*, 91, 79–89.

Lundberg, U., and Frankenhaeuser, M. (1980). Pituitary-adrenal and sympathetico-adrenal correlates of distress and effort, *Journal of Psychosomatic Research*, 24, 125–130.

McClelland, D. C. (1961). *The Achieving Society*, Van Nostrand, New York.

McClelland, D. C., Atkinson, J. W., Clarke, R. W., and Lowell, E. L. (1953). *The Achievement Motive*, Appleton Century Crofts, New York.

Miller, S. M. (1979). Controllability and human stress: method, evidence and theory, *Behaviour Research and Therapy*, 17, 287–304.

Mills, I. H. (1973). Biological factors in international relations. In *The Year Book of World Affairs*, Vol. 27, The London Institute of World Affairs, Stevens and Sons Ltd., London.

Mouton, R. (1965). Effects of success and failure on level of aspiration as related to achievement motives, *Journal of Personality and Social Psychology*, 1, 399–406.

Mowrer, O. H., and Viek, P. (1948). An experimental analogue of fear from a sense of helplessness, *Journal of Abnormal Social Psychology*, 43, 193–200.

Parkes, K. R. (1980). Occupational stress among nurses: 1, *Nursing Times*, 76, 113–116. Occasional Paper No. 25.

Paulhus, D., and Christie, R. (1981). Spheres of control. In *Research with the Locus of Control Construct*, Vol. I, *Assessment Methods* (Ed. H. Lefcourt), Academic Press, New York.

Pervin, L. A. (1963). The need to predict and control under conditions of threat, *Journal of Personality*, 31, 570–587.

Peterson, C. (1982). Learned helplessness and attributional interventions in depression. In *Attributions and Psychological Change* (Eds. C. Antaki and C. Brewin), Academic Press, London, New York.

Poulton, E. C. (1978). Stress and blue collar work. In *Stress at Work* (Eds. C. Cooper and R. Payne), John Wiley, New York.

Prociuk, T. J., and Breen, L. J. (1976). Machiavellianism and locus of control, *Journal of Social Psychology*, 98, 141–142.

Rapoport, R., and Rapoport, R. (1965). Work and the family in contemporary society, *American Sociological Review*, 30.

Rotter, J. B. (1954). *Social Learning and Clinical Psychology*, Prentice Hall, Englewood Cliffs, N.J.

Rotter, J. B. (1966). Generalized expectancies for internal versus external control of reinforcement, *Psychological Monographs*, 80.

Rotter, J. B., and Mulry, R. C. (1965). Internal versus external control of reinforcements and decision time, *Journal of Personality and Social Psychology*, 2, 598–604.

Seeman, M. (1963). Alienation and social learning in a reformatory, *American Journal of Sociology*, 69, 270–284.

Seeman, M., and Evans, J. W. (1962). Alienation and learning in a hospital setting, *American Sociological Review*, 27, 772–783.

Seligman, M. E. P. (1975). *Helplessness: On Depression Development and Death*,

    Freeman, San Francisco, Calif.
Van Harrison, R. (1978). Person–environment fit and job stress. In *Stress at Work* (Eds. C. L. Cooper and R. Payne), John Wiley, London.
Warr, P., and Wall, T. (1975). *Work and Well-being*, Penguin Books, Harmondsworth, U.K.
Weiss, J. M. (1968). Effects of coping responses on stress, *Journal of Comparative and Physiological Psychology*, **65,** 251–266.
Welford, A. T. (1960). *Ergonomics of Automation. Problems of Progress in Industry*, No. 8, HMSO, London.
White, R. W. (1959). Motivation re-considered: the concept of competence, *Psychological Review*, **66,** 297–333.

PART TWO

Stressful Working Conditions and Situations

Job Stress and Blue Collar Work
Edited by C. L. Cooper and M. J. Smith
© 1985 John Wiley & Sons Ltd

Chapter 4

Machine-paced Work and Stress

Michael J. Smith

Department of Industrial Engineering,
University of Wisconsin, Madison, Wis., USA

INTRODUCTION

Paced work goes back to the earliest of people's endeavours to engage in activities together. When people and/or machines are linked together, they have had to adjust their rate of work to each other. This is the essence of teamwork—adjusting to your coworker's capabilities. Thus, the stonemasons of ancient Egypt had to coordinate their rate of work with the stonecutters and the ox-cart drivers. The galley slave rowers of ancient Rome and Greece had to keep their rowing tempo coordinated or face a disastrous result in battle. Coordinating with other persons seems to be a natural fact of life in community living and working, and is accepted by almost everyone. Coordinating with inanimate objects such as machines, however, particularly regarding the rate of activity, is a different matter. Most people dislike having to modify their activities to meet the demands of a machine. The machine that defines the rate of work and possibly even the methods of work does not provide the same sense of control as a tool over which the person exerts influence. In this instance, the person loses control of how and when they will do work and becomes an appendage of the machine. This is the major detraction of machine-paced work—the loss of a sense of controlling the work process.

CLASSIFICATION OF PACED WORK

Salvendy (1981) has classified paced work by the demand that it places on the worker. He defines two major categories, human-paced and machine-paced work, each of which has four subclassifications:

Human-paced work:

1. Unpaced work in which there is no external pairing or no personal

motivational characteristics that impose a speed demand. This is work performed at a 'freely chosen pace' preferred by the worker.

2. Socially paced work which has no external machinery or management imposed rate, but there is peer group pressure to perform at set paces.
3. Self-paced work which has no external machine-generated rate but is paced by management objectives. In this type of pacing the worker can vary the rate of work over the course óf the work cycle (day, week, month, project) to meet objectives set for the end of the work cycle.
4. Incentive-paced work which has two components, neither of which is determined by the machinery. The first component is a self-paced aspect that allows for personal variation in the rate over the work cycle to meet management objectives. The second is a personal motivational component that determines the self-paced rate based on the worker's desire to earn wages.

Machine-paced work:

1. Work-cycle-paced activities define the rate of work by the cycle time of each machine operation. With shorter cycle times (seconds, a few minutes) there is less opportunity for a worker to vary the rate of performing specific tasks. With longer cycle times this machine-paced activity approaches the human-paced condition of self-paced work.
2. Paced work with buffer stocks is a situation in which machine operators have a supply of materials to work on and are not linked to other operators. Thus, if a machine cycle is missed only the machine is affected, not a large number of linked machines.
3. Continuous paced operations are those in which the machine operates by machine actuation such as a conveyor assembly line. In such operations the worker is tied to other workers and a failure to perform his task will influence their ability to perform.
4. Discrete paced operations can be either a single operator or linked operators and can be self-actuated by the operator or by the machine actuation. They differ from continuous paced operations in that there are discrete breaks in the actuation cycle. This allows operators time to build a stockpile to be used if they are linked to other operators and miss a cycle or two for rest periods, or stockpiles can be used for added incentive pay. These discrete breaks may alternatively be used for preparatory work for the next cycle if materials are not available for stockpiling or for rest breaks.

This classification of paced work allows us to compare the characteristics of various paced systems to define potential problem areas in each and to establish the strengths and weaknesses of each. Remembering that loss of control over the work process is a major stressor for workers, it is observed that various forms of paced work influence the amount of worker control quite differently. For instance, short cycle time machine-paced work seems to afford the least amount of worker control, especially if the process is machine actuated. In such a case, the operator works mainly as a high-speed feeder of stock into the machine. There is no opportunity for controlling the machine actuation, for taking a break, or for developing a stock buffer. When this process is tied to a conveyor linking workers together, the added pressure to not miss a cycle enhances the stress on the worker. Contrastingly, self-paced work allows the opportunity for the worker to define the rate of work and also allows the worker to exert control over the process. The worker, in essence, can use any work techniques desired. This opportunity extends the benefits beyond control of the process, to acquiring personal satisfaction in carrying out the process and completing the end product.

That the issue of control over the work process is central to the examination of paced work is exemplified by a taxonomy of paced work proposed by Dainoff, Hurrell, and Happ (1981). In this taxonomy the initialization and duration can be controlled by the operator or by the machine or a combination of both. The extent to which the operator exerts control defines the potential stress effects. Unpaced work is that in which the operator controls both the initiation and duration of the work cycle. In one type of paced work the tasks are initiated by the machine but the duration of the cycle time is controlled by the operator. Dainoff, Hurrell, and Happ (1981) suggest that an example of this type of activity is a telephone switchboard operator since the machinery initiates the process and the operator controls the length of the call. However, for this example, it is known that management imposes call-time limits and a quota of calls to be processed which are limiting factors in the operator's control of the call duration. As Salvendy (1981) has demonstrated, it is not only the machinery that influences the pacing process, but also management policies and personal motivation. Thus, a more appropriate example might be an air traffic controller who responds to a request from the radio and radar screen for an airplane to land, but who has control over the timing of the landing process.

In a second type of paced work, the operator determines the initiation of the task, but the machinery determines the duration of the work cycle time. Murrell (1963) provides an example of this type of work:

> This type of pacing is found when girls feed machines with parts which simply have to be picked up from a bin and placed in an appropriate position. The operator feeds parts into a waiting machine; the machine then processes it while the operator is prevented from loading another part.

The third type of paced work is that most often associated with pacing, in which the machinery controls both the initiation of the work cycle and its duration. Using Murrell's (1963) example of the girls feeding the machine, the operator loads stock into the machine, but at a pace that the machine sets, because it is self-actuating. Thus, they have no control over the rate of actuation or the machine cycle time and are only the feeding extension of the machine. This is the most meagre of work, devoid of content and meaning and threatened by extinction due to improved technology such as automated machine feeders and robots.

As can be seen, paced work can be defined in various ways based on the influences on the work process, such as cycle time, and control over the process, such as in the initiation of the process. It can also be defined by its effects on the workers in the various paced processes.

SELECT EPIDEMIOLOGICAL FINDINGS ON THE EFFECTS OF PACED WORK

The influence of paced work on employee safety and health can best be illustrated by examining select studies involving work systems with different pacing characteristics which demonstrate various effects. These include physiological stress reactions, biomechanical strain, health complaints, and psychological mood disturbances.

Frankenhaeuser and Gardell (1976) studied sawmill workers exposed to various levels of machine-paced work and varying workloads. Expert ratings of ergonomic conditions were used to classify stress-related characteristics of the work. Worker self-reports of psychological strain and ill health were collected along with urine samples to measure worker excretion of adrenaline and noradrenaline. These measures were felt to give a total picture of stress exposure and resultant strain effects as they included third party ratings of stress, as well as worker perceptions, and physiological indices. Additionally, the working population was in a rural area of Sweden, isolated from the rigours of urbanlife. This was felt to be a perfect setting to study the impact of the production technology without the extreme stress of urban living. In addition, the participants were a healthy group of workers.

Two groups of sawmill workers were studied to compare the influence of the work pacing and workload. One group consisted of 14 paced workers with highly repetitive tasks requiring heavy physical activity. This was a job with high attention demands, heavy workload, short cycle time, and machine control of work pace. A second group of 10 workers were engaged in jobs that allowed for freedom to make decisions; they were not tied to machines so their work pace was self-controlled, as was their workload. Both groups were two shift workers and all workers were paid on a group incentive.

Results of data evaluation indicated that the machine-paced workers had higher levels of adrenaline over the course of the workday. In fact, there tended to be a build-up in adrenaline over the course of the day for the paced workers, while the non-paced workers showed a decrease in adrenaline excretion over the course of the day. While this study did not examine the adrenaline excretion pattern off the job, in a later study of paced workers Johansson (1981) demonstrated that paced workers maintain higher levels of adrenaline during the off-the-job hours. In the current study paced workers complained of an inability to 'unwind' or relax after working all day. Additionally, they reported being too tired to interact with their spouse and children after working all day.

A central factor in the worker reactions to the machine-paced work appeared to be the degree of repetitiveness of the work. Using workers self-reports of repetitiveness, comparisons were made in the level of adrenaline excreted. As the worker's perception of repetitiveness increased, so did the level of adrenaline excreted. A related effect was observed for worker well-being. Workers reporting lower levels of repetition reported the highest ratings of personal well-being. Interestingly enough, there did not seem to be a similar finding between strain measures and work cycle time, with one exception. Those cycle types requiring less than 5 seconds to complete were related to higher adrenaline excretion. However, this influence could be confounded by a higher workload in these operations which would increase adrenaline outputs.

Overall, the results of this study demonstrate that machine-paced workers report more psychological strain and greater psychophysical reactions than non-paced workers. These effects can be traced to the worker's lack of control over the work processs and the repetitious nature of the job tasks.

Broadbent and Gath (1981) studied workers in a British auto assembly plant to determine if work pacing had adverse mental health consequences. This study was undertaken because medical records at the plant indicated that there were more patients from the assembly-line operation reporting 'anxiousness' than from elsewhere in the plant. As an initial effort they decided to use a mental health questionnaire (The Middlesex Hospital Questionnaire) to design an interview instrument to examine anxiety levels in the assembly-line workers. The interview form also had questions about the extent of pacing, repetition, cycle time, physical effort, and other general questions about the task activity.

Interviews were made by trained female health care staff of paced and unpaced workers from two auto manufacturing plants. As there were paced and unpaced workers in each plant, comparisons were made between workers within each plant. In total there were 285 men interviewed, representing various degrees of repetitive work and paced work. Two main mental health factors, job dissatisfaction and anxiety, were evaluated for differences between repetitive work and non-repetitive work, and for pacing effects within repetitive work.

The results in the first plant indicated that repetitive work produced greater job dissatisfaction than non-repetitive work, but that pacing did not influence job dissatisfaction. However, for anxiety a different pattern emerged. Repetitive work only had an influence for paced assembly workers, but not for semipaced or unpaced assemblers. The findings from the second plant confirmed this result in that repetitive paced assemblers reported greater job dissatisfaction and anxiety than non-repetitive, unpaced workers. Another important finding was that the cycle time of the operation had no influence on worker job dissatisfaction or anxiety.

My colleagues and I at the National Institute for Occupational Safety and Health have conducted a number of evaluations of machine-paced work (Arndt, Hurrell, and Smith, 1981; Hurrell and Smith, 1981; Smith, Hurrell, and Murphy, 1981; Stammerjohn and Wilkes, 1981; Wilkes, Stammerjohn, and Lalich, 1981). These studies have concerned the biomechanical and psychological stresses imposed by paced work. Smith, Hurrell, and Murphy (1981) and Hurrell and Smith (1981) studied over 3000 machine-paced letter-sorting machine operators and over 3000 unpaced workers using a psycho-social questionnaire that evaluated working conditions, personal character-istics, job demands, and health complaints (physical and mental). Machine-paced mail sorting is of particular interest because of the short cycle time, the repetitive nature of the task, and the total control of the process by the machinery. Operators are automatically fed a piece of mail at approximately one every second and have to make the appropriate keying response to get the letter sorted to the proper bin. Sometimes the response is simply to key three or four digits of the zip code from the envelope. Other times the operator must memorize a keying code to sort sets of zip codes to the same bin or different bins. Thus, the cognitive complexity of the task changes, but the specific demands in terms of pace remain constant, as does the control of the process by the machinery.

The results of various studies (Arndt, Hurrell, and Smith, 1981; Hurrell and Smith, 1981; Smith, Hurrell, and Murphy, 1981) show a similar pattern of stress and strain in the paced operators. That is, they show high levels of visual and muscular strain that can be related to the task demands, as well as high levels of dissatisfaction, work pressure, and psychosomatic complaints. In the Smith, Hurrell, and Murphy (1981) evaluation, the machine-paced workers reported greater physical complaints about sore eyes, tired eyes, neck pain, and sore wrists than non-paced workers, as well as more psycho-somatic complaints. These included nervousness, fatigue, heartburn, stomach pains, and gas pains. They also reported greater work pressure, more task dis-satisfaction, and more job dissatisfaction. However, they reported greater satisfaction with their employer than non-paced workers, an unpredictable result.

Arndt, Hurrell, and Smith (1981) also studied mail-sorting machine operators, but looked at a small group (approximately 50) prospectively over a period of three years. As with the Smith, Hurrell, and Murphy study, Arndt, Hurrell, and Smith found both physical and psychosomatic problems. It was also found that job satisfaction decreased over the three years, while boredom increased. When employees were asked about the amount of pacing they would like in their work, the amount desired became less and less each year, which could be a demonstration of a decreased tolerance for pacing with greater paced work experience. Psychological mood states as measured through standardized tests showed a great deal of variability throughout the study. There were no consistent changes in adrenaline or nonadrenaline measurements. Thus, the results showed increased physical disorders, varying psychological moods, and inconsistent biological effects with increased job dissatisfaction and pacing dissatisfaction.

Stammerjohn and Wilkes (1981) used a similar questionnaire survey instrument as the Smith, Hurrell, and Murphy (1981) study to evaluate paced work in an assembly-line paced inspection task. Workers studied were over 400 paced poultry inspectors carrying out government mandated health inspections of processed chickens and approximately 200 workers with lesser exposure to the paced inspection procedures. Using data from just the 400 paced inspectors, the investigators examined the relationship between perceived stress and strain using a P–E fit model (French and Caplan, 1970) in which employees were asked to rank the work pace, and then various effects of pacing (such as job dissatisfaction) were compared for workers who had different perceptions of the work pace (too high, about right, too low).

The results indicated that workers who felt that the pace was too fast reported more job dissatisfaction, more boredom, and more workload dissatisfaction. When psychological effects were examined, both the workers who felt the pace was too fast or too slow reported more anxiety, depression, and anger, with those reporting too fast a pace having the highest scores.

Wilkes, Stammerjohn, and Lalich (1981) compared health effects and the extent of exposure to pacing by using the number of hours worked per week at the paced job as a measure of exposure. Results showed that the greater the exposure to paced work the higher the level of self-reported psychological and somatic complaints. Full-time paced workers reported greater workload, more underutilization of their abilities, and more boredom. They also reported higher levels of visual, muscular, and gastrointestinal disturbances. Comparison of the responses of this study group to resposes of 23 other occupations on the same psychological measures (Caplan et al., 1975) indicated that the full-time paced workers showed an almost identical pattern to that of machine-paced assemblers in the prior study, thus demonstrating a consistency in the effects of paced work.

PROBLEMATIC ASPECTS OF PACED WORK

The epidemiological studies are consistent in pinpointing aspects of machine-paced work that contribute to employee dissatisfaction, stress, and ill health. These aspects are (1) lack of control over the work process, (2) the repetitious nature of the work task, and (3) the amount of work pressure felt by the employee which is directly related to the rate or pace of the work.

Lack of control

The need to exert control over the environment through self-regulation of perceptual-motor and cognitive processes in a basic human need that is continually striven for (Smith and Smith, 1966). This need is reflected in our neurophysiological make-up and our behavioural mechanisms for exerting control over our environment. Cognitive feedback and motives direct our actions while sensory feedback guides our responses to the desired goal. These basic mechanisms have important temporal and spatial relationships that must be adhered to within very strict limits or our ability to perform is seriously degraded. Thus there is a critical relationship between our environment and the temporal consistencies demanded by the organism. Disruption of these intricate timing mechanisms produce behavioural disturbances such as reduced performance and can have profound effects on psychological processes. Reduction in the ability to control the timing of work processes because of pacing may produce disruption in these basic temporal mechanisms and cause undesired behavioural and/or psychological effects.

These critical timing functions are well known to be influenced by shift work and overtime work (Rutenfranz et al., 1977; Cooper and Marshall, 1976). Circadian variations in bodily functions are disturbed by changes in the light/dark cycle (Ashoff, 1981). It is reasonable to assume that these same rhythms can be disrupted by pacing patterns that are not in synchrony with basic body rhythms. It is recognized that the bodily rhythms vary throughout the day. Many pacing systems do not allow for variable activity during the course of the work day; rather they force the operator to maintain a constant performance level throughout the day. This is counter to the natural variation in bodily functions over the course of the day and may produce health problems similar to those of shift workers. Such a pattern seems to emerge from the findings from the epidemiological studies (Broadbent and Gath, 1981; Smith, Hurrell, and Murphy, 1981), which show that paced operators report sleep disturbances and gastrointestinal disorders, two conditions prominent in shift workers.

Karasek (1981) pooled date from various national surveys of cardio-vascular health and job satisfaction, as well as job demand surveys to study the way in which decision latitude and job demands influence cardiovascular disease risk. His findings indicate that jobs with high demand and low decision latitude (job control) have the highest rates of psychological disturbances and coronary heart disease. Thus, paced jobs which also impose high levels of demand and work pressure are at increased risk for cardio-vascular and psychological disturbancess.

In assessing the need for control over the work task and its health consequences, particularly in terms of stress, there is almost universal agreement among experts that lack of control is bad and will influence health adversely. The research evidence for this is not substantial, but the logic is. Averill (1973) stated that lack of control in terms of not being able to make an adequate response is a critical ingredient for stress to occur. Mandler and Watson (1966) defined a similar relationship such that any condition that interrupts organized response patterns and does not provide an alternatively adequate response will produce stress.

These arguments seem to favour short cycle paced systems as they provide for predictable, organized response patterns. Thus such paced systems may allow for greater employee task control by minimizing the complexity of the response and by increasing the predictability of the next response. Clearly, then, it is not just a lack of decision latitude that influences worker perceptions of control, but also an ability to respond in the stimulus condition. Pacing has its negative points when it comes to task control. The search for the critical aspect(s) of paced work that is problematic must look to other factors, as well, such as repetition.

Repetition

Concern about workers becoming cogs in a wheel or mere machine appendages that load and unload machines that perform the sophisticated aspects of the work seem to be well borne out in paced work. Chase (1975) has determined that as assembly lines get longer, they tend to result in more fractionated tasks and therefore permit little flexibility and socialization with fellow workers. It seems that repetition, fractionalization of tasks, cycle time, and rate of pacing are all interconnected, with the greater the task fractionalization, the more the repetition with timing flexibility. As the task becomes more fractionated and repetitive, the timing cycle gets shorter, allowing less opportunity for variable behaviour from workers. The length of the task cycle and the work pace are the prime determinants of the extent of disruption of body rhythms.

While Broadbent and Gath (1981) did not find that cycle time influenced the effects of pacing, their study examined jobs with relatively long task cycles (minutes in length). Thus, one might expect that disruption of basic bodily rhythms and associated health disturbances would be mitigated as they allow for some variation in behaviour within the cycle itself. Frankenhaeuser and Gardell (1976) found that only cycle times of less than 5 seconds seemed to produce increased adverse effects. Smith, Hurrell, and Murphy (1981) and Stammerjohn and Wilkes (1981) studied jobs with very short cycle times (seconds). These studies demonstrated pronounced psychosomatic effects; while the measures in these studies differed from those of Broadbent and Gath (1981), as did the work tasks, it appears that the shorter cycles showed more profound effects. These activities were more fractionated and more repetitive. In fact, their repetitive nature and the frequency of the work cycle are prime suspects in the physical trauma, such as neck and wrist disorders, that plagued these workers.

Another problem with repetition is that the task content is reduced to enhance the ability of workers to perform tasks quickly. This work simplification coupled with repetition has been associated with worker job dissatisfaction, boredom, and alienation from work (Cooper and Marshall, 1976). Gardell (1971) has stated that challenge and pride in work are fundamental psychological needs that can lead to ill health if unmet. He further states that critical aspects of work that influence a worker's perceptions of challenge and pride in work are the ability to exert control over the work and socialization on the job. Frankenhaeuser and Gardell (1976) found that mechanically controlled work pace that contributes to standardized motion patterns and constant repetition of short cycle operations are the prime factors in lack of job control and loss of socialization on the job which lead to worker stress.

Conway (1977) suggests that certain classes of workers, such as introverts, enjoy assembly-line work with short cycle time and constant repetition. This type of work operation produces isolation and thus they are not required to interact with others. However, while their desire for reduced social contact may be met in these operations, there may still be a disruption of basic biological rhythms that could lead to psychosomatic problems.

A crucial aspect of repetition and cycle time is the limitation that these factors place on worker interaction with other workers. In 1947, Merton stated that it is clear that new production processes and equipment inevitably affect the social relations among workers. Changes in work routine modify the immediate social environment such as the size and composition of the work team, the number and type of contacts with coworkers, worker status, and the degree of physical mobility in conducting a task. He concluded his admonition of these changes by identifying two key aspects that contribute to reduced worker socialization. These are the fractionation of tasks on assembly lines and the introduction of pacing in assembly lines. As paced systems produce greater and greater social isolation, their impact on worker stress in terms of direct effects, and reduced buffering of stress is increased. This is becoming more pronounced as high technology is used in assembly-line processes.

A detailed review of research into repetitive work can be found in Cox's chapter (Chapter 6).

Work pressure

A consistent finding in studies examining paced work is that the most affected employees report high levels of work pressure and workloads (Frankenhaeuser and Gardell, 1976; Caplan et al., 1975; Smith, Hurrell, and Murphy, 1981; Wilkes, Stammerjohn, and Lalich, 1981). This is particularly true for job tasks with very short cycle times (seconds). Do short cycle tasks require increased energy expenditure because they involve continuous motion patterns and thus adversely affect employees? This may be the case, since paced workers performing tasks that are not very taxing, such as keying the mail codes, report just as much work pressure or workload (Smith, Hurrell, and Murphy, 1981) as workers in more demanding tasks, such as sawmill workers (Frankenhaeuser and Gardell, 1976) and poultry inspectors (Wilkes, Stammerjohn, and Lalich, 1981). Thus, the level of activity seems to be more significant to the perception of workload and work pressure than the magnitude of exertion required. This suggests that short cycle repetitive tasks may be more detrimental to worker health than tasks requiring higher energy expenditure with longer cycle times. This may be true for both ergonomic consideration of chronic trauma (Smith, Hurrell, and Murphy, 1981) and for psychosocial processes related to worker perception of stress.

Another significant factor related to employee perception of workload and work pressure is the method of worker payment. In particular, incentive pay schemes can be tied to a high level of worker energy expenditure, often above healthful limits. When these schemes are also tied to social considerations, such as with group incentive schemes, then work pressure can be increased through social obligations and pressures. Frankenhaeuser and Gardell (1976) found adverse psychophysiological effects of paced work in workers being paid on a group incentive. This is an unusual work situation as paced workers typically cannot control their own rate of workload; thus incentives have little chance of influencing performance. More often, an unpaced work operation tends to take on the characteristics of a machine-paced situation when incentive pay schemes are introduced. This is due to the simplification of the work tasks to allow for the setting of incentive rates, and the self-imposition of short cycle times and repetitive actions by employees trying to make as much money as they can. As the work system becomes more and more like machine-paced work, the employees will begin to experience the adverse effects of paced work.

CONCLUSIONS

Machine-paced work seems to be an inevitable aspect of industrialized society. It is introduced because many employers do not believe that employees will work fast enough or hard enough for them to make adequate profits. It is easier to plan work systems if greater control in the variability of production pace can be attained. It is easier to control the distribution of raw materials and other resources in a controlled system such as machine-paced operations. It is more efficient to assemble parts in an assembly-line fashion than at individual workstations. In essence, it is an effective way to control the production process and eliminate variability. These benefits of paced work operations have costs for the workers engaged in machine-paced work. There are definite health consequences of paced work such as psychological disorders, biophysiological disturbances, and psychosomatic illness, which tend to become more pronounced with greater machine control and shorter cycle time.

Much like shift work, the effects of paced work are systemic. They influence basic biological processes. It is quite clear that all aspects of our biology and behaviour vary over the course of the day in a natural pattern. This variation called 'diurnal cycles' is the body's way of shifting gear to change speed when energy requirements change or to conserve energy when possible. A major biological problem that machine-paced work introduces is the demand for constant performance throughout the workday. This is unnatural and contrary to the basic biological variability that our bodies strive to achieve. Thus, there can be disruption of biological rhythms with paced work just like that seen in shift work. Disturbances of sleep, psychological disturbances, and gastrointestinal disorders are the result.

Can the effects of machine-paced work be mitigated much like those of shift work? To answer this, the basic problematic features of paced work need to be identified and a determination made to find out if they can be modified. The literature is clear in defining the three most problematic aspects of paced work as (1) short cycle time, (2) repetitious tasks, and (3) high work pressure or production demand. These factors are changeable, but not without some major rethinking about the purpose of machine-paced work. If paced jobs have more variety built in, and cycle times are increased due to an increase in task complexity, and if production pressure can be decreased, then it is possible that a paced work system would not produce ill effects. However, such changes would be major shifts in the basic concepts underlying the use of machine-paced work systems. They are contrary to the basic work simplification concepts that underlie paced work and that fragment tasks to make them easier to perform in shorter cycles. They are contrary to the production mentality that requires squeezing every last ounce of energy out of each employee every day. No, it is not impossible to change machine-paced work systems, to reduce their adverse influences; it is just not very likely to happen, given the principles on which these systems are based.

REFERENCES

Arndt, R., Hurrell, J., and Smith, M. J. (1981). Comparison of biochemical and survey results of a four-year study of letter-sorting machine operators. In *Machine Pacing and Occupational Stress* (Eds. G. Salvendy and M. J. SMith), Taylor and Francis Ltd., London, pp. 311–318.

Ashoff, J. (1981). Circadian rhythms; interference with and dependence on work–rest schedules. In *The Twenty-four Hour Workday* (Eds. C. Johnson, D. Tepor, W. Colquboun, and M. Colligan), National Institute for Occupational Safety and Health, Cincinnati, Ohio.

Averill, J. R. (1973). Personal control over aversive stimuli and its relationship to stress, *Psychological Bulletin*, **80**, 286–303.

Broadbent, D. E., and Gath, D. (1981). Symptom levels in assembly-line workers. In *Machine Pacing and Occupational Stress* (Eds. G. Salvendy and M. J. Smith), Taylor and Francis Ltd., London, pp. 243–252.

Caplan, R. D., Cobb, S., French, J. R. P., Harrison, R. V., and Pinneau, S. R. (1975). *Job Demands and Worker Health*, National Institute for Occupational Safety and Health, Cincinnati, Ohio.

Chase, R. B. (1975). Strategic considerations in assembly-line selection, *California Management Review*, **28**, 17–23.

Conway, K. (1977). *Differential Health and Safety Effects of Paced Versus Nonpaced Work—A Review of the Literature*, National Institute for Occupational Safety and Health, Cincinnati, Ohio.

Cooper, C. L., and Marshall, J. (1976). Occupational sources of stress: a review of the literature relating to coronary heart disease and mental ill health, *Journal of Occupational Psychology*, **49**, 11–28.

Dainoff, M. J., Hurrell, J., and Happ, A. (1981). A taxonomic framework for the description and evaluation of paced work. In *Machine Pacing and Occupational Stress* (Eds. G. Salvendy and M. J. Smith), Taylor and Francis Ltd., London, pp. 185–190.

Frankenhaeuser, M., and Gardell, B. (1976). Underload and overload in working life: outline of a multisisciplinary approach, *Journal of Human Stress*, **2**, 35–46.

French, J. R. P., and Caplan, R. D. (1970). Psychosocial factors in coronary heart disease, *Industrial Medicine*, **39**, 383–397.

Gardell, B. (1971). Alienation and mental health in the modern industrial environment. In *Society, Stress and Disease* Vol. I (Ed. L. Levi).

House, J. S., and Wells, J. A. (1977). Occupational stress, social support and health. In *Reducing Occupational Stress* (Ed. A. McLean), national Institute for Occupational Safety and Health, Cincinnati, Ohio.

Hurrell, J., and Smith, M. L. (1981). Sources of stress among machine-paced letter-sorting-machine operators. In *Machine Pacing and Occupational Stress* (Eds. G. Salvendy and M. J. Smith), Taylor and Francis Ltd., London, pp. 253–260.

Johansson, G. (1981). Psychoneuroendorine correlates of unpaced and paced performance. In *Machine Pacing and Occupational Stress* (Eds. G. Salvendy and M. J. Smith), Taylor and Francis Ltd., London, pp. 277–286.

Karasek, R. (1981). Job design latitude, job design and coronary heart disease. In *Machine Pacing and Occupational Stress* (Eds. G. Salvendy and M. J. Smith), Taylor and Francis Ltd., London, pp. 45–46.

Mandler, G., and Watson, D. L. (1966). *Anxiety and the Interruption of Behavior*, Academic Press, New York.

Murrell, K. (1963). Laboratory studies in paced work, 1 and 2, *International Journal of Production Research*, **2**, 169–185.

Rutenfranz, J., Colquhoun, W., Knauth, P., and Ghata, J. (1977). Biomedical and psychosocial aspects of shift work, *Scandinavian Journal of Work Environment and Health*, **3**, 165–182.

Salvendy, G. (1981). Classification and characteristics of paced work. In *Machine*

Pacing and Occupational Stress (Eds. G. Salvendy and M. J. Smith), Taylor and Francis Ltd., London, pp. 5–12.

Smith, M. J., Hurrell, J., and Murphy, R. K. (1981). Stress and health effects in paced and unpaced work. In *Machine Pacing and Occupational Stress* (Eds. G. Salvendy and M. J. Smith), Taylor and Francis Ltd., London, pp. 261–268.

Smith, K. U., and Smith, M. F. (1966). *Cybernetic Principles of Learning and Educational Design*, Holt, Rinehart and Winston, Inc., New York.

Stammerjohn, L. W., and Wilkes, B. (1981). Stress/strain and linespeed in paced work. In *Machine Pacing and Occupational Stress* (Eds. G. Salvendy and M. J. Smith), Taylor and Francis Ltd., London, pp. 287–294.

Wilkes, B., Stammerjohn, L., and Lalich, N. (1981). Job demands and worker health in machine-paced poultry inspection, *Scandinavian Journal of Work Environment and Health*, Suppl. 4, 12–19.

Chapter 5

Shift Work

Timothy H. Monk
Department of Psychiatry,
University of Pittsburgh,
Pittsburgh, Pennsylvania, USA
and
Donald I. Tepas
Department of Psychology,
University of Connecticut at Storrs,
Storrs, Connecticut, USA

INTRODUCTION

The human being is not naturally a nocturnal creature. Activity is usually concentrated in the daylight hours, with the night given over to rest. Recent research has indicated that human beings have a powerful time-keeping system (or 'body clock') whose primary aim is to enforce regular cycles of sleep and diurnal activity in our behaviour. Night work involves patterns of behaviour that are essentially unnatural.

Clearly, a pattern of behaviour can be unnatural without being harmful. Indeed, many activities of modern life, such as living in air-conditioned rooms or travelling in cars, may be termed unnatural. The harm that such activities may cause does not necessarily result directly from their 'unnaturalness', but, rather, from an inability of the human being to adjust to them. They can be considered potential sources of stress that may in some situations and in some individuals lead to harm. In a similar way, shift work is an unnatural activity which, under some circumstances, can lead to problems and eventually harm.

Although many like to think that shift work is a scourge of the modern age, heralded by the invention of electric light, it has actually been a part of human working life since the days of ancient Rome (Scherrer, 1981). In those days the congestion in the streets was relieved by decreeing that all deliveries be made during the night hours. Similarly, bakers of bread have been working through the second half of the night for many centuries. However, there is a great deal of difference between the small, often elite, group of shift workers characteristic of earlier ages and the vast cohorts of people currently working abnormal hours.

At present it is estimated that over 20 per cent. of the working population in Europe and North America is working some form of shift system (Tasto and Colligan, 1978). Because this percentage is so high, and because of world-wide increases in unemployment, the population of shift workers can no longer be a self-selected one. We are now seeing people being forced by economic necessity to work on schedules with which they feel uncomfortable. This 'discomfort' can range from slight feelings of malaise and social inconvenience to major medical problems and domestic distress.

Clearly, the level of distress that is experienced will depend not only upon factors related to the individual and his/her situation, but also to the precise schedule being worked. Some schedules are relatively benign, requiring little or no night work, while others can be considered harmful in their requirement of unbroken spells of night duty and/or inappropriate shift rotation. Unfortunately, as we shall see later, it is not possible to make overall generalizations as to what is the best shift system. Additional information about the individual, the physical load of the job, and the requirements of the plant must also be considered. It is probably safe to conclude, however, that for many blue collar jobs, the slower the rotation the better, with permanent shifts being easiest to cope with (Tasto and Colligan, 1978). In contrast, some forms of weekly shift rotation or rotation in the wrong direction may be difficult or impossible to cope with. These issues will be discussed further, in reference to factors related to the human circadian system.

THE CIRCADIAN SYSTEM

As common sense tells us, sleep cannot simply be taken 'at will'. There are certain times during the day when we find it very difficult indeed to fall asleep, and even if we eventually do, such sleeps are usually much shorter than the 'standard' 7 or 8 hours. From studies made under carefully controlled laboratory conditions, we know that this is not due simply to daytime noise or light levels keeping us awake, but to the workings of an internal ('endogenous') biological time-keeping system telling our brain and body that 'this is the time for wakefulness'. This endogenous system is referred to as the 'circadian system' (from the Latin; circa—about, dies—a day), since it involves cycles or rhythms that are about 24 hours in length. As we shall see later, the 'circa' part of this label is important, since these rhythms (in the human) are often closer to 25 hours in period when they are totally unrestrained.

Study of the human circadian system is a relatively new phenomenon, with most of the major experiments dating from the 1960s, 1970s, and 1980s. Early studies (e.g. Siffre et al., 1966) involved subjects who lived for several months in caves that completely isolated them from the time cues and temporal demands of the world outside. These studies demonstrated that the pattern of sleeping and waking did not simply fall apart under such conditions, but retained its integrity at a period that was about one hour longer than the 24-hour rotation period of the earth. That finding was confirmed in a large series of laboratory studies which used underground bunkers for isolation rather than a cave. These bunkers provided all the shielding from light, noise, and other daily time cues provided by caves, but with greater comfort and safety for the subject, and a much more sophisticated monitoring system for the experimenter (Wever, 1979). From the study of over 150 subjects in such 'free-running' experiments, the average period was found to be 25 hours with a standard deviation of 0.5 hour (Wever, 1985). Thus, after about three and a half weeks, an average subject might think that he had been underground for 24 days (in terms of his own cycles of sleep and wakefulness) when in fact he had been underground for 25 (calendar) days. Similar findings have come from above-ground time isolation laboratories (Weitzman *et al.*, 1982), confirming the generality of the earlier results.

Zeitgebers

Clearly, in normal real life we do not live on 25-hour cycles, and there must thus be some mechanism that allows our bilogical clock to reset itself, enabling it to stay in synchrony with the 24-hour routine. This mechanism requires that time cues or 'zeitgebers' (from the German for 'time giver') can input to the circadian system, driving it at the required period. Under a normal day-working routine, the zeitgeber mechanism simply makes the minor corrections needed to keep the circadian system running at exactly 24 hours. In shift work, and after cross-time-zone air flights, however, the effect of zeitgebers is more complex. Because the biological circadian system *is* endogenous and self-sustaining, it has a certain resistance to change. Thus, one cannot instantaneously reset the circadian system as one might reset a more conventional clock. As we shall see later on, many days are needed, and during this time the zeitgebers representing the new routine will be trying to assert their influence on the circadian system.

Zeitgebers can be either physical (i.e. natural) or social in origin. Physical zeitgebers include the rising and setting of the sun, and the noises of the natural world, as well as perhaps more subtle influences such as electro-magnetic fields (Wever, 1979). Social zeitgebers include knowledge of clock time, meal timings, traffic noise, and numerous other social factors.

Expert opinion is divided on the issue of which of the two types of zeitgeber is the more important in man. In the 1970s, the dominant view was that social cues were the more important, with the role of daylight being played down. However, more recent research has emphasized the circadian importance of a hormone (melatonin) which is only suppressed when daylight levels of illumination are encountered (Wehr and Goodwin, 1981). Thus, there is a move towards more emphasis being placed on the physical zeitgebers.

This debate is, of course, of more than simply academic interest to the shift worker. Unlike the air traveller, the shift worker is subject to conflicting zeitgeber information. Thus, although the traveller arrives at his/her destination to find that both social and physical cues are working to encourage adjustment of the circadian system to the new routine, the shift worker finds that the physical zeitgebers are *resolutely* opposed to adjustment and, since society is daytime oriented, the social zeitgebers need not be supportive of adjustment either. Since the circadian system takes a week to adjust to a flight-related 6-hour change in routine (Klein, Wegman, and Hunt, 1972), it is not surprising to find that many experts assert that the circadian system never completely adapts to nightwork (Knauth and Rutenfranz, 1976).

From the above discussion, it is clear that we are not yet in a position to give any definitive list of important zeitgebers for man, or an explanation of the exact mechanism by which they impinge on the circadian system. From some basic research on the circadian system (mostly using people isolated from time in chambers and bunkers) we can, however, begin to pinpoint the areas which are important, and thus begin to suggest strategies that the shift worker might find helpful. This research is the subject of the next section.

Basic research

There are four major points about the circadian system that basic research has taught us. From these four points hang a vast array of very much more complex findings which may be vital to our understanding of human physiology and psychology, but which have a less fundamental direct impact on the shift worker.

The first point is that the circadian system is indeed endogenous, i.e. internal to the human being, and not reliant for its existence on changes in the individual's gross behaviour or immediate environment. This is most elegantly shown in a series of experiments by Froberg and his associates (1977) in Sweden, who studied groups of people experiencing 72 hours of sleep deprivation. These studies took place under conditions of temporal isolation, with subjects ignorant of the time of day, mostly sedentary, and fed a monotonous diet, devoid of all time cues. Figures 1 and 2 illustrate typical findings. For both a physiological measure (body temperature) and a psychological one (subjective alertness or vigilance), there was a strong circadian oscillation superimposed on the gradual decline throughout the 72 hours of the vigil. Thus, for example, the circadian oscillation caused the subjects to feel more alert 58 hours into the vigil than they did at 40 hours. Since sleep was prevented and all the other variables were controlled, we can conclude that the oscillations were stemming from an internal (endogenous) process, rather than either an external influence or a simple reaction to changes in behaviour (sleep versus wakefulness). Thus the shift worker should always

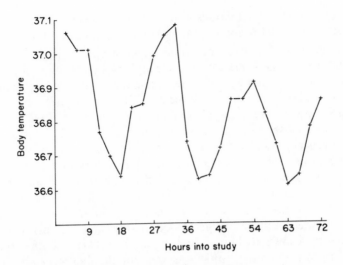

Figure 1 The average body temperature of 15 subjects experiencing 72 hours of sleep deprivation under constant conditions. (After Froberg, 1977)

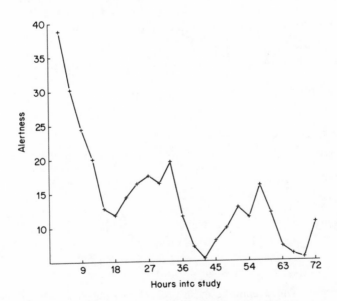

Figure 2 The average subjective alertness of 15 subjects experiencing 72 hours of sleep deprivation under constant conditions. (After Froberg, 1977)

bear in mind that these fluctuations or oscillations will persist to some degree, whatever is being done (or not being done) in terms of routine.

The second point has been mentioned before and is that the circadian system tends to run 'slow' relative to the exact 24-hour rotation of the Earth. This has been determined by longer term temporal isolation experiments, in which sleep is permitted with the subject totally free to select the timing of meals and sleep ('free-running' experiments). As we pointed out, subjective days tend to be closer to 25 hours in length, rather than 24 hours. Figure 3 illustrates the sleep/wake cycle of a 23 year old man who was studied by Weitzman and his colleagues (1982) at the Laboratory of Human Chrono-physiology. The experiment started and ended with 5 days of entrainment to an exactly 24-hour routine, with a two-week period of free-running in between. During the entrainment periods, the subject was in temporal isolation, but was told when to go to bed, get up, and take his meals. That routine was (unknown to him) based on his habitual 'at home' schedule, calculated from a sleep diary that was kept for the two weeks prior to the experiment. During the free-running period, the subject was entirely free to make all decisions regarding sleep and meals.

In the figure, times of sleep (and darkness) are represented by the dark bars, with each day plotted twice, a total of 48 hours being represented across the top. 'Day of study' (marked in minutes) runs down the page from the top, with the last day appearing at the bottom of the figure. The fact that the dark bars during free-running do not line up immediately below each other indicates that the subject's free-running 'days' were not exactly 24 hours in

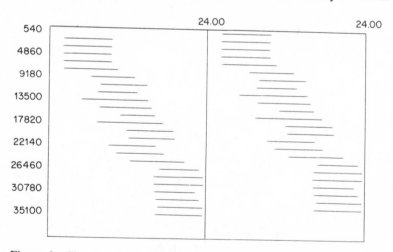

Figure 3   The sleep/wake cycle of a 23-year-old male subject experiencing two weeks of free-running under temporal isolation. This was preceded and followed by 5 days of entrainment to his habitual routine. The solid line represents the time asleep (see text)

length. By fitting a straight line to the beginning of each sleep period, we can obtain an estimate of the period or length of the subject's 'day'. In this example, the period length happened to be 24.7 hours, that is 0.7 hour or 42 minutes slower than 24 hours.

The fact that the human circadian system tends to run slow has important ramifications regarding phase adjustment (i.e. the resetting of the body clock). It suggests that the circadian system would find it easier to cope with changes that cause a phase delay (i.e. a further 'stretching' of the day length) rather than those which cause a phase advance (involving a 'shrinking' of day length). For the air traveller crossing multiple time zones, this would correspond to the prediction that westward flights (phase delays) would involve less of a disruption to the circadian system than eastward ones (phase advances). As Figure 4 shows, this prediction has been verified to a modest degree by Klein and his associates (Klein, Wegman, and Hunt, 1972), who compared 6-hour eastward and westward time zone changes, estimating the rate of phase adjustment in the circadian rhythms of body temperature and performance efficiency.

For the rotating shift worker, the prediction would be that the forward direction of rotation (from mornings to evenings to nights to mornings) would be easier for the circadian system to cope with than the backward direction (from mornings to nights to evenings to mornings). Unfortunately, there has not been a study of shift workers that definitively tests this prediction,

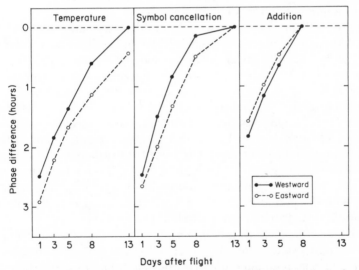

Figure 4   The phase adjustment of the circadian rhythms in body temperature and performance on different tasks to westward and eastward 6-hour time zone transitions. (After Klein, Wegman, and Hunt, 1972. Reproduced by permission of Elsevier Biomedical Press from Folkard and Monk, 1982)

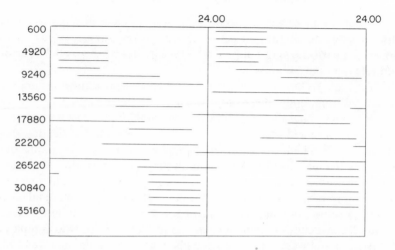

Figure 5 The sleep/wake cycle of a 22-year-old male subject experiencing two weeks of free-running under temporal isolation. This was preceded and followed by 5 days of entrainment to his habitual routine. The solid line represents the time asleep (see text)

although Czeisler, Moore-Ede, and Coleman (1982) in their potash plant study, did show that a change from backward to forward rotation *when combined with a slowdown in shift rotation speed* did produce improvements in employee well-being and production efficiency.

The third finding is concerned with the multifaceted nature of the circadian system. Although the preceding discussion has emphasized the regularity and integrity of the circadian system, there are individuals and situations in which the sleep/wake cycle can appear to be very irregular, with extremely long or short sleep periods occurring. This is referred to as 'spontaneous desynchronization', and often occurs at the end of an otherwise regular free-running episode. An illustration of spontaneous desynchronization, observed in a 22 year old man, is given in Figure 5. Contrary to initial impressions, this desynchronization does not represent a chaotic breakdown of the circadian system. Rather, it appears to represent a condition in which the cycles of sleep/wake and body temperature simply break apart, running at different periods, with the period of the sleep/wake cycle being considerably longer than that of the body temperature rhythm. The importance of this to the shift worker is that it demands a less simplistic view of the factors governing an individual's sleep/wake cycle. Thus, there is not just one controlling oscillator in the circadian system, but (at least) two—one primarily responsible for the sleep/wake cycle, the other for the body temperature rhythm. Thus there is not one biological clock that needs resetting, but many; evidence that one component of the circadian system has adjusted to night work, for example, does not necessarily indicate that the whole system has.

The fourth finding is that these two oscillator systems are not independent. Isolation studies show that the two oscillators can influence each other, with the duration of the sleep episode correlated with the temperature phase at sleep onset (Czeisler *et al.*, 1980). This relationship can be crucially important for the shift worker, who may often try to fall asleep at 'inappropriate' phases of the circadian temperature cycle. Thus, at some times of the day *biological principles alone* may shorten or interrupt sleep episodes. Additionally, as Moses *et al.* (1978) have confirmed, there are some phases of the circadian system in which naps are 'expected' by the circadian system and are thus more restorative to the individual.

Basic research has thus demonstrated that the circadian system is a multifaceted one, with at least two endogenous oscillators or sets of oscillators governing the observed rhythmicity. The oscillator governing the temperature rhythm is referred to as the 'Group I' (Wever, 1975) or 'X' (Kronauer *et al.*, 1982) oscillator and that responsible more for the sleep/wake cycle as the 'Group II' or 'Y' oscillator. The former is considerably less labile than the latter, taking many days to adjust fully to a change in routine. Additionally, the two oscillators operate in an interactive way, so that the duration of a sleep episode depends upon the state of the temperature oscillator at sleep onset. Finally, it appears that both oscillators tend naturally to run 'slow', suggesting that shift rotation in a phase-delay direction might be more easy for the circadian system to cope with than shift rotation in the phase-advance direction.

PERFORMANCE

Not surprisingly, the circadian fluctuations in physiology which we have discussed are reflected in equivalent fluctuations in mood and performance efficiency. Studies of diurnal variation in human performance predate the invention of the terms 'free-running' and 'circadian' by about half a century. Early studies were concerned primarily with the scheduling of school timetables, and used cognitive tasks such as memory for prose and mental arithmetic. Although their findings were not uniformly consistent (see Lavie, 1980, for an excellent review), Gates (1916) concluded that 'in general, the forenoon is the best time for strictly mental work ... while the afternoon might best be taken up with school subjects in which motor factors are predominant'. Gates' conclusion is interesting both in postulating a morning superiority in cognitive (mental) performance, and in differentiating between cognitive and motor tasks. The afternoon inferiority in cognitive performance was held to result from a build-up in mental fatigue, and these early studies thus considered diurnal variation in performance to result from a 'time since waking' effect. The differentiation between cognitive and simple repetitive tasks is particularly important when contemporary studies are considered.

A rather different approach to the study of circadian performance rhythms was pioneered by Kleitman (1939, revised 1963) who was particularly impressed by the parallelism that appeared to exist between the circadian variation in performance and that in body temperature. In contrast to the early school timetabling studies, Kleitman's research favoured tasks with a low cognitive load, such as card dealing and choice reaction. In a series of studies, Kleitman found that performance on these tasks tended to follow the temperature rhythm, even during the process of phase adjustment to an acute change in routine. He thus concluded that there was a causal relationship between temperature and performance. In a later, much more extensive series of studies, Colquhoun and his associates (Colquhoun, Blake, and Edwards, 1968a, 1968b, 1969) confirmed this finding, although they were careful to emphasize *parallelism* between temperature and performance, rather than a causal link. Again, Colquhoun's tasks were mainly those requiring either the maintenance of vigilance, or a simple throughput of information. Interestingly, when a more cognitive digit-span task was used, a very different time of day function emerged, with performance peaking about 12 hours earlier than the temperature peak (Blake, 1967). Conceptually, however, performance was still tied to the temperature oscillator using the mechanism of an 'arousal rhythm' which was held to be parallel to the temperature rhythm, with some tasks suffering a decline over the waking day due to 'super-optimal arousal' (Hockey and Colquhoun, 1972).

During the last ten years, this notion of a single performance rhythm tied exclusively to the temperature rhythm (and thus its oscillator) has been cast in doubt. In 1975, Folkard found a mid-day superiority in verbal reasoning performance and later Folkard *et al.* (1976) were able to radically affect the time of day function by systematically varying the memory load of a task. Neither of these results fitted perfectly with the 'arousal rhythm' model (Monk, 1982). More important in terms of oscillatory control was the finding that intertask differences in phase (time of peak) were also reflected in differences in the *rate* at which circadian performance rhythms phase-adjusted to a change in routine (Monk *et al.*, 1978; Folkard and Monk, 1982). Such rate differences are unlikely to be explicable in terms of simple control by the deep oscillator.

Very recently, groups at both Erling-Andechs (Folkard, Wever, and Wildgruber, 1983) and New York (Monk *et al.*, 1983b, 1984) have sought to investigate the oscillator control aspect directly by causing the two oscillators to run at different periods. Such experiments have revealed that while simple repetitive (e.g. motor) tasks are indeed under deep oscillator control, different processes are involved when more cognitive tasks are considered. Such processes can either involve shorter circadian periodicities (Folkard, Wever, and Wildgruber, 1983; Monk *et al.*, 1984) or simply a strong measure of control from the more labile sleep/wake oscillator (Monk *et al.*, 1983b).

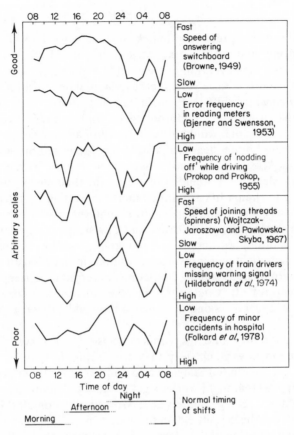

Figure 6   Variation in job performance over the
24-hour period. (After Folkard and Monk, 1979)

From the point of view of blue collar shift worker performance, however, it is probably safe to conclude that for many tasks the performance rhythm will parallel the body temperature rhythm, thus showing decrements during the night hours. This conclusion is confirmed when the circadian variation in actual 'on-the-job' performance is measured for various tasks. Figure 6 illustrates a collection of such tasks, and there is clear evidence that performance at night is inferior to that during the day (Folkard and Monk, 1979). It should be remembered, however, that this effect might be caused by more than simple circadian performance rhythms. There is also likely to be a partial sleep deprivation effect (see below), and also performance decrements due to the shift work equivalent of 'jet-lag'. Shift differences may also exist in the working environment. Ambient lighting levels, supervision levels, machine maintenance, and the actual type of work done are sometimes very different at night.

SLEEP

Sleep is the major preoccupation of most shift workers (Rutenfranz et al., 1977). Indeed, some shift workers assert that if only they could solve their sleep problem, then everything else would be quite tolerable. However, as we have seen from the basic research described above, disrupted sleep may be both a *symptom* of shift work maladjustment and a *cause* of it. Thus, it is unlikely that a simple soundproofing of shift workers' bedrooms (even if economically feasible) would provide much of an improvement in sleep. This is demonstrated quite clearly in a study by Tepas and his associates (Walsh, Tepas, and Moss, 1981) who brought actual shift workers into a sound attenuated, electrically shielded bedroom for their sleeps, with the subjects commuting to their work from the laboratory, rather than from home. Even in this closely shielded sleep environment there was a highly significant difference in sleep length between the day sleeps of night workers and the night sleeps of day workers. These polygraphic studies of sleep indicate that for permanent night workers these reductions in sleep length include changes in the pattern of sleep staging (sometimes referred to as sleep microstructure or architecture). It would appear that for most night workers these differences in sleep staging are what one would expect if they were sleep-deprived.

These laboratory findings confirm those from surveys in which shift workers report how much sleep they are getting. In both Europe (Knauth et al., 1980) and the United States (Tasto and Colligan, 1978; Tepas et al., 1981) it would appear that night workers get about 5 to 7 hours less sleep per week than their day-working counterparts. Most workers on all shifts sleep longer on days off, but there is little data to suggest that workers as a rule are able to totally make up for workday sleep loss in this manner. As a result of this, the partial sleep deprivation of workdays becomes a *chronic* state of partial sleep deprivation for many experienced night workers (Tepas, 1982a). Thus, *in addition* to the mood and performance efficiency fluctuations associated with the circadian system, night work may lead to performance decrements associated with sleep deprivation. The negative effects of sleep deprivation on performance and mood have been well demonstrated. Just as different tasks show different circadian fluctuations, the effects of sleep deprivation on various tasks differs (Williams, Lubin, and Goodnow, 1959). For some tasks, the *interaction* of circadian and sleep deprivation effects may result in very large decrements in night work on the job performance and safety.

It is important to remember that the sleep deprivation of night work has two major origins: firstly, circadian system fluctuations which make sleeping more difficult at some times of the day and, secondly, the self-selected strategies for off-the-job sleep which are used by workers. In most cases, workers are not educated as to how to cope with night work. The strategies which they pick may not be the best ones for them or in keeping with professional recommendations for good sleep and chronohygiene. It is reasonable to argue that the magnitude of sleep deprivation effects might be reduced if workers were provided with educational programmes which show them some of the potential problems associated with sleep and circadian variations, as well as alternative ways of coping with such factors (Tepas, 1982b). Informational programmes of this sort are one way an employer can make efforts to minimize the degree to which a worker's domestic and social factors affect shift work productivity.

DOMESTIC AND SOCIAL ADJUSTMENT

Hitherto we have mainly concentrated on the biological aspects of sleep and circadian rhythms. Human beings are, however, social creatures, and one could argue that the social and domestic factors are at least as important as the biological ones (Walker, 1978, 1985). Both are heavily interrelated, though, and many of the domestic frictions that arise may stem from the shift worker's problems of getting enough sleep, blaming household noises for disruptions that are often more endogenous in origin. Not all the night worker's problems come from circadian disruption, however. For example, while few people would consider visiting or telephoning a day worker at 1:00 a.m., few would avoid doing so to a night worker at 1:00 p.m. Thus the night worker lacks the social taboos that serve to protect the day worker's sleep. Moreover, there are also domestic pressures that can erode a shift worker's sleep time. Most common of these are the child care and household management tasks that are often expected of a female shift worker.

This is illustrated in a study of 50 night nurses conducted by Folkard, Monk, and Lobban, and reported in Monk and Folkard (1985). Half of the nurses were part-time (two nights per week) with 96 per cent. of them having children living with them at home; the other half were full-timers (four nights per week) with only 36 per cent. of them having children at home. The study took place over the first two nights of a run of duty following some time off. From the sleep logs of the two groups (Figure 7) it is clear that the full-timers were getting more sleep than the part-timers, with the latter even taking naps during their 'lunch' break in order to try and catch up.

Another aspect of domestic disruption concerns the role of the shift worker as spouse and parent. With regard to the former, there are three major spouse roles that are affected: sexual partner, social companion, and protector/care giver. All three roles are compromised, and very often the problems are trivialized by a concentration on the first of the three, whereas the other two are often much more important to the couple involved. Feelings of loneliness and insecurity in a wife left alone at home every night, for example, are for many much more chronic and insoluble than those connected with the timing of lovemaking. Similarly, the afternoon/evening shift, which has minimal

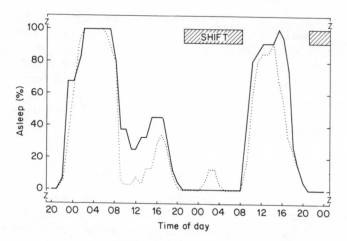

Figure 7   The percentage of full-time (solid line) and part-time (dotted line) night nurses asleep before, during, and after the first of a period of successive night shifts. (After Monk and Folkard, 1985)

impact on the sleep and circadian factors, can have a crushing impact on the role of the shift worker as social companion. With regard to the family role of parent, the afternoon/evening shift is again often disruptive if it means that during the school year the shift worker will not see his children for days on end. Additionally, both spouse and parent roles are heavily disrupted when the shift worker is required to work at weekends.

In addition to disrupted family roles, the shift worker often suffers from social isolation from day-working friends and community organizations that work under the expectation that evenings and/or weekends will be free for meetings and activities. Clearly, the extent to which that is a problem will depend very much on the particular individuals involved, but one can advance the view that perhaps a shift worker who is denied access to community meetings and social and political associations is as much disadvantaged as a handicapped person who is denied wheelchair access to a museum. Certainly it is clear that in certain 'company towns', where shift work is the rule rather than the exception, with social and community life geared accordingly, shift work seems to be very much better tolerated (Wedderburn, 1967).

The impact of shift work on domestic and social life is not always a negative one. Some shift workers report that they preferred their schedule when their children were of a pre-school age, since it allowed them to spend more time with them during their waking hours. Single parents with older children sometimes prefer the night shift since it makes it easier for them to arrange for other people to monitor their children while they are at work. For continuing education courses of all kinds, it may be fairly easy for a permanent night shift worker to schedule classes; it would be impossible for a rotating shift worker to attend any class on a regular basis. Hourly workers may have to suffer a loss in wages or vacation time when they need to visit a doctor or lawyer who offers only daytime hours, whereas a night worker can easily visit a doctor or lawyer during the work week without a loss of income or vacation time. For most workers the overall impact of shift work on their social lives is probably a negative one, but for a select few it may be the one way they can cope with their problems. Even when shift work is the best coping method for a particular worker, one must continue to recognize that the bulk of society is daytime-oriented and thereby prevents this worker from living a 'normal' life.

HEALTH

The health consequences of shift work are important, and there are a number of good reviews in the literature (e.g. Rutenfranz et al., 1977; Rutenfranz, Haider, and Koller, 1985). Obviously, a healthy worker will find shift work more easy to cope with than a sick one. There are, however, several different ways in which health factors can operate. Firstly, and most important, is the general loss of strength and well-being that occurs in ill-health. As discussed later in reference to age, shift work can be considered as a stressor, and additional stressors may lead to a breakdown in the individual that might not have appeared had multiple stressors not been coincident (Monk and Folkard, 1983). The second way in which health factors can operate is through sleep. Many diseases are associated either directly or indirectly with a disruption of the sleep process. These disruptions can occur in several ways: disruptive effects of disease symptoms such as pain and coughing, which arouse the person from sleep and thus have sleep disturbance as a secondary symptom; some sleep disorders such as narcolepsy and sleep apnea have sleep disruption as a major feature; other diseases of the central nervous system (e.g. Parkinson's disease) can have sleep disruption as a major direct symptom; some medicines (e.g. antihypertensive medications) can either directly or indirectly interfere with sleep; many psychiatric disorders (e.g. depression) have sleep disruption as a symptom; and drug and alcohol abuse can quite severely disrupt the sleep process.

Also, the effects of the shift work itself may exacerbate certain diseases. Epileptic seizures, for example, are more frequent under sleep deprivation, and for that reason might preclude the patient from doing shift work. Also, since gastrointestinal distress is sometimes associated with shift work, those suffering from ulcers, or other gastrointestinal complaints, might well be counselled against shift-working (Rutenfranz et al., 1977). Other diseases such as diabetes can require medication on a regular periodic basis which might be interfered with by the changes in schedule that shift work requires.

At the present time there is not sufficient data to support the notion that shift work invariably leads to a specific disease or illness. Furthermore, there is no reason to expect that further research will lead to such a finding. Just as sleep problems result in a variety of health problems and adequate sleep is required for relief from many illnesses, the same should be expected of shift work. The important thing is that both workers and employers should recognize that these diverse potential health hazards do exist so that appropriate preventive action is taken.

AGE

As the shift worker progresses into his/her fifties, one might expect that coping with shift work would start to get easier. Income would probably be increasing with seniority, bringing the opportunity of better housing; the family is likely to have grown up and left home, leaving fewer domestic responsibilities and less daytime noise; less sleep may be needed than when younger; and several decades of experience would have been acquired in mastering the art of coping with shift work. Paradoxically, this is exactly what does *not* happen. Instead, it appears that as the shift worker enters his/her fifties, things start to get dramatically worse. This issue is one of the most crucial to shift work research, since it bears on the whole question of whether or not shift work is 'harmful'.

There is now fairly good evidence that at a 'certain age' in the late forties or early fifties, for some, shift work suddenly becomes intolerable (Akerstedt and Torsvall, 1981). Reinberg characterizes it as the time of life at which glasses become needed for reading. The analogy is a good one, for the change is a combination of a gradual deterioration in physical ability, punctuated by an irrevocable admission of defeat.

It is possible to consider ageing effects within the framework of four possible contributory factors: (1) cumulative adverse shift work effects (since age is usually associated with experience); (2) a general decline in the worker's health and ability to cope with stressors; (3) changes in circadian rhythms; and (4) a tendency towards sleep fragility.

The first factor is potentially the most disturbing, since it suggests that prolonged experience of shift work might, indeed, be harmful. Foret *et al.* (1981) separated out the usually confounded effects of age and experience in relation to sleep hygiene in a sample of about 750 shift workers in an oil refinery. Older (over 40 years) shift workers reported poorer sleep and greater use of sleeping pills than their younger colleagues. More importantly, however, Foret *et al.* showed that, *even within a particular age group*, the longer the experience with shift work, the poorer the sleep measures. Thus, experience with shift work does have an effect on sleep quality and sleeping pill use which is *not* simply a function of the increased age of the worker.

The second factor concerns the general deterioration in health and intolerance to change which characterizes the passing of years. This is an aspect of shift work that regards it as a stressor which has the potential for exacerbating any new or existing problems for the shift worker. This has been discussed in the introduction, and probably represents the major influence of age on shift work coping ability. Thirdly, there are marked changes in the circadian system that occur with age. Circadian rhythms in the elderly tend to be flatter and more phase-advanced (i.e. peaking earlier in the day) than those of their younger counterparts (Weitzman *et al.*, 1982). The effect of these changes is to increase the lability of the circadian system, thus creating shift work coping problems for those on rapidly rotating systems (Reinberg *et al.*, 1980, 1984), and to cause the individual to wake earlier in the day (become a 'morning lark'), thus interfering with the morning sleeps that normally follow a night shift.

Finally, there is the general deterioration in 'sleeping performance' that is characteristic of increased age. This deterioration is characterized by a rise in the number of wakenings during sleep and a reduction in the total number of hours slept (Webb, Agnew, and Dreblow, 1981). This can be characterized as a reduced ability to maintain wakefulness during the 'day' and sleep during the 'night'. Moreover, as mentioned above, there is a change, too, in phase, such that wakefulness is harder to maintain in the evening and sleep harder to maintain during the morning. Both effects significantly interfere with the sleep routines commonly adopted by shift workers, and often they are sufficient to outweigh any of the positive aspects of decreased total sleep *need*.

In conclusion, the problem of ageing in shift work is not due to a single underlying factor. Rather, it would appear to be a complex interaction of many different factors tending to affect the circadian system and sleep hygiene of the shift worker, and in many cases negating any positive benefits that might appear in the social and domestic areas. Sadly, with regard to coping with shift work, the factor of experience appears to weigh in as a negative attribute rather than a positive one.

CONCLUSIONS

From the preceding discussion it is clear that shift work represents a major source of 'blue collar stress', and one that is likely to increase rather than diminish. Japanese and European researchers, who have led the way in this area, are beginning to make quite unequivocal pronouncements about the situations in which shift work is and is not justified and about the ways in which night work should be restricted (Rutenfranz *et al.*, 1977; Kogi, 1985). In the United States, shift work issues are beginning to be noticed, and it is likely that there, too, such ideas will take hold. For those who have done shift work research in the field and have met the many individuals whose lives are made miserable by shift work, such a time will not be a day too soon.

REFERENCES

Akerstedt, T., and Torsvall, L., L. (1981). Shift-dependent well-being and individual differences, *Ergonomics*, 24, 265–273.

Blake, M. J. F. (1967). Time of day effects on performance in a range of tasks, *Psychon. Sci.*, 9, 349–350.

Colquhoun, W. P., Blake, M. J. F., and Edwards, R. S. (1968a). Experimental studies of shift work. I: A comparison of 'rotating' and 'stabilized' 4-hour shift systems, *Ergonomics*, 11, 437–453.

Colquhoun, W. P., Blake, M. J. F., and Edwards, R. S. (1968b). Experimental studies of shift work. II: Stabilized 8-hour shift systems, *Ergonomics*, 11, 527–546.

Colquhoun, W. P., Blake, M. J. F., and Edwards, R. S. (1969). Experimental studies of shift work. III: Stabilized 12-hour shift systems, *Ergonomics*, 12, 865–882.

Czeisler, C. A., Moore-Ede, M. C., and Coleman, R. M. (1982). Rotating shift work schedules that disrupt sleep are improved by applying circadian principles, *Science*, 217, 460–463.

Czeisler, C. A., Weitzman, E. D., Moore-Ede, M. C., and Zimmerman, J. C. (1980). Human sleep: its duration and organisation depend on its circadian phase, *Science*, 210, 1254–1267.

Folkard, S. (1975). Diurnal variation in logical reasoning, *British Journal of Psychology*, 66, 1–8.

Folkard, S., Knauth, P., Monk, T. H., and Rutenfranz, J. (1976). The effect of memory load on the circadian variation in performance efficiency under a rapidly rotating shift system, *Ergonomics*, 19, 479–488.

Folkard, S., and Monk, T. H. (1979). Shiftwork and performance, *Human Factors*, 21, 483–492.

Folkard, S., and Monk, T. H. (1982). Circadian rhythms in performance—one or more oscillators? In *Psychophysiology 1980* (Eds. R. Sinz and M. R. Rosenzwig), Elsevier-North Holland Press, pp. 541–548.

Folkard, S., Wever, R. A., and Wildgruber, C. M. (1983). Multioscillatory control of circadian rhythms in human performance, *Nature*, 305, 223–226.

Foret, J., Bensimon, G., Benoit, O., and Vieux, N. (1981). Quality of sleep as a function of age and shift work. In *Night and Shift Work: Biological and Social Aspects* (Eds. A. Reinberg, N. Vieux, and P. Andlauer), Pergamon Press, Oxford, pp. 149–160.

Froberg, J. E. (1977). Twenty-four-hour patterns in human performance, subjective and psychological variables and differences between morning and evening active subjects. *Biological Psychology*, 5, 119–134.

Gates, A. I. (1916). Variations in efficiency during the day, together with practice effects, sex differences, and correlations, *Univ. Calif. Publs. Psychol.*, 2, 1–156.

Hockey, G. R. J., and Colquhoun, W. P. (1972). Diurnal variation in human performance: a review. In *Aspects of Human Efficiency—Diurnal Rhythm and Loss of Sleep* (Ed. W. P. Colquhoun), English Universities Press, London, pp. 39–107.

Klein, K. E., Wegman, H. M., and Hunt, B. I. (1972). Desynchronization as a function of body temperature and performance circadian rhythm as a result of outgoing and homecoming transmeridian flights, *Aerospace Medicine*, 43, 119–132.

Kleitman, N. (1963). *Sleep and Wakefulness*, University of Chicago Press, Chicago, Ill.

Knauth, P., Landau, K., Droge, C., Schwitteck, M., Widynski, M., and Rutenfranz, J. (1980). Duration of sleep depending on the type of shift work, *Int. Arch. Occup. Environ. Health,* **46,** 167–177.

Knauth, P., and Rutenfranz, J. (1976). Circadian rhythm of body temperature and re-entrainment at shift change, *Int. Arch. Occup. Environ. Health,* **37,** 125–137.

Kogi, K. (1985). Introduction to the problems of shift work. In *Hours of Work—Temporal Factors in Work Scheduling* (Eds. S. Folkard and T. H. Monk), John Wiley and Sons, Chichester, pp. 165–184.

Kronauer, R. E., Czeisler, C. A., Pilato, S. F., Moore-Ede, M. C., and Weitzman, E. D. (1982). Mathematical model of the human circadian system with two interacting oscillators, *American Journal of Physiology,* **242** (*Regulatory Integrative Comp. Physiol.,* **11**), R3–R17.

Lavie, P. (1980). The search for cycles in mental performance from Lombard to Kleitman, *Chronobiologia,* **7,** 247–256.

Monk, T. H. (1982). The arousal model of time of day effects in human performance efficiency, *Chronobiologia,* **9,** 49–54.

Monk, T. H., and Folkard, S. (1983). Circadian rhythms and shift work. In *Stress and Fatigue in Human Performance* (Ed. G. R. J. Hockey), John Wiley and Sons, Chichester, pp. 97–121.

Monk, T. H., and Folkard, S. (1985). Individual differences in shift work adjustment. In *Hours of Work—Temporal Factors in Work Scheduling* (Eds. S. Folkard and T. H. Monk), John Wiley and Sons, Chichester, pp. 227–237.

Monk, T. H., Knauth, P., Folkard, S., and Rutenfranz, J. (1978). Memory-based performance measures in studies of shiftwork, *Ergonomics,* **21,** 819–826.

Monk, T. H., Leng, V. C., Folkard, S., and Weitzman, E. D. (1983a). Circadian rhythms in subjective alertness and core body temperature, *Chronobiologia,* **10,** 49–55.

Monk, T. H., Weitzman, E. D., Fookson, J. E., and Moline, M. L. (1984). Circadian rhythms in human performance efficiency under free-running conditions, *Chronogiologia,* **11,** 343–354.

Monk, T. H., Weitzman, E. D., Fookson, J. E., Moline, M. L., Kronauer, R. E., and Gander, P. H. (1983b). Task variables determine which biological clock controls circadian rhythms in human performance, *Nature,* **304,** 543–545.

Moses, J., Lubin, A., Naitoh, P., and Johnson, L. C. (1978). Circadian variation in performance, subjective sleepiness, sleep and oral temperature during an altered sleep–wake schedule, *Biological Psychology,* **6,** 301–308.

Reinberg, A., Andlauer, P., De Prins, J., Malbecq, W., Vieux, N., and Bourdeleau, P. (1984). Desynchronization of the oral temperature circadian rhythm and intolerance to shift work, *Nature,* **308,** 272–274.

Reinberg, A., Andlauer, P., Guillet, P., Nicolai, A., Vieux, N., and LaPorte, A. (1980). Oral temperature, circadian rhythm amplitude, aging and tolerance to shift work, *Ergonomics,* **23,** 55–64.

Rutenfranz, J., Colquhoun, W. P., Knauth, P., and Ghata, J. N. (1977). Biomedical and psychosocial aspects of shift work: a review, *Scand. J. Work Environ. Health,* **3,** 165–182.

Rutenfranz, J., Haider, M., and Koller, M. (1985). Occupational health measures for night workers and shift workers. In *Hours of Work–Temporal Factors in Work Scheduling* (Eds. S. Folkard and T. H. Monk), John Wiley and Sons, Chichester, pp. 199–210.

Scherrer, J. (1981). Man's work and circadian rhythm through the ages. In *Night and Shift Work: Biological and Social Aspects* (Eds. A. Reinberg, N. Vieux, and P. Andlauer), Pergamon Press, Oxford, pp. 1–10.

Siffre, M., Reinberg, A., Halberg, F., Ghata, J., Perdriel, G., and Slind, R. (1966). L'isolement souterain prolonge. Etude de deux sujet adultes sains avant, pendant et apres cet isolement, *Presse Med.*, **74**, 915–919.

Tasto, D. L., and Colligan, M. J. (1978). Health consequences of shift work, Stanford Research Institute Technical Report: Project URU-4426, Menlo Park, Calif.

Tepas, D. I. (1982a). Work/sleep time schedules and performance. In *Biological Rhythms, Sleep and Performance* (Ed. W. B. Webb), John Wiley and Sons, Chichester, pp. 175–204.

Tepas, D. I. (1982b). Adaptation to shift work: fact or fallacy?, *J. Human Ergol.*, **11** (Suppl.), 1–12.

Tepas, D. I. (1982c). Shift worker sleep strategies, *J. Human Ergol.*, **11** (Suppl.), 325–326.

Tepas, D. I., Walsh, J. K., Moss, P. D., and Armstrong, D. (1981). Polysomnographic correlates of shiftworker performance in the laboratory. In *Night and Shift Work: Biological and Social Aspects* (Eds. A. Reinberg, N. Vieux, and P. Andlauer), Pergamon Press, Oxford, pp. 179–186.

Walker, J. (1978). *The Human Aspects of Shift Work*, The Pitman Press, Bath.

Walker, J. (1985). Social problems of shift work. In *Hours of Work—Temporal Factors in Work Scheduling* (Eds. S. Folkard and T. H. Monk), John Wiley and Sons, Chichester, pp. 211–225.

Walsh, J. K., Tepas, D. I., and Moss, P. D. (1981). The EEG sleep of night and rotating shift workers. In *Biological Rhythms, Sleep and Shift Work* (Ed. L. C. Johnson, D. I. Tepas, W. P. Colquhoun and M. I. Colligan). Spectrum Publications, New York, pp. 451–466.

Webb, W. B., Agnew, H. W., and Dreblow, L. (1981). Sleep of older subjects on shift work. In *Night and Shift Work: Biological and Social Aspects* (Eds. A. Reinberg, N. Vieux, and P. Andlauer), Pergamon Press, Oxford, pp. 197–203.

Wedderburn, A. A. I. (1967). Social factors in satisfaction with swiftly rotating shifts, *Occupational Psychology*, **41**, 85–107.

Wehr, T. A., and Goodwin, F. K. (1981). Biological rhythms and psychiatry. In *American Handbook of Psychiatry* (Eds. S. Arieti and H. K. H. Brody) Vol. 7, Basic Books, New York, pp. 46–74.

Weitzman, E. D., Czeisler, C. A., Zimmerman, J. C., Ronda, J. M., and Knauer, R. S. (1982). Chronobiological disorders: analytic and therapeutic techniques. In *Disorders of Sleep and Waking: Indications and Techniques* (Ed. C. Guilleminault), Addison Wesley, California, pp. 297–329.

Wever, R. (1975). The circadian multi-oscillator system of man, *Int. J. Chronobiology*, **3**, 19–55.

Wever, R. (1979). *The Circadian System of Man: Results of Experiments under Temporal Isolation*, Springer-Verlag, New York.

Wever, R. (1985). Man in temporal isolation: basic principles of the circadian system. In *Hours of Work—Temporal Factors in Work Scheduling* (Eds. S. Folkard and T. H. Monk), John Wiley and Sons, Chichester, pp. 15–28.

Williams, H. L., Lubin, A., and Goodnow, J. J. (1959). Impaired performance with acute sleep loss, *Psychological Monographs*, **73**, 1–26.

Job Stress and Blue Collar Work
Edited by C. L. Cooper and M. J. Smith
© 1985 John Wiley & Sons Ltd

Chapter 6

Repetitive Work:
Occupational Stress and Health

Tom Cox

Stress Research, Department of Psychology,
University of Nottingham,
Nottingham, England

Perhaps the most important principle on which the economy of manufacture depends, is the division of labour amongst the persons who perform the work (Charles Babbage, 1835).

This chapter first describes the evolution of industrial repetitive work and attempts an analysis of its stressful aspects. It then considers data which offer some evaluation of this analysis, in terms of studies on workers' job perceptions (reliability) and on worker health (validity). A large proportion of those employed in repetitive work are women, and many of the key studies have considered women workers or subjects.

THE CENTRAL CONCEPT

The issue of the stressful nature of repetitive work has attracted some attention in the scientific literature. In the last 10 years, there have been several relevant reviews. However, although these have dealt with essentially the same source material and data, they have done so under three different heads, or some combination of them: repetitive work, monotony, and boredom.

For example, in 1980 and again in 1982 (Cox, Thirlaway, and Cox, 1982), the author discussed repetitive work, while Salvendy and Smith (1981), in their book *Machine Pacing and Occupational Stress*, were concerned with a similar range of questions. At more or less the same time, O'Hanlon (1981) and Smith (1981) reviewed the literature on boredom, and Thackray (1981) and Davies, Shackleton, and Parasuraman (1983) combined this topic with that of monotony at work. Cursory examination of these authors' reference sections quickly reveals the overlap between the three areas.

A question of definition

Repetive work may be defined in operational terms as work in which a discrete set of task activities are repeated over and over again in the same order without planned interruptions by other activities or tasks. The cycle time for the set of activities may be measured and used as one index of the repetitiveness of work. In many cases, the repetition in work is of a simple and unskilled set of actions.

Monotony usually refers to the nature and impact of the stimulation provided by work. The monotonous work environment is one in which the pattern of sensory and kinaesthetic stimulation is nearly constant or is repetitious and predictable, and of little significance. As a result, it is of low psychological impact due to habituation.

Boredom is an ill-defined scientific concept; it appears to refer to a particular cognitive state with strong emotional correlates.

While there can be some consensus on what constitutes repetition in work, there is less agreement over the nature of monotony, and even less on that of boredom (Davies, Shackleton, and Parasuraman, 1983). Despite this, the three concepts are obviously linked. Repetitive work practices are often associated with, and contribute to, monotonous work environments, and this monotony may in turn determine feelings of boredom. However, it is illogical to suggest that these arguments are necessarily reversible. The aetiology of boredom may be invested in factors other than exposure to monotony, and monotony may arise outside of repetitive work processes.

Whatever the exact relationship between repetitive work, monotony, and boredom, the questions, of relevance here, remain 'in what way is repetitive work stressful?' and 'what are its effects on the worker?'.

CONTEXT: PAST AND FUTURE

The use of short-cycle repetitive tasks in industrial work can be traced back to the beginnings of the Industrial Revolution and the modern factory system, and to the mechanization of work.

The industrial revolution

The factory system in Britain began to develop during the late Tudor period (1559–1640), but made little headway until much later during the eighteenth century. Industry until then was domestic, based on individual craft skills; goods were scarce and expensive, beyond the reach of most of the population. The apprentice system was an essential and much abused part of such industry. The modern factory system was born just after the Napoleonic wars as a part of what has since been termed the Industrial Revolution.

The Industrial Revolution in Britain harnessed inventive genius, religious zeal, and shrewd investment to easily accessible human and natural resources. In a relatively short period of time, these factors combined to make that country the first major industrial power.

The initial impact of the Industrial Revolution was grim. The mechanization of work brought falling wages, inflation, and unemployment, but new levels of profit. In 1797, a highly skilled handloom weaver, in the textile industry, earnt 26s 8d (week), but by 1811, this had dropped to 14s 7d, while the roughly calculated cost of living had risen by up to 85 per cent.

However, the textile indutry eventually boomed. In 1750, it employed some 40,000 workers, but by 1851 this figure had risen to 1,500,000 (out of a population of 21,000,000). The Industrial Revolution eventually created jobs, and it created wealth, albeit increasing the divide between rich and poor. It also created many other problems, particularly for the new working class; many stemming from the type of work that they were required to perform. One major source of difficulty arose from the repetitive work practices that accompanied mechanization and went to make up much of the modern factory system.

The division of labour

The origins of repetitive work can be traced back beyond the publication of Adam Smith's (1776) *The Wealth of Nations*, but there is no doubt that his exposition on the division of labour proved a major force in its development. As an argument, he discussed the production of pins. For relatively unskilled workers, without the aid of machinery, the production of several pins a day would have been praiseworthy. Making pins required a number of essential operations, such as drawing out the wire, straightening it, cutting it to length, pointing it, grinding the top to receive the head, and so on. He described how these operations could be broken up and carried out separately by different workers. Each worker would concentrate on one aspect of the overall task, and the numbers assigned to these different aspects would be decided in a way that ensured the flow of production. Smith (1776) observed that 10 men working in this way could make many thousands of pins a day compared to say 20 or 30 under the old system.

The ideas conceived by Smith (1776) were later brought to term in Charles Babbage's (1835) book *On the Economy of Machinery and Manufacture*. The creation of simple repetitive jobs, he believed:

1. reduced the time required for training,
2. reduced the materials wasted during training,
3. created greater flexibility in manpower planning, and
4. saved lost time due to job transfers.

Furthermore, repetition in work was inevitably associated with simpler jobs. With these simpler jobs, relatively fewer skilled workers had to be employed, and cheaper labour could be used. Babbage (1835) argued that the division of labour allowed these workers to develop their performance to a high degree of excellence and rapidity through the constant repetition of the same task.

Together, these outcomes were among the obvious benefits to organizations. However, while bestowing economic and planning benefits on organizations, these methods arguably degraded work for many of the individuals involved, and have been roundly attacked for this (Braverman, 1974).

Largely following on from Marx's development of the concept of *alienation*, it has been claimed that industrial repetitive work has marked detrimental effects on the worker. Those cited have ranged from lowered job satisfaction and unhappiness to feelings of powerlessness, from poor physical and mental health to absenteeism (Blauner, 1964; Shepard, 1971; Coburn, 1979).

However, many of the early studies in this area have attracted criticism. for example, Kasl (1978) has pointed out that certain of the commonly used criterial measures, such as 'powerlessness' or 'meaninglessness', reflect but do not go far beyond workers' accurate descriptions of their jobs. Furthermore, he has argued that the terms used in conceptualizing these descriptions and perceptions are usually 'value laden' and suggest mental health outcomes without any being independently measured or demonstrated.

The scientific-technological revolution

According to Toffler (1980) the effects of the Industrial Revolution represented the *second wave* of change to which society has had to adapt, the development of agriculture producing the *first wave*. It is apparent that a *third wave* is now well established and accelerating. This has attracted many labels, perhaps the most appropriate being that of the scientific-technological revolution (Daglish, 1972). Not least among its effects are further changes in the nature of work, and many of these are based on the adoption of computer-based technology in the workplace.

Unfortunately, where simple tasks are being computerized, they invariably retain many of their previous repetitive and monotonous features. Moreover, where other more complex jobs are being redesigned, to suit computer technology, deskilling is often involved. The adoption of such technology is thus allowing further job simplification and the creation of more, rather than less, routine and repetitive tasks.

Many of the job design problems initially created by the Industrial Revolution are now being recreated in the context of computer-based work. Thus it is unlikely that the problems of repetitive work will 'go away'; this was the conclusion reached by the author in 1979 (Cox *et al.*, 1979) and repeated in 1984 (Cox and Cox, 1984). Research into the problem of repetition in work as a source of stress, and the discussion of its effects, will remain apposite for some time to come.

ANALYSIS OF STRESSFUL SITUATIONS

An early step in understanding any work-related problem is to conduct some form of job or task analysis (Landy and Trumbo, 1976); in the present case that analysis needs to address the question of the nature and structure of stressful situations. This may be achieved at two levels of description (Cox, 1984). Firstly, jobs or work situations might be described in terms of their underlying psychological and social processes, and secondly, they might be described in terms of specific elements of the job which are identified as sources of stress or dissatisfaction. The former assessment may be more coherent if soundly based in theory, but the latter will require an empirical approach. There are a variety of methods by which these assessments might be made; these are not discussed here, except to note the recommendation (Howell, 1976) that in job analysis it is wise to use a combination of different sources of information and methods of enquiry. The data gathered during such an analysis should be proved reliable and then validated against other independent criteria (Cox, 1984).

An outline is presented below of the application of such a problem-centred job analysis to repetitive work.

UNDERLYING PSYCHOLOGICAL AND SOCIAL PROCESSES

Karasek (1979) has suggested that jobs might be assessed in terms of two independent dimensions: workload and job discretion. The latter refers to an apparent mixture of responsibility and control over work. It has also been suggested that conditions combining high workload with low discretion might be inherently stressful. This type of analysis has been developed by others to include some consideration of the (social) support available to the worker (see, for example, Payne, 1979).

The author (Cox, 1983) has attempted to set such an approach in the context of the *transactional model of occupational stress* (see Cox, 1978; Cox and Mackay, 1981). He has defined the three concepts involved and offered suggestions for their measurement. More relevant here, he has also suggested, like Payne (1979), that 'stress' is experienced (as negative emotion) when the demands of the worker are not matched to their level of skill (or skill potential), and that this state is exacerbated when the worker is constrained in coping or receives little support for coping from others.

The combination of these factors may be used as the basis for assessing and describing potentially stressful situations. For example, the three factors mentioned have been used to categorize the stressful elements of repetitive work reported in a study carried out in the East Midlands (UK), see below.

Stressful elements of repetitive work

In 1976, at the start of a project commissioned by the British Department of Employment, and funded through the Medical Research Council, the author and his colleagues made a series of exploratory visits to companies in the East Midlands (UK) that employed repetitive work practices. During those visits, the researchers talked to management, to local union officials, and where possible toured the shopfloor talking to workers at their place of work. From the 14 different companies visited, a consensus was built up to what, in the mid 1970s, were the problems facing workers engaged in repetitive and associated forms of work. These problems are listed in Table 1. The essence of this list has been published elsewhere (Cox, Thirlaway, and Cox, 1982).

Table 1   Sources of demand, constraint, and support

Demands:	The repetition of a simple, and frequently meaningless, motor act, often asssociated with the underutilization of skill or skill potential, contributing to habituation, loss of ability to attend, and drowsiness
	Restricted levels of stimulation and perceptual repetition (monotonous work environment), giving rist to habituation, loss of ability to attend, and drowsiness
	Incentive pay schemes
Constraints (and lack of control):	
	Physical and task-related constraints on behaviour, high noise levels, high attentional demands, physical layout, machine pacing and high levels of pacing resulting in a relatively isolated work station
	Lack of control over task, little responsibility and autonomy, low participation in company management or product planning
Social support:	Demands and constraints often result in reduced social contact at work, unhelpful work groups and lack of acceptance by group, poor relationship with supervisor

Casual consideration of the description of repetitive work offered in Table 1 suggests that it may readily fulfil the necessary criteria for stressful work: demands not matched to workers' abilities (underutilization of skill), workers with little control over their work, and little discretion in coping with it. In many situations, the work itself may fail to promote a supportive and helpful social or supervisory environment.

It would therefore seem reasonable to propose the hypothesis that repetitive work is potentially stressful. However, various caveats must be added. Firstly, the nature of repetitive work will vary from company to company, and this will effect the applicability of the hypothesis in any particular situation. Secondly, the experience of stress is an individual phenomenon, and thus there will be individual differences in the determination of that experience (and response to it).

EVALUATION

This assessment of repetitive work as potentially stressful may be evaluated against several different types of data obtained from a variety of field and experimental studies. Certain of these data are considered below. Two different types of evidence are considered: firstly, data from other studies on workers' perceptions and descriptions of their jobs which confirm the reliability of the assessment, and secondly, data on what is known of the effects of such work on suboptimum health (Rogers, 1960), overt illness, and disability. This provides some validation of the assessment.

WORKERS' PERCEPTIONS AND DESCRIPTIONS
OF REPETITIVE WORK

Two early studies exist which go some way towards describing workers' perceptions of and reactions to repetitive work (Cox, Dyce Sharp, and Irvine, 1953; Caplan *et al.*, 1975). The first is a study conducted for the now-defunct National Institute of Industrial Psychology (NIIP) in Britain, over 30 years ago, while the other, a somewhat more recent study, was conducted for the National Institute of Occupational Safety and Health (NIOSH) in the United States.

The NIIP study

Cox, Dyce Sharp, and Irvine (1953) carried out detailed interviews with 160 women and 6 men engaged in repetitive work in a variety of British industries. The data from the men were ignored because of the small sample size.

The authors noted several aspects of work which were of importance to the workers interviewed: diversity and variation in work, the degree of attention and skill demanded, the degree to which the organization of work was effective, the degree of teamwork involved, and the physical working conditions. They suggested that some of these could be considered in terms of their impact on the workers' feelings of (1) freedom and constraint, (2) security, and (3) creativeness.

Some degree of freedom appeared to be valued by the workers, although for some the need to feel emotionally secure in their work ran counter to this. Such workers disliked too frequent or too random a change of task; they also disliked moving to unfamiliar tasks and joining strange work teams. The main source of satisfaction in terms of creativeness was that of 'turning out plenty'. Much of the work involved handling unrecognizable and meaningless parts of a product and this appeared to preclude other 'quality-based' satisfactions. One of the most common remarks was: '. . . there is no skill in this job, except doing it fast!' Cox, Dyce Sharp, and Irvine (1953) suggest that manual skill should be considered from the standpoint of 'speed' as well as 'power' (the capacity to do difficult tasks).

A recurrent theme throughout many of the interviews was the complaint of feeling thwarted and of not having skills fully utilized. *Underutilization of skill* was one of the principle factors in the aetiology of mental illnesss mentioned sometime earlier by Fraser (1947) in his study of engineering workers. This was particularly the case among his women workers.

Most of those interviewed disliked pacing, either by machine, conveyor belt, or by others in their workgroup. Many of the workers were paid on piece rate, and some preferred a moderate level of pacing because this allowed them to earn a reasonable bonus. They feared that on self-paced work their rhythm and resolve would soon dissipate, resulting in relatively lower output and consequently lower wages.

Large individual differences appeared to exist in relation to attentional demand. Some workers liked tasks which demanded at least some of their attention, which it was said helped pass the time and reduce boredom; others liked tasks which could be performed automatically, allowing them to daydream or talk with their workmates.

Dissatisfaction was particularly noticeable where the constraints imposed were perceived as unnecessary. On the more positive side, changes in the types of material worked upon, variations in working methods, and job rotation were generally welcomed and regarded as ways of making time pass more quickly.

Some of the points made by the NIIP study are picked up in the more recent NIOSH work.

The NIOSH study

The NIOSH survey was carried out in the 1970s by the Institute for Social Research at the University of Michigan (Caplan *et al.*, 1975; French, Caplan, and van Harrison, 1982) and examined self-reported job demands in a variety of occupational groups, ranging from unskilled through professional. The survey was based on the administration of a questionnaire, and the sample of several thousand obtained consisted of *male* workers only.

Results from this survey indicated that individuals working on assembly-line tasks (including those with repetitive elements) reported high levels of 'stress' in comparison to many other occupational groups. Stress was measured in terms of the *underutilization of skills*, lack of participation, and lack of adequate (preferred) job complexity.

THE NOTTINGHAM STUDY; A MODEL
FOR JOB DESCRIPTIONS

While a good indication of how workers perceive their jobs was provided by the NIIP study, somewhat supported by the NIOSH research, that information might now be dated. Furthermore, it does not allow an overall evaluation of such work in the workers' own terms. In a study conducted from Nottingham, workers' descriptions of their jobs were modelled using principle components analysis applied to data obtained from an adjective checklist.

The reasons behind the adoption of this particular approach have been set out and discussed elsewhere (Cox and Mackay, 1979). It has been widely used and successfully applied in personality research (Masterson, 1975) and in mood research (Nowliss, 1965; Thayer, 1967, Mackay *et al.*, 1978; Cox and Mackay, 1985), as well as in the area of job satisfaction (Locke, 1976).

Method

A list of 60 adjectives was generated by a research committee of occupational and social psychologists, all with experience of shopfloor studies. Several versions of the list were then taken out and discussed with small groups of workers. The workers were asked to indicate which words they might use in everyday conversation about their work, and which they did not understand or would never use in such conversation. They were also asked to suggest words that they or others might use, but which were not included in the lists.

The suggestions made by the workers were considered within the overall research plan, and a list of 55 adjectives was arrived at. In discussion, it also emerged that the adjectives needed to be rated on a (five-point) frequency scale, rather than on an intensity scale. Workers recognized the day-to-day variation in their jobs and their reactions to them, and this made an intensity scale difficult to apply without further instructions and contingencies.

The scale used was:

Never   Rarely   Sometimes   Often   Always

This scale also had a separate 'cannot decide' category (?). The list of adjectives was used in the form of a checklist and administered to over 400 workers in three different companies, each carrying out repetitive or associated forms of work. A light engineering company, a heavy engineering company, and a pharmaceutical company took part in this field study (see Table 2).

Table 2   Companies used in job perceptions study

Company	Light engineering	Heavy engineering	Pharmaceutical
No. of employees	610	2000	1902
Sample size	75	52	301
Work	Assembly Machine operation Inspection Press operation Soldering	Machine operation Inspection	Machine operation Soap moulding Soap packing Confectionary packing Tablet inspection Conveyor belt inspection
Work, hours	40	41.5	40
Overtime, hours	4	1.3	4
Training	2 weeks	4–5 weeks	4–6 weeks
Female: male	M = F	M > F	F > M

The coded responses to the checklists were subjected to principle components analysis. Two analyses were conducted. The initial analysis was described by Cox and Mackay in 1979, and the subsequent analysis was more briefly reported by Cox, Thirlaway, and Cox, in 1982.

Initial analysis

The initial analysis of the checklist data suggested a four-factor orthogonal solution after (varimax) rotation. The four factors were provisionally named: pleasantness, tedium, difficulty, and pressure. The workers' scores on these four factors were calculated and then used to discriminate between groups in terms of (1) the company they worked for, (2) their shift, and (3) their sex. Several different comparisons were made.

Age, experience, and pressure

One interesting finding was that, for women workers, there appeared to be some association between age and the report of pressure. The older women workers reported their jobs as being *less* pressured. This relationship was demonstrated for workers in both the light and heavy engineering companies.

There may have been at least three different explanations for these findings. Firstly, those women who found the job too difficult may have left and thus the negative relationship between age and the report of pressure may have been due to self-selection. Secondly, the older womens' greater experience of previous life events may have provided a contrast to work which made work problems seem less significant. Thirdly, there are particular problems associated with entry to work, and possibly with adolescence or a young family, which influence perceptions of work, and therefore do not affect older women.

A slightly different pattern of effect was demonstrated for women in the pharmaceutical company. Here the women workers were slightly older, but had spent *less* time on their current job. They found their work *more* pressured. This company, in contrast to the others, encouraged previous employees to return to work after having time away for a family. The important factor determining the report of pressure may therefore be related to exposure to work and its associated problems, rather than age per se.

Sex differences

Interestingly, the women in the pharmaceutical company reported their jobs to be both *more* tedious and *more* pleasant than the men employed there. Casual observation suggested that although there was less variety in the womens' work than in the mens', there was more opportunity for socializing at work. the social context for work appeared better for the women employed in the pharmaceutical company than for the men (for the type of work under discussion). These observations led to an investigation of the role of the social environment in determining perceptions of job pleasantness (see later).

It may be an important observation that (women) workers are able to distinguish between task-related characteristics of work and those that are contextual, and make different judgements on them.

Subsequent analyses

More detailed examination of the four-factor model of job perceptions suggested the presence of two relatively major factors and two minor ones; there was also some conceptual overlap between the major and minor factors. The major factors were those of pleasantness and difficulty. The checklist data were therefore reanalysed, against more stringent criteria, and the possibility of a two-factor solution established. As part of this analysis, items (adjectives) with extreme mean scores and restricted variance were rejected. A two-factor orthogonal model was adopted after (varimax) rotation. The factors were bipolar, and were named pleasantness (/unpleasantness) and easiness (/difficulty). This model was preferred for economy, ease of presentation, and statistical rigour. It has been adopted in all later research.

Several studies have been conducted using this *job description checklist* (JDCL), and various data can now be compared (Table 3).

Table 3   Workers' job descriptions (JDCL)

Type of work	Pleasantness	Easiness
Hosiery workers:		
1. Machine operators	35.7	20.3
2. Hand modification and preparation	42.7	24.2
3. Finishing	36.5	20.7
Simulated repetitive work:		
1. Loading	34.1	26.8
2. Sorting	36.0	19.1
3. Machine minding	43.8	20.3
Drivers:		
Bus drivers	35.8	23.4
Train drivers	43.0	25.1

SOCIAL CONTEXT TO WORK

The data collected from the pharmaceutical company suggested that women workers might perceive their tasks to be tedious but still describe their jobs as relatively pleasant. Following testing, casual discussions were held with workers on two different 'lines'. The first line was concerned with packing toiletries, largely soap. The women worked in groups of about six, and largely at their own pace. On the second line, the women worked in groups of four or six, but were examining saline packs for small air bubbles. Again the work was self-paced, but by contrast required close attention.

The women agreed that their work was relatively straightforward and unvarying, and to this extent monotonous. However, those that could socialize and talk with other workers tended to describe their work more positively and as more pleasant than those who could not. The workers packing toiletries were not subject to high attentional demands and had others around them to talk to. Their work was perceived as more pleasant than that of the women inspecting saline packs. They were subject to high attentional demand and could not talk.

The following simple hypothesis was then formulated (Cox *et al.*, 1979; Cox, Thirlaway, and Cox, 1982): tasks which are high in attentional demand are viewed as less pleasant than tasks which are low in such demands. However, it soon became clear that this only holds true in situations where workers had an opportunity to socialize, and concentrating on the task interfered with this social intercourse. This modification of the hypothesis is discussed below.

Hosiery industry study

The usefulness of the proposed model of workers' descriptions of their jobs was examined in a study in the East Midlands hosiery industry. A questionnaire incorporating the job description checklist was distributed to over 200 workers in five hosiery companies.

The original simple hypothesis, relating attentional demand and job pleasantness, set out above, was *not* supported by the data collected. The *greater* the attentional demand the *more* pleasant the job. This finding was immediately understandable. In the jobs studied in the hosiery industry, the majority were subject to constraints and barriers which virtually excluded meaningful contact or conversation with others. These were in addition to those imposed by high attentional demands. They included physical layout of machinery, noise levels, and postural constraints. The hypothesis was therefore modified.

If the workers have the opportunity to talk and generally socialize with other workers, then tasks demanding little attention will be judged more pleasant than those demanding much attention. High attentional demand interferes with social intercourse. If, for other reasons, such socializing is not possible, then tasks which demand much attention may be perceived as more pleasant. This hypothesis is consistent with the earlier observations of Cox, Dyce Sharp, and Irvine (1953).

Job design and job pleasantness

Workers were also asked to provide saliva samples at the beginning and end of their shifts, and to allow their jobs to be categorized. Those categories used in this study were:

1. repetition in work,
2. cycle time,
3. attentional demand,
4. posture,
5. job flexibility, and
6. pay scheme.

Univariate analyses showed that all the various categorizations of work (see above) affected the judgement of job pleasantness, largely in sensible and easily predictable ways. Flat-rate payment was associated with a more pleasant job than piece-rate payment, non-repetitive work was seen as more pleasant than repetitive work, and the longer the cycle time the more pleasant the job. Similarly, jobs with some flexibility were described as more pleasant than those which were relatively inflexible. Tasks where the worker had to stand were described as less pleasant than those where the worker was seated.

The most pleasant tasks were where the workers had the opportunity to vary their position.

Reliability of assessment

The three studies reviewed here go some way in demonstrating the reliability of the initial analysis of the stressful aspects of repetitive work. It is clear from the studies reviewed that an *underutilization of skill* is often associated with repetitive work and that this is a source of complaint. There are also problems associated with lack of participation and lack of adequate job complexity. Often the only 'skill' component is that of speed. There is dissatisfaction with unnecessary constraints, and satisfaction is limited to the speed of work. Short cycle times and inflexible jobs are associated with low reports of job pleasantness. High attentional demands and machine pacing appear to be disliked by some workers, although preferred by others.

The Nottingham study revealed that workers' descriptions of their jobs could be modelled in terms of two (orthogonal) factors: job easiness and job pleasantness. Job pleasantness contained elements of job satisfaction, and was partly determined by aspects of job design. Such perceptions may be part of, or at least contribute to, overall well-being. The following sections consider what is known of the effects of repetitive work on suboptimum health, ill health, and disability.

EFFECTS ON HEALTH

The World Health Organisation (1964) defines health as a state of 'complete physical, mental and social well-being, and not merely the absence of disease or infirmity'. This definition recognizes a state which is neither optimum health (complete well-being) or actual or overt illness or disability. Rogers (1960), in his Health Status Scale, refers to this state as 'suboptimum health'. Rogers (1960) also points out that 'health' is a dynamic concept and health states are in a constant process of change, and that no particular state can be maintained indefinitely. The changes which occur in a state of suboptimum health, broadly defined, are probably what most researchers are concerned with when examining the quality of (working) life. This section will consider the evidence that exposure to repetitive work may influence both suboptimum health and overt illness.

Cox *et al.* (1983) and O'Hanlon (1981) have together reviewed several studies which appear to show that exposure to repetitive and monotonous (boring) work is related to poor health states. However, O'Hanlon (1981) has wisely noted that many of the relevant studies suffer from serious methodological problems, especially those which have concerned mental health outcomes. Despite this, together the various evidences tend to suggest that exposure to such jobs may be associated with impaired health, although it is difficult to determine the extent to which this is driven by factors such as shift working, social class, and sex of worker.

SUBOPTIMAL HEALTH

The evidence that repetitive work may be detrimental to suboptimum health (Rogers, 1960) largely concerns (1) the relationship between boredom at work and mental health, (2) the effects of assembly- and production-line work on the report of general symptoms of ill health, (3) the effects of job incongruence (underload), and (4) the effects of monotony and understimulation on psychological function. However, perhaps one of the most interesting studies is that of Colligan, Smith, and Hurrell (1977) on occupational incidence rates of mental health disorders.

Colligan, Smith and Hurrell (1977) collected data on mental health diagnoses from 22 of the 27 mental health centres in Tennessee (1972–1974). The 8,450 cases were recorded by occupational groups, 130 different groups being defined for this study. The subsequent group data were ranked both according to the estimated admission rates, and by z scores. Z scores were calculated for observed against expected frequencies on the basis of the relative frequency of members of that group in the population. The top 30 of the 130 ranks were reported. Health care workers dominated these rankings, but 'industrial inspectors' ranked fourth (admission rate 20.5/1000; z score 11.4) and operatives ranked twenty-eighth (admission rate 10.2/1000; z score 18.5). With respect to the inspectors, Colligan, Smith, and Hurrell (1977) suggested that because they had received very little attention from researchers, there was still a need to identify the relationship between psychological adjustment and exposure to stress, e.g. underutilization of skill, high need to concentrate, and boredom.

Boredom

The evidence that there are negative mental health outcomes associated with boredom at work has been briefly presented by O'Hanlon (1981). He has concluded that the accumulated evidence only suggests that workers who complain of chronic boredom are also more neurotic and otherwise less mentally healthy than those who do not (Kornhauser, 1965; Gardell, 1971; Hill, 1975; Nachreiner and Ernst, 1978). Chronically bored workers appear to harbour feelings of resentment and repressed hostility (Kornhauser, 1965; Broadbent, 1979), and suffer from feelings of anxiety or depression (Gardell, 1971; Caplan et al., 1975).

Of course, no causality can be implied from these findings. It is as likely that boredom is a result of failure to adapt to work in those who are resentful, anxious or depressed, as it is that boredom contributes to those states.

Assembly- and production-line work

There are several survey-based studies concerned with the effects of assembly- and production-line work on self-reported health. Most have used symptom checklists or questionnaires as criterial measures, although occasionally psychiatric interviews have also been employed. Many of the studies have concerned women workers. The notable exception is the NIOSH study described below (Caplan et al., 1975; French, Caplan, and van Harrison, 1982).

The Lancaster study

A study by Shimmin, McNally, and Liff (1981) considered the pressures reported by women production-line workers and the possible effects of their work on their report of general symptoms of mental strain and ill health. These assessments were made using Goldberg's (1972) general health questionnaire (GHQ). The survey data were compared with the results of normative data from psychiatric interviews (Goldberg, 1972).

Shimmin, McNally, and Liff (1981) described the pattern of effect as follows. Women in the sample worked full-time rather than part-time for financial reasons. These, in turn, arose from their home circumstances. Those whose families were very dependent on their wages, felt that they must continue with their work even though they might dislike it. Thus there appeared to be greater effects of full-time work on mental health than part-time work. Their data showed clear effects of shift on the percentage of high scorers on the GHQ. Day shift workers showed more effects on mental health than morning or afternoon shift workers, and evening shift workers appeared the least effected. There were also associations between mental health scores, so determined, and household dependence on the woman's earnings and her feelings about her job.

The Nottingham study

A somewhat similar questionnaire-based survey was conducted from Nottingham, by the author and his colleagues. They considered workers in three British companies in the food and drinks and pharmaceutical sectors. In all three companies, one in five of the workers studied were also briefly interviewed. In one company pre- and post-shift urine samples were taken in an attempt to describe the urinary catecholamine response to work. However, the conditions under which this proved feasible could not be sufficiently controlled and the data were thus rendered meaningless.

Two different and major analyses of the available questionnaire data have been conducted. The first concerned the effects of job design of perceived job pleasantness, post-shift reports of stress (Mackay *et al.*, 1978; Cox and Mackay, 1985), and symptom levels (Cox *et al.*, 1983), while the second (see Cox, Thirlaway, and Cox, 1984) concerned the effects of sex and marital status on symptom levels. Essentially a hierarchical model for analysis of covariance was employed in both analyses, with controls for any effects of age of the worker.

The data showed that generally repetition in work, lack of job rotation, and short cycle time detrimentally affected perveived job pleasantness, post-shift stress, and self-reported symptom levels. However, the degree of attention demanded by the job was less clearly related to these particular outcome measures. The data also suggested that women workers reported more symptoms of ill health than their male coworkers, and that married women appeared *more* healthy, by this criterion than single women.

The Oxford study

A recent well-controlled survey by Broadbent and Gath (1981) has considered the mental health of workers in two British car plants. In both, workers engaged in repetitive tasks showed lower levels of job satisfaction than those engaged in non-repetitive work; interestingly, they did not necessarily show poorer mental health. However, those engaged on paced assembly lines showed higher levels of anxiety than those who were not. There was no difference in job satisfaction between the two jobs. Broadbent and Gath (1981), in comparison to most studies, report no effects of cycle time over the range found in these plants.

The NIOSH study

Perhaps one of the major studies on job demands and worker health was carried out by NIOSH in the United States (Caplan *et al.*, 1975; French, Caplan, and van Harrison, 1982). Over 2000 male workers, in a wide range of jobs, were surveyed. Several blue collar groups were included, and the data from these can be compared with that from their supervisors and relevant white collar groups (see Table 3).

The overall sample means were calculated for a variety of measures, and the scores for each occupational group were then expressed in terms of how far they were from this mean. Steps of $\frac{1}{3}$ standard deviation were used to mark this comparison.

Table 3 reveales the contrast between the effects of machine-paced

Table 3   Jobs and worker well-being

Group	N	Anx	Dep	SoC	Irrit	JobD	Bore
Assembly							
Machine-paced	79	+	+	++	0	++	+++
Self-paced	69	0	0	+	0	+	++
Machine minding	34	+	+	+	+	++	++
Supervisor	178	0	0	0	0	0	0
Engineer	110	0	0	0	0	0	0

The scores are expressed in terms of $\frac{1}{3}$ standard deviations from the overall sample mean ($n = 2,010$): $+\frac{1}{3}$ s.d. above, $++\frac{2}{3}$ s.d. above (etc.), and 0 within $\frac{1}{3}$ s.d. from mean. (Anx, anxiety; Dep, depression; SoC, somatic complaints; Irrit, irritability; JobD, job dissatisfaction; Bore, boredom.)

assembly work and machine minding, on one hand, and supervisory and white collar work, on the other. Interestingly, the effects of self-paced assembly work are somewhat intermediate. The most obvious differences concerned boredom at work, job dissatisfaction, and somatic complaints.

Job incongruence and underload

Coburn (1979) has studied the relationship between job–worker incongruence and mental and physical health. Over a thousand Canadian male workers, in a variety of jobs, completed a postal questionnaire which attempted to assess the degree of work overload or underload (job incongruence), attitudes towards the job, and health status. The Langer (1962) index of psychophysiological symptoms was used as a measure of psychological well-being, and physical health was assessed by self-rating scales and a measure of incapacity.

Coburn's (1979) data suggested that excessively complex work, although not necessarily disliked, was associated with poorer psychological well-being and physical health. Somewhat by contrast, overly simple work was disliked and associated with poor psychological well-being, but not with impaired physical health. The influence of job congruence on physical health was most noticeable for men who feel that their work was too complex for them to handle adequately. Coburn's (1979) evidence suggests that *perceived* job incongruence has much larger effects on health than *objective* incongruence.

Monotony and understimulation

A study by Martin and her colleagues (1980), albeit using a cross-sectional design, appears to show that exposure to repetitive and monotonous work may be associated with an impairment of intelligent problem-solving behaviour. The authors surveyed a group of predominately female (Swiss) watchmakers, who had worked for varying periods of time at the same repetitive tasks. A significant negative correlation (–0.55) was found between workers' verbal intelligence (paragraph completion test) and the duration of their exposure to 'boring work'.

The real possibility exists that the more intelligent workers had self-selected or been promoted out of this repetitive work. However, before dismissing this finding, there are other studies which suggest that part of the effect might be due to exposure to unstimulating situations.

An early study by Myers and his colleagues (U.S. Human Resources Research Office: cited by Cooper, 1968) concerned military personnel placed in sensory isolation for 96 hours; this group was compared to a control group who experienced no confinement. Tests of mental ability were given before, during, and after confinement. The tests used assessed immediate memory, numerical ability, verbal fluency, successive subtraction, and inductive reasoning. After confinement, scores on the latter two tests were significantly lower for the isolated men than for the controls.

The ability to introspect on mood may be impaired by exposure to repetitive work (Cox, 1978); this may be consistent with Benyon and Blackburn's (1972) observation that 'switching off' and 'letting your mind go blank' are used as strategies for coping with repetitive and monotonous tasks by car assembly workers. In the same vein, Nilsson (1975) has reported that Swedish sawmill workers on repetitive tasks with short cycle times often reported somnolescence, daydreaming, and occasionally hallucinations. The need to expend effort in overcoming these effects was held responsible for commonly expressed feelings of mental fatigue among such workers. A somewhat similar conclusion has been reached by Soviet scientists in a review of the literature on the psychophysiological effects of monotonous work. They suggest that the main cause of stress in such work is 'the conflict between the inhibition (or reduction) in activation which is associated with monotonous work, and the volitional effort required to continue working'. This type of explanation has been developed by both O'Hanlon (1981) and by the present author (Cox, 1980; Cox, Thirlaway, and Cox, 1982).

ILL HEALTH AND DISABILITY

One of the first major studies of the effects of repetitive work on physical health was carried out by Samoilova (1971) in the Soviet Union. She compared morbidity patterns in Russian women working on repetitive machine-paced tasks (such as punch press operation, fabric cutting, or bottling) with those on less repetitive self-paced work (packing or upholstering). Overall, the health of the repetitive workers was considerably poorer. They appeared to suffer up to 3 to 5 times the incidence of cardiovascular disease, 4 to 7 times the incidence of disorders of the peripheral nerves (e.g. neuritis), 2 times the incidence of gastritis, and 2 to 3 times the incidence of diseases affecting the musculoskeletal system. The workers engaged in repetitive tasks were absent from work for medical reasons up to 5 times as often as those with less repetitive jobs.

Other studies

Studies by Laville and Teiger (1975) in France, by Nerell (1975) in Sweden, and by Ferguson (1973) in Australia have lent support to Samoilova's (1971) findings. Together these, and other studies (such as Kuorinka, 1979; Vihma, Nurminen, and Mutanen, 1982), have suggested detrimental effects of repetitive and associated forms of work. These studies are briefly described below.

Posture and musculoskeletal problems

Obviously, the physical demands of repetitive work (movement patterns and postural requirements) could account for much of the pattern of effect described by Samoilova (1971) and others.

Upper limbs and neck

Kuorinka (1979), in Finland, has described how repetitive movements can directly affect musculoskeletal systems, especially in the upper limbs and neck, and how extreme postures are associated with damage in the relevant regions. Kuorinka (1979) discussed these effects in terms of mechanical over-strain. Such effects may be particularly obvious when the work is short cycle and the muscles do not have adequate time to relax.

In the clothing industry, the early development of mass-production methods caused work once done by seamstresses to be completed by sewing machine operators. A high prevalence of musculoskeletal complaints has been observed in many studies on sewing machine operators (Teiger, Laville, and Duraffourg, 1973; Vaneckova et al., 1977; Sillanpaa and Frilander, 1980; Vihma, Nurminen, and Mutanen, 1982). In Finland, for example, Vihma, Nurminen, and Mutanen (1982) have studied the possible occupational origin of musculoskeletal (rheumatic) complaints among such operators. The subjects for their study were chosen by random sampling and comprised 40 sewing machine operators with short work cycles (30 to 60 seconds) and 20 seamstresses as a reference group. The two groups were matched with respect to age and length of service. A survey of their working postures revealed that in the sewing machine operators work there was a greater static load on both the neck and shoulders, and on the lower limbs (Teiger, Laville, and Duraffourg, 1973; Vihma, 1978). These were the anatomical sites where musculoskeletal complaints occurred more frequently among these operators than seamstresses.

Legs

On the same theme, Winkel (1979) has shown how sedentary work may be associated with poor circulation in the legs. In a pilot study, albeit on only three healthy Swedish women, he compared lower leg swelling when they sat performing light work with and without rest pauses involving leg movement (walking). Without rest pauses, the women experienced more tension and tiredness in their legs, and about twice as much swelling.

Other problems

In Australia, Ferguson (1973) surveyed telegraphists who had, among other things, complained about extreme task monotony. He compared these telegraphists with clerical, maintenance, and supervisory personnel in the same offices. In the busiest office studied (Sydney), the telegraphists were more likely to be 'neurotic', and suffered more frequently from trunk myalgia and exaggerated tendon reflexes. They also had a higher incidence of asthma and bronchitis.

Disorders of the digestive system

The study by Laville and Teiger (1975) concerned French assembly workers, and attempted to assess the incidence of a range of disorders among that group. Sadly, they did not use a control group for comparison purposes; however, the incidence of gastritis and sickness in their sample was about 75 per cent., much above what would normally be expected. Somewhat similarly, Nerell (1975) showed that between 33 and 60 per cent. of different groups of Swedish sawmill workers were receiving treatment for peptic ulcers or gastritis at the time of his study.

It is possible that disorders of the digestive system may, to some extent, be associated with shift working (see later; Rutenfranz, 1982).

Behaviour problems

Various behavioural problems have been cited in the literature, including hysterical reactions, insomnia, hypersensitivity to noise and light, regular drinking, and excessive smoking. For example, in their study of French assemblers, Laville and Teiger (1975) found that approximately three-quarters experienced occasional hysterical reactions. Half experienced regular insomnia and nearly all occasionally manifested some form of psychological problem, such as hypersensitivity to noise and light, extreme emotional lability, or anxiety. These workers' morbidity patterns appeared to be extremely aberrant.

Ferguson's (1973) survey of telegraphists, who complained about extreme task monotony, showed they were more regular drinkers and smoked excessively, compared to their controls.

Kosmider and Pilawski (1979) compared two groups of women workers in the Polish garment industry. Their 'experimental' group was comprised of seamstresses; their 'control' group consisted of similar women doing far less monotonous work. The women were given written tests and gynaecological examinations. Serious aberrations of psychosexual behaviour were found to be more frequent among the seamstresses. These effects appeared to be partly related to the constraints on movement and posture imposed by their work, in particular by their work seats (Pilawski, Olszewska and Lazar, 1979). These constraints had an adverse effect on the womens' genital organs, including hypertropic changes, through a syndrome of pelvic congestion.

CONFOUNDING FACTORS

There are several different factors which are predictive of health, and which are associated with repetitive work; e.g. shift working, social class, and sex of worker. These are discussed below.

Shift work

In most industrialized countries, about one-fifth of the work force is engaged in shift working. Much of the repetitive work carried out in the manufacturing sector is subject to shifts, and some of the apparent health effects of repetitive work might be due to shift working.

There is insufficient space to review the occupational health literature on shift work. However, authorative reviews by Harrington (1978) and Rutenfranz (1982) suggest that the main source of problems is night work, and its effects are most obviously expressed through sleep disturbance. Shift work involving nights and permanent night shifts are associated with high frequencies of complaint about sleep disturbances. For example, in a study of 322 railway workers, Rutenfranz et al. (1974) reported complaints in about 80 per cent. of that sample.

In addition, there is some suggestion that digestive and gastric disorders may also be associated with shift working, although in conjunction with other aggravating factors. This may be partly linked to a disruption of eating habits, which also appears to accompany shift work involving nights (Rutenfranz, Knauth, and Angersbach, 1981).

Both Harrington (1978) and Rutenfranz (1982) conclude that as far as other diseases are concerned, a significant hypermorbidity caused by shift work is unlikely. Studies of mortality in relation to shift working are rare. However, in a careful comparison of mortality rates in shift and day workers, Taylor and Pocock (1972) could find no differences in rates.

Harrington (1978) states that, at present, there is no evidence to suggest that women are more vulnerable to shift work than men, although he also notes that there are very few relevant studies. The possibility thus remains that sex differences might exist in adaptation to shift work; the most likely areas of concern relate to endocrinological disturbance and disruption of family and social life for married women with children.

Women's work and women's health

Many of those employed in the manufacturing sector on repetitive work are women. Therefore a description of the occupational health of repetitive workers may be similar in some respects to a discussion of 'women's work and women's health'.

About 15 per cent. of all women workers work in industrial (blue collar) jobs, mostly in the textile and clothing industries. There are, however, large numbers of women employed as inspectors, packers, and assembly-line workers. Stellman (1977) briefly summarizes the hazards that such women are exposed to, but does not, in this context, directly address the important question of possible sex differences in response to those hazards. The obvious area in which, by physiological necessity, such differences must exist is that of reproductive health. It would appear that women of child-bearing age are vulnerable to certain chemical and physical hazards, both before, during, and after pregnancy (while breast-feeding), and that any ill effects might be expressed through the foetus. It is possible that postural and physical demands might also threaten the pregnant mother.

An interesting question arises if women are particularly vulnerable while of child-bearing age to certain job demands and hazards. Should they be protected by law, or common practice, or should they be allowed the responsibility for deciding their own health and that of the foetus? If they are subject to protection, albeit well meaning, at what point does such protection operate as discrimination?

In this context, Root, Lindell, and Miller (1984) reach several interesting conclusions from their review of employment policies for female industrial workers in the United States. They agree that some form of prudent protective action is required for women of child-bearing potential, when making the work environment totally safe from embryo/foetotoxic hazards is not an economic proposition. However, some employers appear to use such exclusionary policies as a pretext for discriminating against female workers. They note that exclusionary practices appear to operate mainly in male-dominated industries where women are not a primary part of the work force. Where they are, exclusionary policies are often noticeable by their absence.

Social class

Social class is a strong predictor of both morbidity and mortality patterns. For men (OPCS, 1978), the differences between social classes in mortality rates is apparent whether they are measured by crude death rates, by direct age-standardized death rates, or by standardized mortality ratios. Unskilled and semiskilled workers show standardized mortality ratios (SMRs) of 137 and 114 respectively, compared with SMRs of 77 and 81 for professional and intermediate groups. This difference is consistently maintained across all causes of death. It appears most marked for infective and parasitic diseases, mental disorders, and diseases of the respiratory system. Much of the explanation of these differences necessarily concerns conditions of housing, sanitation, and diet; however, the nature of the person's job, their income, and exposure to hazards and climate may contribute directly, as well as indirectly, to their poorer state of health. This fact of social class effects will confound many between-group comparisons.

Comments on health data

There are many problems associated with collecting reliable data on health in an occupational setting, and many more if this information has then to be related to particular job problems or features of job design.

Perhaps the most common approaches are based on surveys or regularly collected data from health screening. However, possibly the most adequate information comes from experimental studies, although the scope for such research is severely limited for practical, ethical, and legal reasons. Much of the published statistics must therefore be interpreted with caution. However, and despite this, there appears to be some reason for believing that 'repetitive' and associated workers show poorer health than those not engaged in such tasks (in terms of both suboptimum health states and frank illness or disability). However, this may relate to features of job design outside of the fact of repetition, e.g., shift work and working posture, or it may only indirectly reflect job factors and be confounded to some extent by social class and sex of worker as predictors of morbidity.

Whatever the complete explanation, it is relatively clear that workers engaged in repetitive work practices suffer poorer health than most other occupational groups. This may be particularly so for those engaged in shift work which involves night working.

CONCLUDING REMARKS

This chapter has attempted to describe the problems and sources of stress associated with repetitive and associated forms of work. It has offered a model to describe workers' perceptions of such jobs, and has explored the health-related costs of this work. Together, it is suggested, this evidence supports the hypothesis that repetitive work is potentially stressful, and can, for certain individuals, threaten the quality of life and their health.

It must be the shared responsibility of managers and workers to explore ways of improving job design with respect to repetitive work or of providing workers with strategies by which they can cope with exposure to such work and ameliorate its effects.

REFERENCES

Babbage, C. (1835). *On the Economy of Machinery and Manufacture*, Charles Knight, London.
Benyon, H., and Blackburn, R. M. (1972). *Perceptions of Work: Variations within a Factory*, Cambridge University Press, Cambridge.
Blauner, R. (1964). *Alienation and Freedom: The Factory Worker and His Industry*, University of Chicago Press, Chicago.
Braverman, H. (1974). *Labour and Monopoly Capital*, Monthly Review Press, London.
Broadbent, D. E., and Gath, D. (1981). Ill-health on the line: sorting myth from fact. *Employment Gazette*, **89**, (3).
Caplan, R. D., Cobb, S., French, J. R. P., van Harrison, R., and Pinneau, S. R. (1975). Job demands and worker health, U.S. Department of Health, Education and Welfare, Publ. No. NIOSH 75-160, Washington, D.C.
Coburn, D. (1979). Job alienation and wellbeing, *International Journal of Health Services*, **9**, 41–59.
Colligan, M. J., Smith, M. J., and Hurrell, J. J. (1977). Occupational incidence rates of mental health disorders, *Journal of Human Stress*, **1977**, September, 34–39.
Cooper, R. (1968). The psychology of boredom, *Science Journal*, **4**, 38–42.
Cox, D., Dyce Sharp, K. M., and Irvine, D. H. (1953). Women's attitudes to repetitive work, National Institute of Industrial Psychology, Report No. 9, London.
Cox, T. (1978). *Stress*. Macmillan, London.
Cox, T. (1980). Repetitive work. In *Current Concerns in Occupational Stress* (Eds. C. L. Cooper and R. Payne), John Wiley and Sons, Chichester.
Cox, T. (1984). Psychosocial and psychophysiological factors in the design and the evaluation of working conditions within health care systems. In *Breakdown in Human Adaptation to Stress* (Eds. J. Cullen and J. Siegrist), Martinus Nijhoff Publ., The Hague.
Cox, T., and Cox, S. (1984). Job design and repetitive work, *Employment Gazette*, **92**, 97–100.
Cox, T., and Mackay, C. J. (1979). Impact of repetitive work. In *Satisfactions in Job Design* (Eds. R. Sell and P. Shipley), Taylor and Francis, London.
Cox, T., and Mackay, C. J. (1981). A transactional approach to occupational stress. In *Stress, Work Design and Productivity* (Eds. Corlett and P. Richardson), John Wiley and Sons, Chichester.
Cox, T., and Mackay, C. J. (1985). The measurement of self reported stress and arousal, *British Journal of Psychology*, **76**, 183–186.
Cox, T., Thirlaway, M., and Cox, S. (1982). Repetitive work, wellbeing and arousal, *Advances in the Biosciences*, **42**, 115–135.
Cox, T., Thirlaway, M., and Cox, S. (1984). Occupational well-being: sex differences at work, *Ergonomics*, **27**, 499–510.

Cox, T., Thirlaway, M., Cox, S., and Mackay, C. J. (1979). Job stress: the effects of repetitive work, *Employment Gazette*, **87**, 1234–1237.

Cox, T., Thirlaway, M., Gotts, G., and Cox, S. (1983). The nature and assessment of general well-being, *Journal of Psychosomatic Research*, **27**, 353–359.

Daglish, R. (1972). *The Scientific and Technological Revolution: Social Effects and Prospects*, Progress Publishers, Moscow.

Davies, D. R., Shackleton, V. J., and Parasuraman, R. (1983). Monotony and boredom. In *Stress and Fatigue in Human Performance* (Ed. G. R. J. Hockey), John Wiley and Sons, Chichester.

Ferguson, D. (1973). A study of occupational stress and health, *Ergonomics*, **16**, 649–663.

Fraser, R. (1947). The incidence of neurosis among factory workers, Industrial Fatigue Research Board, Report No. 90, HMSO, London.

French, J. R. P., Caplan, R. D., and van Harrison, R. (1982). *The Mechanisms of Job Stress and Strain*, John Wiley, New York.

Gardell, B. (1971). Alienation and mental health in the modern industrial environment. In *Society, Stress and Disease* (Ed. L. Levi), Vol. 1, Oxford University Press, New York.

Goldberg, D. (1972). *The Detection of Psychiatric Illness by Questionnaire*. Oxford University Press, Oxford.

Harrington, J. M. (1978). *Shift Work and Health. A Critical Review of the Literature*, HMSO, London.

Hearnshaw, L. S. (1949). What is industrial psychology?, *Occupational Psychology*, **23**, 1–8.

Hill, A. B. (1975). Work variety and individual differences in occupational boredom. *Journal of Applied Psychology*, **60**, 128–131.

Howell, W. C. (1976). *Essentials of Industrial and Organisational Psychology*, The Dorsey Press, Homewood, Ill.

Karasek, R. A. (1979). Job demands, job decision latitude, and mental strain: implications for job redesign, *Administrative Science Quarterly*, **24**, 285–308.

Kasl, S. V. (1978). Epidemiological contributions to the study of work stress. In *Stress at Work* (Eds. C. L. Cooper and R. Payne), John Wiley and Sons, Chichester.

Kornhauser, A. (1965). *Mental Health of the Industrial Worker*, University of Chicago Press, Chicago, Ill.

Kosmider, M., and Pilawski, Z. (1979). Psychosexual disturbances among women employed in the garment industry, Paper presented to International Ergonomics Association, Warsaw (August), *Ergonomics*, **22**, 732 (abstract).

Kuorinka, I. (1979). Occupational strain from working movements, Paper presented to International Ergonomics Association, Warsaw (August), *Ergonomics*, **22**, 732 (abstract).

Landy, F. J., and Trumbo, D. A. (1976). *Psychology of Work Behaviour*, The Dorsey Press, Homewood, Ill.

Langer, T. S. (1962). A 22 item screening scale of psychiatric symptoms indicating impairment, *Journal of Health and Human Behaviour*, **3**, 269–276.

Laville, A., and Teiger, C. (1975). Sante mentale et conditions de travail, *Therapuetische Umschau*, **32**, 152–156.

Locke, E. A. (1976). The nature and causes of job satisfaction. In *Handbook of Industrial and Organisational Psychology* (Ed. M. D. Dunnette), Rand McNally, Chicago.

Mackay, C. J., Cox, T., Burrows, G., and Lazzerini, A. J. (1978). An inventory for the measurement of self reported stress and arousal, *British Journal of Social and Clinical Psychology*, **17**, 283–284.

Masterson, S. (1975). The adjective checklist technique: a review and critique. In *Advances in Psychological Assessment* (Ed. P. MacReynolds), Jossey-Bass, San Francisco.

Martin, E., Ackerman, U., Udris, I., and Dergeli, K. (1980). *Monotonie in der Industrie*, Hans Huber Verlag, Bern, Germany.

Nachreiner, F., and Ernst, G. (1978). Monotony and satiation as a person situation interaction. Paper presented to: XIXth International Congress of Applied Psychology, Munich.

Nerell, G. (1975). Medical complaints and findings in Swedish sawmill workers. In *Ergonomics in Sawmill and Woodworking Industries* (Eds. B. Thunell and B. Ager), National Board of Occupational Safety and Health, Stockholm.

Nilsson, C. (1975). Working conditions in the sawmill industry: a sociological approach based upon subjective data. In *Ergonomics in Sawmill and Woodworking Industries* (Eds. B. Thunell and B. Ager), National Board of Occupational Safety and Health, Stockholm.

Nowliss, V. (1965). Research with the MACL. In *Affect, Cognition and Personality* (Eds. S. S. Tomkins and C. E. Izard), Springer, New York.

O'Hanlon, J. F. (1981). Boredom: practical consequences and a theory, *Acta Psychologica*, **49**, 53–82.

OPCS (1978). *Occupational Mortality (1970–1972)*, Decennial Supplement, Office of Population Censuses and Surveys, HMSO, London.

Payne, R. (1979). Demands, supports and constraints, and psychological health. In *Response to Stress: Occupational Aspects* (Eds. C. J. Mackay and T. Cox), IPC Science and Technology Press, Guildford.

Pilawski, Z., Olszewska, D., and Lazar, W. (1979). Ergonomic analysis of work seats used by seamstresses in the garment industry, Paper presented to International Ergonomics Association, Warsaw (August), *Ergonomics*, **22**, 735 (abstract).

Rogers, E. H. (1960). *The Ecology of Health*, Macmillan Press, New York.

Rutenfranz, J. (1982). Occupational health measures for night and shift workers, *Journal of Human Ergology*, **11** (Suppl.), 67–86.

Rutenfranz, J., Knauth, P., and Angersbach, D. (1981). Shift work research issues. In *Advances in Sleep Research* (Eds. L. C. Johnson, D. I. Tepas, W. P. Colquhon, and M. J. Colligan), Vol. 7, Spectrum Publications, Medical and Scientific Books, New York.

Rutenfranz, J., Knauth, P., Hildebrandt, G., and Rohmert, W. (1974). Nacht- und Schichtarbeit von trriiebfarhzeugfuhrern. 1. Mitt: Untersuchungen uber die tagliche Arbeitszeit und die ubrige Tagesufteilung, *Int. Arch. Arbeitsmed.*, **32**, 243–259.

Salvendy, G., and Smith, M. (1981). *Machine Pacing and Occupational Stress*, John Wiley and Sons, Chichester.

Samoilova, A. J. (1971). Morbidity with temporary loss of working capacity of female workers engaged in monotonous work, *Sovetskia Zdravaakhranenie*, **30**, 41–46 (in Russian).

Shepard, J. M. (1971). *Automation and Alienation*, MIT Press, Cambridge, Mass.

Shimmin, S., McNally, J., and Lift, S. (1981).Pressures on women engaged in factory work. *Employment Gazette*, **89**, 344–349.

Sillanpaa, J., and Frilander, P. (1980). Work load in the manufacture of textiles and the manufacture of wearing apparel, Part I. Tampere Regional Institute of Occupational Health, Tampere (in Finnish).

Smith, A. (1776). *The Wealth of Nations*. Reprinted by Penguin Books, Harmondsworth, Middlesex (1970).

Smith, R. P. (1981). Boredom: a review, *Human Factors*, **23**, 329–340.

Stellman, J. M. (1977). *Women's Work, Women's Health*, Pantheon Books, New York.

Taylor, P. J., and Pocock, S. J. (1972). Mortality of shift and day workers 1956–68, *British Journal of Industrial Medicine*, **25**, 106–118.

Teiger, C., Laville, A., and Duraffourg, J. (1973). Taches repetives sous contrainte de temps et charge de travail. Laboratoire de Physiologie du Travail et d'Ergonomie, Rapport No. 39, Paris (in French).

Thackray, R. I. (1981). The stress of boredom and monotony: a consideration of the evidence, *Psychosomatic Medicine*, **43**, 165–176.

Thayer, R. E. (1967). Measurement of activation through self report, *Psychological Reports*, **20**, 663–678.

Toffler, A. (1980). *The Third Wave*, Pan Books, London.

Vaneckova, M., Tihelkova, D., Chmelar, J., and Mokry, Z. (1977). The study of working positions at the operations of various types of industrial sewing machines, Occupational Safety and Health Series, ILO 35, ILO, Geneva.

Vihma, S. (1978). The work of sewing machine operators, Finnish Board of Labor Protection, Tampere (in Finnish).

Vihma, T., Nurminen, M., and Mutanen, P. (1982). Sewing-machine operators' work and musculo-skeletal complaints, *Ergonomics*, **254**, 295–298.

Winkel, J. (1979). Swelling of the lower leg in sedentary work, Paper presented to International Ergonomics Association, Warsaw (August), *Ergonomics*, **22**, 737 (abstract).

Job Stress and Blue Collar Work
Edited by C. L. Cooper and M. J. Smith
© 1985 John Wiley & Sons Ltd

Chapter 7

Stress and Quality Control Inspection

Colin G. Drury

Department of Industrial Engineering,
State University of New York
at Buffalo, Amherst, NY, USA

INTRODUCTION

As with many other industrial activities, quality control is undergoing a period of rapid change. Increased quality demands from customers show the need for accuracy of quality information, both to protect the customer from defective products and to provide the feedback needed to keep costly processes running at their optimum points. At the same time, pressure on cost containment is leading to emphasis on throughput. The inspection function of quality control, and particularly the inspector, is increasingly the focus of these two pressures.

As the demands are increasing on the human inspector, the response of engineers has been to progressively automate the inspector's job. Sophisticated microprocessor-controlled optical scanning and gauging devices have been developed which remove some of the aspects of inspection from the inspector's direct control. However, automation is not without its human problems.

The inspection function of quality control is carried out by human inspectors, often aided by instruments and machinery. However, the human inspector is prone to error. For example, Sinclair (1970) reviews a large number of studies and concludes that inspectors typically make 10 to 30 per cent. type 2 errors (failing to detect defects) while at the same time making 1 to 10 per cent. type 1 errors (rejecting items which are good). Two books on the human inspector (Harris and Chaney, 1969; Drury and Fox, 1975) show measurements of inspection error in many industries, ranging from electronic components through glass and steel sheets to food products. In many studies of the human inspector, the emphasis has been on performance, i.e. how to reduce inspector error, neglecting the effect this performance has on the inspector, i.e. inspector stress. This chapter will review the inspector's job from two points of view, performance and stress, to show how they are closely related and how factors affecting one can affect the other.

If stress and quality control are to be examined, then the obvious inter-section of these two fields is in the job of the inspector. This section will review what is known about performance and stress in inspection. Many studies (e.g. reviews in Harris and Chaney, 1969; Drury and Fox, 1975) have shown that stressors such as degraded lighting, poor instructions, and lack of job aids affect inspection performance. It is not intended to review these effects as recent reviews of inspection (e.g. Drury, 1982, 1984) have covered them in considerable detail. However, studies of the effect of inspection on human well-being are notably lacking in the literature.

To review this area, a concept and definition of stress is needed. Again, more detail can be found elsewhere in this volume, but two quotations will serve to provide a framework. First, Cox and Mackay (1977) state:

Stress. . . arises as a result of an imbalance between the person's perceptions of the demands made upon him, and his perception of his ability to cope when coping is important.

Similarly, Caplan *et al.* (1975) state:

. . . 'stress' refers to any characteristics of the job *environment* which pose a threat to the individual . . . either *demands* which he may not be able to meet or insufficient *supplies* to meet his needs. . . On the other hand 'strain' refers to any deviation from normal responses *in the person* (a) *psychological strains* . . . (b) *physiological strains* . . . (c) *behavioural symptoms of strains.*

Both emphasize the role of the objective environment (actual external world, actual personal capabilities) and most particularly the subjective environment (perceived external world, perceived personal capabilities) in deter-mining stress and hence strain.

A distinction needs to be made at this stage between the job of inspection and the tasks of inspection. Typically, an inspection job is defined as what an inspector does during the working day. This job can be broken down into a series of tasks, which can then be isolated and studied. However, the central tasks of inspection such as locating defects, judging severity of defects, or record-keeping do not comprise the whole job. For example, inspectors have job relationships with the workers whose output they inspect, with super-visors, with sales and production management, and with other inspectors. Hence two rather distinct stresses can arise: those associated with the central tasks of inspection and those associated with the broader job of the inspector. This is a key distinction because task stresses may be studied in the labora-tory whereas job stresses may not.

THE INSPECTION TASK

Task performance

Inspection in industry is of two types, inspection by variables and inspection by attributes. For variables inspection, a measurement of a variable (length, resistance, viscosity, etc.) is made on an interval scale and is used to determine whether the item inspected (and the batch from which it came) is acceptable or not. Inspector error in such an inspection system can consist of bias (wrong mean value) and/or imprecision (added variability). Automation here is relatively simple, as the output from the measuring device, a number, can easily be compared with another number representing the standard. The inspection decision is relatively trivial, even though the measurement process may represent the pinnacle of laser-and-microchip technology.

Attributes inspection, on the other hand, is where items are classified as 'good' or 'faulty', based on the existence of a discrete blemish, such as a surface finish defect or a damaged integrated circuit chip.

For attributes inspection, almost all inspection jobs involve the following four tasks (Drury, 1978):

1. Present pre-selected item for inspection.
2. Search the item to locate possible faults ('flaws').
3. Decide whether each flaw is sufficiently bad to be classified as a fault.
4. Take the appropriate action of acceptance or rejection.

Whether these four tasks are performed by human or mechanical means, they are liable to error. The errors in the first and last task are usually very small, consisting of misdirected movements or fumbles. Human performance in such tasks as picking items up, manipulating them, and putting them aside is relatively well known (e.g. Konz, 1982). It is the search and decision-making tasks in inspection which take a large proportion of the time and contribute greatly to inspection error.

The most usual search for defects is visual, e.g. searching glass plates for inclusions (Drury, 1975) or trays of baked goods for malformed goods (Chapman and Sinclair, 1975).

Almost all of the information taken in by the inspector in visual search is taken in during the fixations, which average about one-third of a second in duration and account for over 90 per cent. of the search time. Eye movements between fixations are extremely rapid and the time they take is so short compared with the fixation time that they are usually ignored. This has led to models of visual search as a sequence of fixations. In each fixation, an inspector can detect faults in an area of the item, called the visual lobe, around the centre of the fixation. This area varies with the conspicuity of the fault and is *not* simply the most sensitive part of the retina, called the *fovea centralis*.

The area of this visual lobe is a function of the luminance of the object inspected, the contrast between the object and the fault on the object, the size of the fault, and the distance of the fault from the inspector's eyes. It is possible to derive detailed mathematical expressions for how much a person can see in one fixation, given exact values of all these factors (e.g. Greening, 1975), but this has rarely been performed quantitatively for industrial inspection.

Eye movement studies of inspectors show that they do not follow a simple pattern in searching an object (Megaw and Bellamy, 1979). Some tasks have very random-appearing search patterns while others show some systematic search components in addition to this random pattern. However, all who have studied eye movements agree that performance, measured by the probability of detecting a fault in a given time, is reasonably predictable assuming random search (Drury, 1978). The equation relating probability (P_i) of detection of the fault in a time (t) to that time is

$$P_t = 1 - \exp\left(-\frac{t}{\bar{t}}\right)$$

where $\bar{t}$ is the mean search time, predictable from fixation duration, search area, and visual lobe size.

The pure decision component of inspection can be measured by concentrating on tasks which require no search. Many such tasks have been measured in the factory and in the laboratory; e.g. the studies reviewed in Drury and Fox (1975). The general conclusion of such studies is that they are one of those rare tasks where a human being behaves like a rational economic decision-maker, balancing the costs and payoffs involved to arrive at an optimum performance. Hence many authors (e.g. Wallack and Adams, 1969; Drury and Addison, 1973) have treated inspection decisions by the theory of signal detection (TSD). TSD shows how an inspector can balance the two possible errors of inspection, misses and false alarms, against each other in response to the prior probability of a fault and the payoff matrix implied in the task.

A model of the inspection process (Figure 1), combining search and decision-making, has been proposed (Drury, 1978) and found to predict well the speed/accuracy trade-off in inspection in a large number of industrial studies (Drury, 1975). This model has been conceptually useful in improving inspection performance by improving search and/or decision-making as well as in analysing human and automated inspection performance in the same terms (Drury and Sinclair, 1983). It is also of value in determining the tasks of inspection, so that the literature on the stresses generated by these tasks may be interpreted in an inspection context.

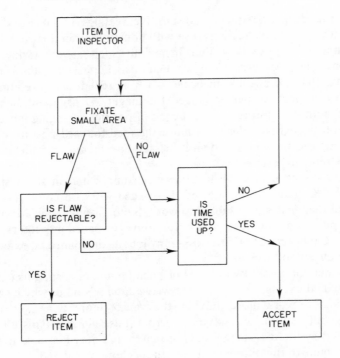

Figure 1   Model of inspection task performance

Task stress

In order to perform an inspection task, an inspector must use senses (usually vision), a search procedure, and decision-making. Each can be shown to be related to task stress. The visual stress of prolonged inspection on a simulated conveyor belt was shown by Brozek *et al.* (1950). Under low illumination conditions, critical flicker fusion frequency (CFFF) decreased after 2-hour and 4-hour work periods. No opthalmological measures changed, but complaint scores increased significantly. In a visual search task, Inomata (1977) found stress indicated by decreased heart rate variability using a number of different methods. Decision-making tasks have long been associated with decreased heart rate variability (e.g. Kalsbeek, 1973). Thackeray, Jones, and Touchstone (1974) gave a monotonous serial-reaction task for 40 minutes to subjects and measured heart rate mean (which showed a slight decrease over time) but an increase in heart rate variability, suggesting a gradual relaxing over time-on-task.

   Prolonged vigilance for rare events has often been compared to industrial inspection for rare defects (e.g. Swets, 1977). There is considerable evidence (e.g. Mackie, 1977) relating vigilance to stress measures and some evidence relating prolonged inspection to stress. For example, Kishida (1973) and Saito

(1972) found that frequency of positive feelings about work fell while frequency of negative feelings rose with hours of inspection. In addition, the frequency of non-work-related behaviour such as chattering, changing positions, yawning, and arranging hair also increased with working time (Kishida, 1973), especially in paced work. A recent study relating postural stress to inspection performance (Bhatnager, Drury, and Schiro, 1984) showed both discomfort and frequency of position changing increasing with time-on-task, perhaps due to a more slumped-forward posture over the $2\frac{1}{2}$ hours. Errors and time per item inspected also increased with time-on-task, despite frequent rest pauses.

Pacing of the inspection task has been implicated in stress studies. For example, Kishida's study showed that paced work on conveyors was more stressful than self-paced table-top work. Saito, Tanaka, and Maruchi (1969) found increased absenteeism rates for conveyor-paced inspectors. The major study of Caplan et al. (1975) across many jobs again confirmed external pacing as a significant job stressor.

In inspection tasks, two effects of pacing must be distinguished: speed of working and pacing. Drury (1973) reviewed many studies which showed that as inspectors work more quickly, they make more type 2 errors (missed defects) but may make less type 1 errors (false alarms). This effect can be explained by the two-stage model of search and decision-making (Figure 1). Pacing refers to the difference between machine-paced and self-paced work. The same speed effect appears to be found for all inspection tasks, whether speed is changed by instructions (self-pacing) or by external means (machine-pacing). If pacing is by conveyor, speed appears to have the largest effect (Purswell, Greenhaw, and Oats, 1972; Buck, 1975), but there are other effects of movement speed and spacing on the conveyor.

Studies of paced versus unpaced inspection have not usually controlled for speed of working and, perhaps because of this, have obtained contradictory results. For example, Fox and Haslegrave (1969) found paced and unpaced performance no different in a screw-sorting task while Fox and Richardson (1970) found twice as many errors with machine-pacing in a simulated inspection task. McFarling and Heimstra (1975) in a different simulated inspection task found self-pacing to be better than machine-pacing, both in terms of performance and subjective assessment. Machine-pacing was seen by the subjects as more demanding and less controllable, suggesting a different motivational structure for paced inspection. This was confirmed by Eskew and Riche (1982) who showed no pacing effect in an inspection task but did show an interaction between pacing and the locus of control personality variable.

Liuzzo and Drury (1980) used heart rate variability to measure job stress in blink inspection, i.e. where the images of a perfect item and an unknown item are blinked rapidly onto a single screen in front of the inspector. While no differences in heart rate variability were found between self-paced performance under the blinking and stationary conditions, performance did differ. In a later study (Coury and Drury, 1982; Coury, 1983), a complex, rapid inspection task was studied under several pacing conditions. Performance remained constant as pacing speed increased, but stress, as measured by heart rate variability, showed a complex effect of pacing. These can both be interpreted as the inspector allocating more or less processing demands to the various tasks, following the active processing model of Kahneman, 1973. Thus increased stress could give a performance decrement, as in the Liuzzo and Drury (1980) study, or a physiological change, as in the Coury (1983) study, dependent upon whether the inspector decided to allocate the same resources to the task or increase the level of resources allocated. In a second study, Coury (1983) found that for severely paced conditions a near-linear relationship existed between performance and heart rate variability, indicating that under extreme time pressures both stress and performance may be seen to change as the total resources available are no longer sufficient.

Confirmation of this was seen in an experiment performed for a local steel company by Narayanaswamy and Drury (1981) and reported in Drury (1982). In an inspection task involving mainly search with some decision-making, subjects under faster pacing conditions found more flaws per unit time (increased resource allocation), but showed increasing stress as measured by heart rate variability. The pattern of heart rate variability changed between paced and unpaced performance. During paced performance, heart rate variability changed for the worse throughout each test period and failed to recover to its initial value. In unpaced performance, heart rate variability eased in each test period and recovered completely after work (Figure 2), a pattern similar to the Liuzzo and Drury (1980) study. Clearly, pacing in inspection can be particularly stressful.

A more recent study of inspection aided by automation was reported by Kleiner and Drury (1984). A video comparator was used as an aid to inspection of circuit boards for faults such as missing, damaged, or mis-inserted components. The comparator shows two alternating images on a colour monitor—one of a part of the board being inspected and the other of the equivalent part of a known perfect board. In this way, differences between the inspected and perfect boards appear to flash on and off when the monitor is viewed. Comparison of use of this automation aid with unaided inspection showed some performance advantages but no changes in stress as measured either by CFFF or heart rate variability. The findings of these two measures confirmed previous results of a gradual decrease in CFFF with time-on-task and a gradual increase in heart rate variability, as shown in the self-paced condition of the Narayanaswamy and Drury (1981) study.

From these various studies of stress in the inspection task, it appears that certain aspects, such as poor lighting, decision-making, and external pacing are certainly stressful. Others, such as time-on-task, may be stressful, but

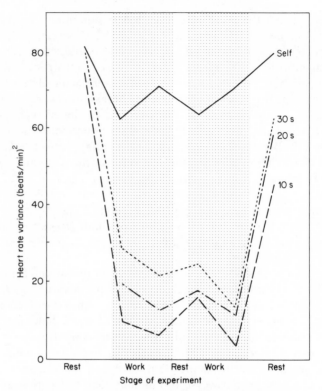

Figure 2 Heart rate variability in unpaced inspection and paced inspection at three different times per item (10, 20, and 30 seconds). *High* heart rate variability is indicative of *low* mental load

usually only when combined with conditions such as pacing or poor lighting.

THE INSPECTION JOB

For the job of inspection, as opposed to its constituent tasks, it is more difficult to separate performance and stress. Indeed, the early authors in this field made no such distinction and will be quoted directly for the relevance of their observations, even to modern inspection jobs.

Two early reviews by Raphael (1942) and McKenzie (1958) have a considerable amount to say about the inspection job. For example, Raphael's comments link stress and performance closely together:

> All inspection involves the making of constant small decisions. Doubt is always an unpleasant emotional state; therefore the easier the decision 'should this be passed?' is made, the better both for the accuracy of the inspection and the ease of the inspector....Routine inspection is probably the most trying type of repetition job, for, unlike most other routine work, constant attention is

essential. This concentrated attention is particularly difficult to maintain if there are very few rejects. If faults are found every few minutes they cause a certain variety, but if a reject only occurs once or twice a day it is hard to keep alert.

Perhaps the most telling description of inspection is by McKenzie:

> In the factory, inspection is always, if implicitly, of people; inspection decisions about a man's work directly reflect on him.

He also makes the point that inspectors have the responsibility for quality but rarely the authority to enforce quality. The old quality control dictum that

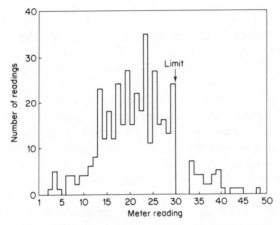

Figure 3   Distribution of inspectors recorded values of lamp filament resistance. Note each of values just beyond the standard of 30 units. (Adapted from Juran, 1945)

'you can't inspect quality into a product' is partly true; the inspector in the feedback role is improving the quality of output, but at some social cost.

The point needs to be reemphasized that stress on the inspector and inspection performance are difficult to separate for at least three reasons:

1. The ratio of actual performance to maximum performance is a measure of mental load, and hence contributes to task stress.
2. Inspection performance perceived as poor or inconsistent by others is a fruitful source of friction within many industries (McKenzie and Pugh, 1957).
3. Performance measures on their own may reveal pressures on the inspectors. For example, Juran (1935) plotted the distributions of numbers of defects found in samples and actual measured meter readings in an inspection job. He found a distinct gap in the distributions just beyond the allowed limits and interpreted this as showing that the inspectors were unwilling to classify items or whole batches as 'just defective' (Figure 3).

To help justify their decisions they attempt to make the evidence appear more clear-cut than would be expected statistically.

McKenzie and Pugh (1957) define the classic dilemma of the inspector in terms of:

> ... relations between the production department and inspection department, that is, between two groups of people that have to work with each other yet do not have exactly the same immediate interests.... One basic point is that cooperation can hardly be looked for if the situation is an essentially competitive one.

The dilemma is also seen by Jamieson (1966), who showed that improved inspection consistency and performance occurred when the inspection department was separate from production—a highly stressful situation as shown by McKenzie and Pugh (1957). Paradoxically, the best situation for inspection performance may be the worst for production performance. Van Beek (1964) showed that by reorganizing a complex assembly line for electrical equipment so that inspectors were incorporated into the production system, the earlier feedback of results improved quality. Additionally, he found higher morale with the smaller working groups obtained. Maher *et al.* (1970) reorganized process inspectors into 'enriched' jobs in a new quality control department. This opposite change also gave great improvements in throughput and attitudes.

When the inspection department is separate, McKenzie (1958) says that inspectors see themselves as leagued against a hostile world. In more detail:

> Underlying all this is the general structure of the relationship of inspection with production. Each department has its own interests and its internal loyalties. Within the inspection department these ties may be very close. One reason is that inspectors are comparatively thin on the ground—outnumbered probably ten times by production people. Also, intercommunication between inspectors is intensive; the argument is that an inspector must know about any snag that has occurred in an earlier process so that he can be alert for its possibly causing unusual faults in a later one. Moreover, inspectors tend to have more chances of getting around the works than the production man, whose movements are much more restricted.
>
> Inspectors need this solidarity because their relations with production are often strained. This is hardly surprising, since inspection is a control function relative to production, with the task not only of seeing whether work does or does not conform to specifications, but also of accepting or rejecting it. Rejection obviously makes it harder for production people to reach their output schedule and to meet their cost budget. What is more, inspection also has to report to higher authority what level of conformity production is achieving: this reporting function does not endear the inspector to the production man. Again, inspection differs from other control functions such as output schedules and cost budgets in that it concerns itself with the actual performance of the work rather than with the limits of time and cost in which it must be done. So

inspection's control is a rather intimate one with considerable likelihood of running up against people's feelings of self-esteem.

In total, the dice are loaded against easy relations between inspection and production so long as inspection is given all these functions. Moreover, although the inspector has a superordinate function, he does not have the direct authority which would support it.

Similarly, Thomas and Seaborne (1961) show yet another source of pressures—sales:

> However, the rejections made by an inspector in order to exert control successfully must have meaning to the production department over whom control is to be exerted. This, in effect, amounts to a demand for a certain degree of consistency in his performance, but the total production pressure is not towards complete consistency. In his role as a member of the industrial organization as a whole, the inspector is concerned with the maintenance of a certain production flow. When the production department is having difficulties there will be a considerable pressure to maintain a certain output by accepting some of those components which in more favourable circumstances he would be inclined to reject. On the other hand, of course, when output is high and of good quality the tendency is to raise the quality standard and this can be done at this time without unfavourable repercussions from the production department. . . .
>
> In certain inspection situations the main pressure may not come from production but from the sales department. The performance of the inspector again need not be completely consistent but should match the demands made by the changing customer requirements and market conditions and interpreted by the Sales Department. These pressures from production and sales may be at least partially conflicting. They impinge on the total inspection function, and the extent to which either of these will affect an individual inspector will depend on the structure of the inspection organization and his place in it.

Both McKenzie and Pugh (1957) and Thomas and Seaborne (1961) note that a vital part of the inspection/production interface is the perceived accuracy and consistency of the inspectors. Inspectors can be easily shown to be less than perfect, and this fact is often used by a production department to justify to themselves their own apparent low quality, as a way of saving face.

The small working group improvements of McKenzie and Pugh (1957) as well as Van Beek (1964) can be extended to cover much of the motivational literature. Harris and Chaney (1969) show that group goal-setting, participating leadership, and group-oriented problem-solving all increase quality and satisfaction, although these are strictly for production workers not inspectors. Rubenstein (1971) found positive attitude changes after introduction of problem-solving groups and rotating workers between production and inspection. Limits to the motivational approach to improving quality are cogently argued by Juran (1966) in an attack on the then-current 'zero-defects' programmes.

What these authors on job stresses are saying is that inspectors respond in predictable ways to the pressures placed on them, but that these pressures may well be rather subtle. Similar evidence comes from studies explicitly examining the 'payoff matrix' of an inspector—i.e. the costs and rewards contingent upon accepting or rejecting good and faulty items or batches. These payoffs and costs define the utility of each choice to the inspector and, given a knowledge of the *a priori* fault probability, any utility-maximizing device will behave in predictable ways. It is becoming more common to model the human inspector as such as a utility-maximization device (e.g. Wallack and Adams, 1969; Drury and Addison, 1973). As noted earlier, TSD has been applied to problems of vigilance, decision-making, and inspection. While many authors have reservations about its strict applicability (Weiner, 1975), it does have considerable predictive value.

The problem of predicting performance thus reduces in part to measuring the pressures on the inspector and finding where this causes the inspector to place acceptance/rejection criterion, according to the 'resultant' of these perceived pressures. The inspector will obviously choose a criterion nearer to that desired by management if given better knowledge of both the types of fault likely to occur (feedforward information) and the relative proportions of errors being made (feedback information). It is interesting to note that both of these techniques for improving criterion adjustment also enhance overall performance as measured by the apparent signal-to-noise ratio of faults (Sheehan and Drury, 1971; Drury and Addison, 1973). This confirms previous industrial studies that both the informational aspects and motivational aspects of feedback are important, although in a large study of the effects of quality feedback on production operators, Stok (1965) found no evidence of increased motivation.

A very direct way to control the payoff matrix of inspectors is by financial incentive schemes. Raphael (1942) rejects direct incentive based on throughput, but suggests feedback of errors and promise of promotion as better alternatives. Murrell (1965) offers support for this view. The problem with feedback of errors, for motivational or incentive purposes, is that their measurement implies a further inspection of the products, which may be impractical. From experience in the glass industry, the author has found that a sample, check, inspection costs little when compared with the cost of errors, and both feedback and incentive schemes have been successfully implemented on this basis.

There are two additional factors showing pressures on the inspector which can be discussed in terms of the payoff matrix: conformity and standards. Many of the early authors (e.g. McKenzie, 1958; Seaborne, 1963) have shown that there are definite inspection 'norms' within a group. Indeed, McKenzie quotes Mitchell (1935) as finding that when production of a product doubled, so did apparent quality. The inspectors were attempting to keep the same norm for number of rejects per day despite the increased output. Drury and Addison (1973) found a similar tendency for inspectors to aim for a fixed amount of rejection despite changes in quality. In payoff-matrix terms, they behaved as if this was their primary criterion of success. Seaborne (1963) showed very clearly the effects of conforming to group rejection norms in an extended laboratory simulation of group inspection. Konz and Redding (1965) report similar effects.

The setting of external standards against which to inspect is a central problem in quality control. The usual recommendation is to have agreed 'limit standards' at the workplace so that the inspector's judgement is relative rather than the notoriously unreliable absolute. The difficulty with this recommendation is that it usually fails. The author has seen many limit standards jealously guarded to the point of gathering dust in cupboards instead of being at the inspection point. Again some standards are just too heavy or clumsy to use (McKenzie, 1958). Also Belbin (1957) shows that standards in the factory may bear little relationship to reasons for customer complaint; customers change their quality requirements frequently. For example, a strike, production stoppage, or poor sales by a customer will often cause increased rejections of material from the supplier, whereas in the opposite situation almost any quality is acceptable. Belbin suggests ways of isolating the inspector and the payoff matrix from these external conditions. Limit standards are supplied for grading of items, not for accept/reject decisions. Thus each item is given a letter grade, invariant in time, while final accept/reject decisions are based on the currently acceptable letter grade for a particular customer. Belbin also provides details of training schemes to go with this plan. Seaborne and Thomas (1964) give many examples of the development and change in subjective inspection standards.

Summarizing the job factors there is evidence that the inspection job is, in the words of Cavanagh and Rodger (1962) one with high status but not popular. The competing pressures of production, sales, peers, and customers have usually been studied in their effect on performance. It is entirely possible that these same pressures contribute a large amount to inspection stress.

A CASE STUDY

There have been very few studies which have set out to examine specifically the effect of an inspection job on inspector stress. Stress is typically measured in component tasks or as a byproduct of a study whose typical aim is performance measurement. One exception is the NIOSH-sponsored study by Wilkes, Stammerjohn, and Lalich (1981) of poultry inspection.

As shown by Chapman and Sinclair (1975), inspection of chicken carcasses is performed at high speed, often less than 4 seconds per carcass. The job demands constant attention and considerable judgement. Typically, performance is considerably below perfection (Chapman and Sinclair, 1975). The

Wilkes, Stammerjohn, and Lalich (1981) study was requested by government and unions to identify stresses and health effects of inspection. About 800 inspectors were surveyed and classified as having high exposure (full-time), medium exposure (part-time), variable exposure (relief inspectors), or low exposure (supervisors) to the stresses of inspection. Full-time inspectors worked 8-hour days with approximately 30 minutes of total breaks and 30 to 45 minutes lunch. Work was machine-paced and often uncomfortable because of the poor workplace ergonomics.

Job stresses were measured using the methodology developed by Caplan *et al.* (1975), while health outcomes were assessed on a symptom checklist.

The results confirmed many of the findings in this review. Inspectors, particularly full-time inspectors, had high perceived quantitative workloads but low utilization of their abilities. Their workload was perceived as highly variable and their future as uncertain. Role ambiguity and role conflict was typical of paced workers in general, although less than administrators. Social support from supervisors and others at work was particularly low. Job dissatisfaction, workload dissatisfaction, and boredom were high and somatic complaints frequent. These latter were mainly from the visual, gastrointestinal, and musculoskeletal areas. 'The high visual demands of the task were reflected in the visual complaints', as the authors note.

Clearly, the inspectors see themselves in much the same light as researchers have painted their predicament. The task itself is visually demanding, paced and in need of constant attention to decision-making, all aspects associated with stress measures. The job is ambiguous and demands can be conflicting, recalling the observations about conflicting pressures of production and sales. The inspector is poorly supported by the rest of the factory population, again reinforcing the impression of inspectors leagued together against a hostile world. Finally, there is confirmation that inspection is quantitatively a stressful job; health complaints are high compared with other jobs studied by Caplan *et al.* (1975). Given that inspection is stressful, further study of the stresses of the components of the job may give valuable clues to the use of automation not just to improve performance but to improve performance with reduced inspector stress.

REFERENCES

Belbin, R. M. (1957). New fields for quality control, *British Management Review*, **15**, 70–89.

Bhatnager, V., Drury, C. G., and Schiro, S. G. (1984). The effect of time-at-task on posture and performance in inspection, *Proceedings of 1984 International Conference on Occupational Ergonomics*, Toronto, May, Vol. 1, pp. 289–293.

Brozek *et al.* (1950). Changes in performance and in occular functions resulting from strenuous visual inspection, *American Journal of Psychology*, **63**, 51–66.

Buck, J. R. (1975). Dynamic visual inspection: task factors, theory and economics. In *Human Reliability in Quality Control* (Eds. C. G. Drury and J. G. Fox), Taylor and Francis, London.

Caplan, R. D., Cobb, S., French, J. R. P., van Harrison, R., and Pinneau, S. R. (1975). Job demands and worker health, NIOSH Research Report, HEW Publications No. NIOSH 75-160.

Cavanagh, P., and Rodger, A. (1962). Some hidden determinants of inspectors' judgements, *Occupational Psychology*, **36**, 152–158.

Chapman, D. E., and Sinclair, M. A. (1975). Ergonomics in inspection tasks in the food industry. In *Human Reliability in Quality Control* (Eds. C. G. Drury and J. G. Fox), Taylor and Francis, London.

Coury, B. G. (1983). The impact of extended work periods on performance and response in paced conditions. Final report on NIOSH Contract No. 821591—Impact of extended effort on paced, decision-making inspection.

Coury, B. G., and Drury, C. G. (1982). Stress, pacing and inspection. In *Machine Pacing and Occupational Stress* (Eds. G. Salvendy and M. Smith), Taylor and Francis, London.

Cox, T., and Mackay, C. (1977). A psychological model for occupational stress. In *Mental Stress in Industry*, Medical Research Council Meeting.

Drury, C. G. (1973). The effect of speed of working on industrial inspection accuracy, *Applied Ergonomics*, **4**, 2–7.

Drury, C. G. (1975). Inspection of sheet materials: model and data, *Human Factors*, **17**, 257–265.

Drury, C. G. (1978). Integrating human factors models into statistical quality control, *Human Factors*, **20**(5), 561–572.

Drury, C. G. (1982). Improving inspection performance. In *Handbook of Industrial Engineering* (Ed. G. Salvendy), John Wiley, New York, Chap. 8.

Drury, C. G. (1984). Ergonomics in quality control, *Proceedings of 1984 International Conference on Occupational Ergonomics*, Toronto, May, Vol. 2, pp. 47–55.

Drury, C. G., and Addison, J. L. (1973). An industrial study of the effects of feedback and fault density on inspection performance, *Ergonomics*, **16**, 159–169.

Drury, C. G., and Fox, J. G. (1975). *Human Reliability in Quality Control*, Taylor and Francis, London.

Drury, C. G., and Sinclair, M. A. (1983). Human and machine performance in an inspection task, *Human Factors*, **25**(4), 391–400.

Eskew, R. T., and Riche, C. G. (1982). Pacing and locus of control in quality control inspection, *Human Factors*, **24**(4), 411–415.

Fox, J. G., and Haslegrave, C. M. (1969). Industrial inspection efficiency and the probability of a defect occurring, *Ergonomics*, **12**, 713–722.

Fox, J. G., and Richardson, S. (1970). *The Complexity of the Signal in Visual Inspection Tasks*, Unpublished paper, University of Birmingham, Department of Engineering Production, England.

Greening, C. P. (1975). Mathematical modelling of air-to-ground target acquisition, *Human Factors*, **18**, 111–148.

Harris, D. H., and Chaney, F. B. (1969). *Human Factors and Quality Assurance*, John Wiley, New York.

Inomata, O. (1977). An evaluation of heart rate variability in different levels of mental loading, *Journal of Human Ergology*, **6**(2), 208–210.

Jamieson, G. H. (1966). Inspection in the telecommunications industry: a field study of age and other performance variables, *Ergonomics*, **9**, 297–303.

Juran, J. M. (1935). Inspectors' errors in quality control, *Mechanical Engineering*, **57**, 634–644.

Juran, J. M. (1966). Quality problems, remedies and nostrums, *Industrial Quality Control*, **22**, 647–653.

Kahneman, D. (1973). *Attention and Effort*, Prentice-Hall, Englewood Cliffs, N.J.

Kalsbeek, J. W. H. (1973). Do you believe in sinus arrhythmia?, *Ergonomics*, **16**, 99–104.

Kishida, K. (1973). Temporal change in subsidiary behavior in monotonous work, *Journal of Human Ecology*, **2**, 75–89.

Kleiner, B. M., and Drury,. C. G. (1984). A comparison of blink aided and manual inspection using laboratory and plant subject, *Proceedings of the Human Factors Society 28th Annual Meeting*, October, San Antonio, Tex., pp. 670–674.

Konz, S. (1982). *Work Design: Industrial Ergonomics*, Grid Publishing Co., Columbus, Ohio.

Konz, S., and Redding, S. (1965). The effect of social pressure on decision-making, *The Journal of Industrial Engineering*, **16**(6), 381–384.

Liuzzo, J., and Drury, C. G. (1980). An evaluation of blink inspection, *Human Factors*, **22**, 201–210.

McFarling, L. H., and Heimstra, N. W. (1975). Pacing, product complexity and task perception in stimulated inspection, *Human Factors*, **17**, 361–367.

McKenzie, R. M. (1958). On the accuracy of inspectors, *Ergonomics*, **11**, 258–272.

McKenzie, R. M., and Pugh, D. S. (1957). Some human aspects of inspection, *Journal of Institution of Production Engineers*, **36**, 378–388.

Mackie, R. R. (Ed.) (1977). *Vigilance*, Plenum Press, New York.

Maher, J., et al. (1970). Enriched jobs improve inspection, *Work Study and Management Services*, **1970**, 821–824.

Megaw, E. D., and Bellamy, L. (1979). Variables that affect search patterns. In *Search and the Human Observer* (Eds. J. N. Claire and N. A. Sinclair), Taylor and Francis, London.

Mitchell, J. H. (1935). Subjective standards in inspection for appearance, *The Human Factor*, **9**, 235–239.

Murrell, K. F. H. (1965). *Ergonomics*, Chapman and Hall, London, Chap. 18.

Narayanaswamy, S., and Drury, C. G. (1981). The effect of pacing speed on inspection performance, Report to Bethlehem Steel Co., on Grant No. 150-2440-N.

Purswell, J. L., Greenhaw, L. N., and Oats, C. (1972). An inspection task experiment, *Proceedings of the Human Factors Society 16th Annual Meeting*, pp. 297–300.

Raphael, W. (1942). Some problems of inspection, *Occupational Psychology*, **16**, 157–163.

Rubenstein, S. P. (1971). Participative quality control, *Quality Progress*, **4**, 24–27.

Saito, M. (1972). A study on bottle inspection speed, *Journal of the Science of Labour*, **48**, 395–400.

Saito, M., Tanaka, T., and Maruchi, N. (1969). A study on movement of eyeballs in empty bottle inspection, Paper presented at the 16th International Congress on Occupational Health, Tokyo.

Seaborne, A. E. M. (1963). Social effects on standards in gauging tasks, *Ergonomics*, **6**, 205–209.

Seaborne, A. E. M., and Thomas, L. F. (1964). *Subjective Standards in Industrial Inspection*, HMSO, London.

Sheehan, J. J., and Drury, C. G. (1971). The analysis of industrial inspection, *Applied Ergonomics*, **2**, 74–78.

Sinclair, M. A. (1970). The use of performance measures on individual examiners in inspection schemes, *Applied Ergonomics*, **10**(1), 17–25.

Stok, T. L. (1965). *The Worker and Quality Control*, University of Michigan Press, Ann Arbor, Mich.

Swets, J. A. (1977). Signal detection theory applied to vigilance. In *Vigilance* (Ed. R. R. Mackie), Plenum Press, New York.

Thackeray, R. I., Jones, K. N., and Touchstone, R. M. (1974). Personality and physiological correlates of performance decrement on a monotonous task requiring sustained attention, *British Journal of Psychology*, **65**, 351–358.

Thomas, L. R., and Seaborne, A. E. M. (1961). The socio-technical context of industrial inspection, *Occupational Psychology*, **35**, 36–43.

Van Beek, H. G. (1964). The influence of assembly line organization on output, quality and morale, *Occupational Psychology*, **38**, 161–172.

Wallack, P. M., and Adams, S. K. (1969). The utility of signal detection theory in the analysis of industrial inspector accuracy, *AIIE Transactions*, **1**, 33–44.

Weiner, E. L. (1975). Individual and group differences on inspection. In *Human Reliability in Quality Control* (Eds. C. G. Drury and J. G. Fox), Taylor and Francis, London.

Wilkes, B., Stammerjohn, L., and Lalich, N. (1981). Job demands and worker health in machine-paced poultry inspection, *Scand. J. Work Envir. Health*, 7(4), 12–19.

Job Stress and Blue Collar Work
Edited by C. L. Cooper and M. J. Smith

Chapter 8

Alternative Work Schedules: Flextime and The Compressed Work Week

Joseph J. Hurrell, Jr., and Michael J. Colligan

National Institute for Occupational Safety and Health,
US Department of Health and Human Services,
Cincinnati, Ohio, USA

There is a considerable body of research indicating that the temporal scheduling of work can have a significant impact on the physical and psychological well-being of the individual worker. Permanent night and rotating shift work, in particular have been linked to a variety of health complaints and problems involving social/familial adjustment (e.g. Rutenfranz *et al.*, 1977; Winget, Hughes, and LaDou, 1978; Johnson *et al.*, 1981; Tepas, Walsh, and Armstrong, 1981). For the most part, these shift-related complications have been attributed to the disruption of physiological and social circadian rhythms associated with working at hours which are dyssynchronous with the normal diurnal activity cycle (Aschoff, 1981; Wever, 1981).

From the workers' perspective, however, concerns regarding the effects of work hours on the overall quality of their lives take on a much broader focus. At issue here is not only the direct and immediate influence of the hours of work on physiological and psychological functioning, but also their effects on leisure time and off-the-job family activities. Such concerns coupled with the increasing frequency, in both the United States and Europe, of dual-worker families have stimulated experimentation with a number of novel work schedules. Two varieties of such alternative schedules currently receiving considerable speculative and increasing empirical attention are flextime and the compressed work week. Both types of schedules have been touted as being capable of lessening experienced time pressure and thereby improving not only job performance and organizational effectiveness, but also the quality of life for workers and their families. This chapter attempts to examine what is known concerning the advantages and disadvantages of these two alternative work schedule systems and to identify future research needs.

FLEXTIME

Flextime is a work schedule that leaves the standard number of working hours unchanged but allows workers some degree of freedom on when to start and stop work. Flextime arrangements are referred to by many names (e.g. floating day, flexitour, gliding time, maxiflex) and, in fact, there is no standard flextime arrangement (Lieb, Lefkowitz and Associates, 1981). Rather, programmes are typically tailored to the individual organization, its workers, and the community in which they function. As Golembiewski and Proehl (1978) have noted, flextime arrangements may vary along seven different dimensions: (1) band width, which refers to the number of hours between the earliest starting time and the latest permissible finishing time; (2) core hours, referring to a period of time within the band width during which employees must be at work; (3) flexible hours, meaning the number of hours in a workday that are left to the workers discretion; (4) workweek length, referring to the greatest number of hours a worker is permitted to work in one week; (5) banking, meaning how many hours a worker can carry forward or owe; (6) variability freedom, indicating the degree to which the workers can vary their schedules without approval; and (7) supervisory role, meaning how approvals are granted and under what circumstances management might preempt the system to suit organizational needs.

From its origins in West Germany in the late 1960s, flextime in various forms spread rapidly across Europe. McEwan Young (1981), for example, has estimated that in the United Kingdom in 1980 about a million workers were working flextime schedules who 10 years previously had worked fixed work hours. While precise data on the present use of flextime in Europe are difficult to obtain, it has been estimated that as many as 40 per cent. of workers in Switzerland and 35 per cent. of workers in France use flextime (Haldi Associates, Inc., 1975; Sharko and Price, 1976).

While somewhat slower to gain acceptance in the United States (Nollen and Martin, 1978), flextime has become tremendously popular. According to a Bureau of Labour Statistics (1980) survey (*Current Population Survey*), approximately 7.6 million or about 12 per cent. of workers employed in full-time, non-farm wage and salary jobs were on schedules that permitted them to vary the time they begin and end their workdays. In this survey, the standard industrial classifications of finance, insurance, and real estate (17.1 per cent.), trade (14.7 per cent.), and public administration (15.2 per cent.) led the industry groups in the proportion of full-time workers permitted to vary their work hours. According to these same data, nearly 25 per cent. of federal workers (excluding postal workers) and 14 and 9 per cent. of state and local government workers respectively were on flextime schedules. By 1990 it is estimated that 25 per cent. of all full-time non-farm workers in the United States will be on flextime work schedules (Work in America Institute, 1981).

In terms of occupational use, flextime appears to be most widespread among sales personnel managers, professional workers, and transportation equipment operatives—occupations in which the practice is long-standing and often informal (U.S. Bureau of Labour Statistics, 1981). Flextime is difficult to arrange and therefore least often found in jobs such as receptionists, retail sales clerks, workers in shipping rooms and mail rooms, nurses, bus drivers, security guards, machine-paced assemblers, and in very small work units (Nollen, 1979).

The advantages attributed to flextime have been both numerous and diverse in nature. Flexible work hours have been viewed as a method to raise morale; reduce lateness, absenteeism, and turnover; increase productivity; improve corporate image; reduce overtime; facilitate recruitment; provide opportunities for scheduling educational, recreational, social, and family pursuits; reduce gasoline consumption and peak-load residential energy use; and improve air qualities (see Swart, 1978; Nollen, 1979).

Potential disadvantages of flextime have been discussed by Allenspach (1975), Nollen (1979), Swart (1978) and Ronen (1981), and include the following: (1) worsened internal and external communications; (2) difficulty in scheduling the coverage of certain jobs at needed times; (3) increased energy costs; (4) difficulty in scheduling meetings; (5) reduction in services to the public; (6) additional planning and organization; (7) increases in stock as a buffer for assembly lines; and (8) impaired job performance owing to non-work activities.

Unfortunately, however, there have been very few systematic investigations which have attempted to examine the effects of flextime. As both Pierce and Newstrom (1983) and Orpen (1981) have noted, a majority of flextime literature is descriptive, anecdotal, and highly speculative. Indeed, a recent analysis of some 183 references to flextime (Lee, 1984) found that only 7 per cent. could be characterized as research in nature. The following section will examine that research which deals with the effects of flextime on, firstly, the work organization (in terms of factors such as absenteeism, productivity, and job satisfaction) and, secondly, the community (in terms of its impact on factors associated with transportation to and from work). This section is followed by a discussion of the impact of flextime on the well-being of individual workers and their families.

Flextime: organizational and community effects

One of the most consistently studied aspects of flextime has been its relationship to absenteeism. The first systematic investigation of this relationship appears to have been conducted by Golembiewski, Hilles, and Kugno (1974). In this quasi-experimental study, a group of 43 scientists, hourly workers, and supervisors participating in a pilot flexible work hours programme showed a 35 per cent. decrease in paid absences at a one-year post test. By comparison, a similar control group of 41 subjects showed a 15 per cent. increase over the same period. Not all studies, however, report such dramatic effects. An early study by Fields (1974) of some 22 clerical employees of a large life insurance company, for example, found only a 7.6 per cent. decrease in absences after a 6-month period. In the Fields (1974) study, however, employees were not permitted to bank or borrow hours.

More recent studies of flextime and absenteeism have been somewhat more sophisticated in that they have attempted to examine variables that might moderate the flextime–absenteeism relationship. Krausz and Freibach (1983), for example, investigated the moderating effects of marital status and parenthood upon unauthorized and unpaid absences in a large insurance company in Israel. The experimental group consisted of 148 women from departments working under a schedule of flexible working time while the control group consisted of 129 women from departments with rigid schedules. Absence rates were found, in the two-month period of study, to be significantly lower under the flexible than the rigid work schedule. As anticipated by the authors, married women and mothers were found to have the lowest rates of absenteeism when employed under a flexible schedule. It is interesting to note that mothers of young children, in this study, felt that the beneficial effects of flextime in the workplace are often offset by non-flexible arrangements of their non-work life caused by home obligations and by their dependence upon others such as babysitters whose life and work arrangements are not flexible.

Similarly, Pierce and Newstrom (1983) investigated the moderating effects of perceived autonomy for scheduling work and non-work time on the flextime–absenteeism relationship in some 188 clerical workers in five insurance companies. While main effects of flextime were noted, no perceived autonomy–work schedule interaction was found.

A host of less rigorous survey studies of both company officials and employees has tended to support the contention that flextime has beneficial effects on absenteeism rates. Many of these studies have been reviewed by Nollen (1979).

Studies of the effects of flextime on performance have been somewhat less consistent in their findings. While surveys of employer and employee perceptions of performance have been favourable (Nollen and Martin, 1978; Nollen, 1979), more rigorous and controlled studies have given mixed results. The Pierce and Newstrom (1983) study described above, for example, found a positive association between work schedule flexibility and performance appraisals given by immediate supervisors. Schein, Maurer, and Novak (1977), however, using a sample of 247 clerical workers in a large life insurance company, found only limited evidence for increased productivity. Using comparisons with productivity outcomes (e.g. number of claims processed and percentage of work completed in 5 days) during the same period the previous year, Schein found increases in only one of four groups of workers studied. This increase, according to Schein, may not have resulted from flextime but rather from other structural and technological changes occurring during the experiment. No change in productivity was found in the other three groups. A recent study by Orpen (1981), however, found no evidence for a flextime performance relationship. Using a pre-test and post-test control group design, 64 female clerical workers in a large federal agency in South Africa were randomly assigned to either flexible or fixed working hours for 6 months. No major differences between the two groups were found on either supervisor-assessed performance or actual work output. Clearly more research is needed using multiple measures of performance and a greater diversity of job tasks.

Reports of job satisfaction and morale in companies and work units using flextime have generally been quite positive (see Swart, 1978; Nollen, 1979). These investigations, however, as Pierce and Newstrom (1983) note, have tended to use non-systematic data-collection strategies and non-standardized research scales which cast doubt on their validity. More rigorous studies of job satisfaction, like the studies of flextime and performance, have produced mixed results. The Orpen (1981) study, discussed above, for example, found flextime caused a significant increase in satisfaction as measured by the Index of Job Satisfaction (Brayfield and Roth, 1951), but the reasons for the increase were unclear. Krausz and Freibach (1983), however, found no differences in satisfaction (as measured by a six-item index) among their sample of clerical workers. Likewise, the Pierce and Newstrom (1983) study, also using clerical workers, found no significant relationship between work schedule flexibility and job satisfaction as measured by the Minnesota Satisfaction Questionnaire (Weiss et al., 1976). They did find, however, that perceptions of time autonomy play an important intervening role in the flexible work schedule–job satisfaction relationship. It seems obvious that future studies need to be directed towards the identification of features of flexible work hour systems that may impact satisfaction.

As indicated previously, flextime has the potential for having a substantial community impact. In particular, flextime may reduce rush-hour use of public and private transportation and thereby reduce commuting time, gasoline consumption, accident rates, and improve air quality. It is also possible that flextime may lead to a reduction in peak-load residential use of electricity and natural gas (see Kohlenberg, Phillips, and Proctor, 1976). Unfortunately, very little empirical evidence exists concerning these issues. A study (Ott, Slavin, and Ward, 1980) conducted by the U.S. Department of Transportation, however, does provide some limited insight. This study was conducted at a government research facility in Boston which employed over 600 persons. Based on the results of a survey administered to employees, it was estimated that 90 per cent. of the workers shifted modes of transportation to work due to flextime. The percentage of respondents driving alone dropped from 42.4 to 39.8 per cent. while car-pool participation increased from 35.4 to 37.4 per cent. Transit patronage also increased slightly. Over 50 per cent. of the auto drivers and car-poolers who had not changed modes reported travel time savings due to flextime. All those switching to driving alone and car-pooling reported travel time savings. These travel time savings were estimated to have resulted in fuel savings of about 5 per cent. for vehicles driven to work. A smaller study conducted with two federal agencies in the Washington, D.C., area (see Winett and Neale, 1981) also found a significant decrease in commuting time for workers who entered a flextime programme which allowed them to start work earlier.

Flextime: individual and family effects

Perhaps the least explored aspect of flextime has been its impact on the lives of workers and their families. This is a curious irony in that flextime arose as a means of allowing workers greater freedom and more opportunities in scheduling educational, recreational, social, and family pursuits.

Perhaps the first in-depth investigations of how flextime affects individuals and their families were conducted by Winett and Neale (1980, 1981). This study, as noted above, was conducted in two federal agencies in the Washington, D.C., area and involved the completion of time-activity logs by 26 control subjects and a group of 24 workers who volunteered, and subsequently participated, in a flextime programme. This programme allowed workers to start work at an earlier time. Analyses of these time-activity logs revealed that the group of workers changing to an earlier schedule showed a significant increase in the amount of time spent with their children in the evening. These workers also reported (on other collection instruments) that the increase in p.m. time alleviated some of the difficulties involved in co-ordinating various work and home life situations. These findings seem to be consistent with data presented in the Ott, Slavin, and Ward (1980) study (discussed above), indicating that more than 75 per cent. of those surveyed felt that flextime allowed them to increase participation in non-work activities. However, Winett and neale (1981) found no pre-post differences in time spent in activities such as exercising, watching television, and eating dinner. Thus what non-work activities are participated in (other than child rearing) is unclear.

A more recent study by Lee and his colleagues at Loughborough University (see Lee, 1983) has attempted to expand upon the work of Winett and Neale (1980, 1981). In this study 100 employees (75 male and 25 female) in a single organization were surveyed before and 6 months after the implementation of flextime. Participants were queried as to their actual conjugal role activities, their perceptions of stress related to these activities, and the contextual factors likely to affect role demands. Results of the study showed that for women there was no major change in housework activities. Males, however, spent a larger amount of time in car maintenance activities. In terms of child-related activities, there was no change for females; however, males reported taking on an increasing share of child socialization activities. Lee (1983) concludes that the major change to be brought about by flextime is an improvement in the amount of time fathers spend with their children.

Several studies have attempted to examine the effects of flextime on psychological strains in working women, but have provided contradictory results. The Krausz and Freibach (1983) study, discussed earlier, found no differences in psychosomatic symptoms or depression between women employed in flextime arrangements and those working rigid hours. Differences in depression were reported by Barling and Barenburg (1984). In this study, conducted in Johannesburg, South Africa, 21 working mothers employed in a flextime arrangement were compared to 33 non-flextime working mothers. Compared to their non-flextime counterparts, mothers working full-time in a flextime system reported less behavioural depression. No differences in either ideational or psychological depression were noted, however. Flextime mothers also reported less parent-spouse and parent-self role conflict.

In summary, there is a tremendous need for well-controlled research on the effects of flextime on workers, their families, their work organizations, and their communities. Previous research has focused primarily on the organizational consequences of flextime, and has produced few consistent findings. Clearly more conceptual work is in order which seeks to identify differences in flextime arrangements capable of producing the kinds of inconsistencies reported above.

COMPRESSED WORK WEEK

Compressed work week refers to a schedule in which the standard 40-hour week is condensed to three or four working days rather than the customary five. While it is commonly believed that such schedules are a recent development, the compressed work week has in various forms existed for many years (Poor, 1970). Its use, however, has increased dramatically since the early 1970s (Nollen, 1979).

According to the BLS *Current Population Survey* (US Bureau of Labour Statistics, 1980), approximately 1.9 million or 2.7 per cent. of full-time non-farm American workers are on some form of compressed work week. The most popular schedule is the 4.40, consisting of four consecutive 10-hour workdays, followed by three days off. A variant of this routine is the 'rolling 4-10' with four 10-hour workdays, followed by four days off. Thus in the former system a worker is on the job for 40 hours in every 7-day period, with the same days of the week off each week. With the rolling 4-10, the worker is on the job for 40 hours in every 8-day period, and the off days roll forward by one weekday every week (Leib *et al.*, 1981). Common users of these schedules include service workers (6.7 per cent. of all employed in this job category), transportation equipment operatives (4.4 per cent.), and factory operatives (3.3 per cent.), according to Bureau of Labour Statistics data (Leib *et al.*, 1981).

One of the earliest industries to implement compressed work week schedules was the petroleum/chemical industry, and it has thus been the focus of most of the evaluation research (Campbell, 1980; Tepas and Tepas, 1981). Here the most popular schedule has involved the 12-hour work shift, largely possible as a result of the continuous nature of the production process, and the fact that the work involves primarily vigilance/monitoring tasks rather than intense physical labour. As described by Northrup, Wilson, and Rose (1979), most of the plants on 12-hour shifts use one of three schedules: (1) one which allows for every other weekend off (EOWEO), in which the individual alternates work/rest days on a 3/2, 2/3 basis; (2) a three-on, three-off rotating schedule; or (3) a four-on, four-off rotating schedule. Of these three systems, the EOWEO appears to be the easiest to implement and is the most popular among the workers because of the regularity and frequency of long weekends. Because of their popularity, and the fact that most of the available research deals with the 4/40 and 12-hour shifts, the remainder of the discussion will focus on these work regimes.

Perceived advantages of compressed schedules include: (1) the increase of 'usable leisure' time in terms of long weekends and blocks of 'off days'; (2) a reduction of commuting time, automobile and gasoline usage, etc., as a result of the cutback in workdays; (3) a reduction in work-related costs (e.g. child care expenses, commuting fares, lunch, etc.); and (4) anticipated increases in productivity arising from reduced absenteeism, reduced start-up/shut-down times relative to operating times, and the keying of work schedules to operating/processing functions rather than standard work times (Hedges, 1971). The expansion of consecutive free days also permits the shift worker a longer recuperative time and increases the probability that at least one of his/her off days will overlap with that of other family members and friends.

In addition to these potential advantages, however, the compressed work week may have some rather serious disadvantages. These include:

1. The reduction of available leisure time on scheduled workdays.
2. The potential fatigue effects of working extended hours and the implications this might have for overall health and accident susceptibility.
3. The potential problems associated with prolonged exposure (i.e. 10 or 12 hours) to levels of physical and chemical hazards in the workplace which have time-related exposure standards predicated on the more traditional 8-hour workday.

As with flextime, discussions of the relative pros and cons of the compressed work week have been primarily speculative, and little systematic research has been conducted to evaluate its effects on individual and organizational functioning. Case reports of worksites using alternative schedules have relied upon anecdotal observations or self-report surveys from 'grab' samples to evaluate employee adjustment and are thus subject to criticism on methodological grounds. Controlled laboratory studies, on the other hand, have tended to focus on extended intensive performance under atypical work/rest conditions (e.g. Chiles, Alluisi, and Adams, 1968; Alluisi and Morgan, 1982). Generalizing from these situations to the 'real world' in which individuals work at a less strenuous level but on a work/rest schedule which may remain fixed for years appears unwarranted. It is not surprising, then, that after reviewing the literature on the performance effects of commonly used work schedules, Alluisi and Morgan (1982) state 'there have been no conclusive studies, and, with few exceptions, no well-controlled experimental attempts to examine the long term effects of atypical schedules' (p. 183).

The following section examines the available research involving the organizational impact of the compressed work week in terms of efficiency, productivity, and worker satisfaction. This is followed by a review of the studies which have been concerned with the individual effects (including health and productivity) of the compressed work week.

The compressed work week: organizational effects

Research into the impact of the compressed work on organizational efficiency has been summarized by Nollen (1979) and can best be characterized as inconclusive. With respect to productivity, Calvasina and Boxx (1975) analysed weekly output data for workers in a pair of garment manufacturing plants which had switched from a 5-day/40-hour per week schedule to a 4-day/38-hour work week. Pre- and post-switch comparisons made a year later indicated no change in weekly output. Campbell (1980) surveyed 72 hydrocarbon processing plants which had switched from 8- to 12-hour shifts and found 27 sites indicating an increase in plant efficiency, 23 sites reporting a decrease, and 22 reporting no change. Ivancevich (1974) compared the questionnaire responses of two plants of workers on a 4/40 work week with a standard 5-day control plant and found that supervisors reported higher levels of productivity and effectiveness under the compressed work week regime one year after implementation. In a later study, using a larger period of observation and a larger sample, Ivancevich found that the improvements in productivity after a conversion to a 4/40 work week that were apparent at 13 months did not hold up after 25 months (Ivancevich and Lyon, 1977). Thus while there is no evidence to indicate that the compressed work week impairs performance, there is some suggestion that the initial improvement in efficiency following conversion to a shortened work week may reflect Hawthorne-type effects. Future research is needed which permits repeated measures of performance over longer periods of time.

Studies examining the impact of the compressed work week on morale and job satisfaction have found such schedules to produce generally favourable effects (e.g. Maklan, 1977; Nollen and Martin, 1978). As might be expected, however, worker demographic characteristics play a significant role in moderating this finding. Thus younger workers seem to be more satisfied with the compressed work week than older workers (Dunham and Hawk, 1977; Allen and Hawes, 1979), males more than females (Dickinson and Wijting, 1975; Allen and Hawes, 1979), and new workers at low wage grades more than experienced, higher paid workers (Dunham and Hawk, 1977; Northrup, Wilson, and Rose, 1979). As noted by Mahoney, Newman, and Frost (1975), the critical factor influencing a worker's satisfaction with the compressed work week involves not physical fatigue or work-related concerns, but rather the use of leisure time. To the extent that the individual's life style and personal/family needs require blocks of free time each day, the compressed schedule becomes a source of conflict. For younger, unmarried workers, on the other hand, the long weekends afforded by the compressed work week may more than compensate for a slightly longer workday. A complete understanding of the impact of compressed schedules on worker adjustment, therefore, requires a broad prospective which focuses on both personal and work-related activities. For the present, it would appear that worker reaction to the compressed work week has been generally positive, resulting in greater job satisfaction and organizational morale (Campbell, 1980; Northrup *et al.*, 1979).

The compressed work week: Individual effects

As previously noted, an initial concern with the compressed work week (and extended workday) is the fact that threshold limits of exposure to various chemical and physical hazards in the workplace presuppose an 8-hour workday. The effects of exposures to these same hazards for periods of 10 to 12 hours have yet to be determined, but obviously would vary as a function of job- and hazard-specific standards. Northrup, Wilson, and Rose (1979) discuss the problem in some detail and suggest, as one solution, the establishment of exposure limits based on total weekly hours of work rather than on a daily basis. Some progress has been made in this regard. The National Institute for Occupational Safety and Health, for example, now states recommended standards for exposure in terms of time weighted average concentrations for up to a 10-hour workday in a 40-hour work week. There is, however, a critical need for industry (and hazard) specific research aimed at examining the specific effects of exposure to a wide range of carcinogenic and other hazardous substances during compressed work week schedules.

The sparse research pertaining to the potential health effects of compressed schedules reported in the literature deals mainly with absentee-ism. Thus Campbell (1980), based on the survey responses of 71 petroleum refineries which had converted from a traditional 40-hour week to a 12-hour/day schedule, reports 13 locations showing an increase in absenteeism, 30 locations experiencing a decrease, and 28 indicating no change. Nollen and Martin (1978) found that 71 per cent. of a sample of 156 organizations using some form of compressed schedule reported a decrease in the rate of absenteeism relative to a 5-day/40-hour schedule. Gardner and Dagnall (1977) tracked a sample of 356 men employed in an oil refinery for a one-year period before and after switching from a 5/40 to a 12-hour/day schedule and found no change in sickness absence. Similar results were reported by Northrup, Wilson, and Rose (1979) following interviews with management representatives of 50 oil refinery plants on compressed work schedules. Nord and Costigan (1973) prospectively surveyed a group of workers employed as machine operators and inspectors in the manufacture of pharmaceutical products who were on a $9\frac{1}{2}$ hours/day, 4-day schedule. There was a 10 per cent. reduction in absenteeism immediately after the adoption of the compressed work week, followed by an additional 10 per cent. reduction one year later. There was also a slight, but statistically significant, reduction in the sleep of workers on the shortened week from an average of 7.05 hours/night on the 5-day week to 6.72 hours/night on the 4-day schedule.

In a more intensive study of the effects of the 4/40 schedule on physiological functioning, Volle et al. (1979) compared two groups of workers from two different factories (one on a 4/40 schedule, the other on a 5/40) engaged in light manufacturing work on a number of biomedical/physio-logical parameters. Measurements taken before and after the first and last day of the work week indicated no significant differences between the two groups in terms of heart rate, blood pressure, body temperature, respiratory volume, O_2 consumption, and CO_2 production. It thus appears that there are no dramatic health effects associated with the compressed work schedule. It should be noted, however, that the studies reported to date have examined a small number of gross health indices among workers in light industry who had been on the new schedule for a year or less. Long-term prospective studies using a multivariate design are needed.

Perhaps the most obvious a priori concern about the potential impact of the 10- and 12-hour workday on the individual worker is that of fatigue. Thus, in a survey of approximately 450 assembly workers on a traditional 5/40 schedule, it was found that the most salient anticipated disadvantage of conversion to a 4/50 schedule was the worker's concern about excessive fatigue. Lack of efficiency due to fatigue was also one of the primary reasons for not adopting a 4-day work week given by a sample of approximately 800 members of the American Management Association reported by Wheeler, Gurman, and Tarnowieski (1972). Hodge and Tellier (1975), based on 223 responses of employees of twelve 4-day companies, found that the primary sources of dissatisfaction were the longer workday and increased feelings of fatigue. Nevertheless, the employees reported a substantial increase in job satisfaction following adoption of the compressed work week schedule. The same results were reported by Maklan (1977) who found that, while 22 per cent. of his sample of male blue collar 4/40 workers reported feeling very tired after work, the compressed work week sample was significantly more satisfied with their work schedule than 5/40 men. It appears, then, that the longer workday results in a greater *perception* of fatigue among workers on compressed schedules, but that they feel this is offset by the advantages of extended off-days and blocks of liesure. Finally, it remains to be determined whether the subjective fatigue experienced by the workers on compressed schedules actually translates into objective outcomes, whether such fatigue is a transitory psychological stage in the adaption process, or whether reported fatigue may reflect expectancy or something akin to demand characteristics. Of the 70 petroleum refineries responding to Campbell's (1980) survey, five sites reported an increase in accidents, eight sites a decrease, and 57 no change after converting from a 5/40 to a 12-hour/day schedule. Northrup, Wilson, and Rose (1979) reported that none of the 50 petrochemical plants in their survey reported an increase in accidents as a result of adopting 12-hour shifts. Volle *et al.* (1979), in addition to the physiological data previously described, included a variety of performance tests in their assessment of the effects of 4/40 work schedules on a sample of workers engaged in the manufacture of kitchen equipment. Relative to a control group of 5/40 workers performing similar work, the workers on a compressed schedule showed no differences in simple and choice reaction time, left-hand grip strength, or performance on the Omega 37 test of psychological creativity, in measures taken before and after their regular work week. There were, however, significant differences on measures of right-handed grip strength and critical flicker fusion, with the performance of workers on the traditional 5/40 schedule being more efficient.

Finally, Colquhoun, Blake, and Edwards (1969) examined the performance of 22 male naval recruits assigned to 12-hour shifts for 12 consecutive days in a laboratory study designed to simulate shipboard conditions. The tasks included auditory and visual monitoring resembling certain sonar operations and a calculation test involving the addition of a series of two-digit numbers. The same study design had been previously used with a sample of naval recruits on a standard 8-hour shift (Colquhoun, Blake, and Edwards, 1968), thereby allowing a comparison of the effects of these two schedules on performance. Since such an analysis was not intended by the original study design, however, any inferences derived from this comparison should be treated tentatively.

Consistent with the Volle *et al.* (1979) study, there were no dramatic fatigue effects evidenced by the 12-hour group relative to the traditional 8-hour group. During the forenoon period (08.00 to 11.30 with a 10-minute rest

break at 9.40) performance efficiency at both tasks (vigilance and calcu-
lations) rose gradually in each group to the same extent, thus reflecting the
normal circadian effect (e.g. Colquhoun, 1971). Following lunch (11.30 to
12.30), both groups evidenced the expected 'post-lunch dip' in performance
with efficiency declining from the morning level during the 12.30 to 14.10 and
14.20 to 16.00 sessions. Despite a light meal break (16.00 to 16.30) performance in the 12-hour group rose gradually during the extra 4-hour session to
the 'expected' (i.e. based on circadian norms) maximum level. The general
circadian pattern for the 8- and 12-hour groups were similar, with no obvious
fatigue effects attributable to the longer work session. Colquhoun did note
that the 12-hour group took longer to recover from the 'post-lunch dip', both
in terms of task performance and pulse rate, and speculates that the latter
finding may be due to an inadvertent confounding of work schedule with
introversion/extraversion. Post-study examination of the results of the Heron
Personality Inventory (administered to the subjects prior to the experiment)
indicated that the 12-hour group scored considerably lower in introversion
and neuroticism than the 8-hour groups. This suggests that personality factors
might be important in influencing adaptation to the compressed work week.

Examination of performance over the 12-hour/day period indicated a 49
per cent. increase in mean calculation speed among the 8-hour group relative
to a 30 per cent. increase among the subjects working 12 hours/day—this
despite the fact that the latter group, by definition, received 50 per cent. more
practice during the course of the study. There were no differences between
the two groups in error rates. Given that the 8-hour group showed greater
relative improvement over the 12-day test period than the 12-hour group, it is
possible that significant performance differences may have appeared.

Finally, Monk and Embry (1981) studied six process control workers at a
British chemical plant using a 12-hour rapidly rotating shift system to assess
the relationship between the circadian body temperature rhythm and
performance on low and high memory load tasks. Low memory load performance was positively correlated with the body temperature rhythm, peaking in
the afternoon and ebbing in the pre-dawn/early morning hours. High memory
load performance, on the other hand, was inversely related to body temperature, peaking at around 02.00 to 04.00 hours and falling off into the
afternoon. In addition, there was a sharp decrease in efficiency on the high
load memory task for the last two hours of the night shift, whereas for the low
memory load task, the drop-off in performance occurred on the last two
hours of the day shift. Whether this time of day–task interaction is a 'pure'
circadian effect or involves additional moderating effects associated with
fatigue arising from a 12-hour work schedule cannot be ascertained without
an 8-hour and no-work baseline group. Nevertheless, there is a clear
indication that the effects of an extended workday schedule on performance
depends upon 'time of day' and task characteristics. The fatiguing effects of

extended shifts, if any, might be expected to vary with the nature of the work being performed and the starting and ending time of the shift. To date, this work has not been done.

In summary, there is a need for well-controlled research investigating the physical and psychological impact of alternate compressed work week schedules. Previous field research has focused on global indices of safety (e.g. accident rates) and health (e.g. absenteeism), and has generally found no dramatic detrimental effects associated with the longer workday. There is some indication that personal and demographic characteristics (e.g. age, sex, marital status) and life style factors (e.g. hobbies, leisure pursuits, etc.) may influence satisfaction with, and adaptation to, compressed schedules.

The laboratory (e.g. Colquhoun, Blake, and Edwards, 1969) and quasi-experimental (Volle *et al.*, 1979) studies directly relevant to concerns with the longer workday have indicated subtle performance changes (critical flicker fusion, speed calculation, post-lunch dip recovery) indicative of pscycho-logical fatigue. Colquhoun, Blake, and Edwards (1969) also suggest that personality factors (e.g. intraversion/extraversion) may be significant moderating variables in predicting adaptation to a compressed work regime. The work of Monk and Embry (1981) suggests that diurnal effects and memory load characteristics may affect performance on the extended schedules. The implications of these findings for worker health and safety performance have yet to be determined.

REFERENCES

Allen, R. E., and Hawes, D. K. (1979). Attitudes toward work, leisure, and the four day work-week, *Human Resources Management*, **18**, 5–10.
Allenspach, H. (1975). *Flexible Working Hours*, International Labor Office, Geneva.
Alluisi, E. A., and Morgan, B. B. (1982). Temporal factors in human performance and productivity. In *Human Performance and Productivity*, Vol. 3, *Stress and Performance Effectiveness* (Eds. E. A. Alluisi and E. A. Fleishman). Erlbaum, Hillsdale, N.J.
Aschoff, J. (1981). Circadian rhythms: interference with and dependence on work-rest schedules. In *The Twenty-Four Hour Workday: Proceedings of a Symposium on Variation in Work–Sleep Schedules* (Eds. L. C. Johnson, D. I. Tepas, W. P. Colquhoun, and M. J. Colligan), DHHS (NIOSH) Publication No. 81-127, US Government Printing Office, Washington, D.C.
Barling, J., and Barenburg, A. (1984). Some personal consequences of flextime work schedules, *Journal of Social Psychology*, **123**, 137–138.
Brayfield, A., and Roth, H. (1951). An index of job satisfaction, *Journal of Applied Psychology*, **35**, 307–311.
Campbell, L. H. (1980). Can new shift schedules motivate?, *Hydrocarbon Processing*, **April 1980**, 249–256.
Calvasina, E. J., and Boxx, W. R. (1975). Efficiency of workers on the four-day work week, *Academy of Management Journal*, **18**, 604–610.

Chiles, W. D., Alluisi, E. A., and Adams, O. S. (1968). Work schedules and performance during confinement, *Human Factors*, **10**, 143–196.

Colquhoun, W. P. (Ed.) (1971). *Biological Rhythms and Human Performance*, Academic Press, London.

Colquhoun, W. P., Blake, M. J. F., and Edwards, R. S. (1968). Experimental studies of shift work. II: Stabilized 8-hour shift systems, *Ergonomics*, **11**, 527–546.

Colquhoun, W. P., Blake, M. J. F., and Edwards, R. S. (1969). Experimental studies of shift work. III: Stabilized 12-hour shift systems, *Ergonomics*, **12**, 856–882.

Dickinson, T., and Wijting, J. P. (1975). An analysis of workers' attitudes toward the 4-day, 40-hour work week, *Psychological Reports*, **37**, 383–390.

Dunham, R. B., and Hawk, D. L. (1977). The four-day/forty-hour week: Who wants it?, *Academy of Management Journal*, **20**, 644–655.

Fields, C. (1974). Variable work hours—the experience, *Personnel Journal*, **53**, 675–678.

Gardner, A. W., and Dagnall, B. D. (1977). The effect of twelve-hour shift working on absence attributed to sickness, *British Journal of Industrial Medicine*, **34**, 148–150.

Golembiewski, R. T., Hilles, R., and Kugno, M. S. (1974). A longitudinal study of flexi-time effects: some consequences of an OD structural intervention, *Journal of Applied Behavioral Sciences*, **10**, 503–532.

Golembiewski, R. T., and Proehl, C. W., Jr. (1978). A survey of the empirical literature on flexible workhours: character and consequences of a major innovation, *Academy of Management Review*, **3**, 837–853.

Haldi Associates, Inc. (1975). *Alternative Work Schedules: A Technology Assessment*, National Technical Information Service, Springfield, Va.

Hedges, J. N. (1971). A look at the 4-day work week, *Monthly Labor Review*, **October 1971**, 33–37.

Hodge, B. J., and Tellier, R. D. (1975). Employee reactions to the work week, *California Management Review*, **18**, 25–30.

Ivancevich, J. M. (1974). Effects of the shorter work week on selected satisfaction and performance measures, *Journal of Applied Psychology*, **59**, 717–721.

Ivancevich, J. M., and Lyon, H. L. (1977). The shortened work week: a field experiment, *Journal of Applied Psychology*, **62**, 34–37.

Johnson, L. C., Tepas, D. I., Colquhoun, W. P., and Colligan, M. J. (Eds.) (1981). *The Twenty-Four Hour Workday: Proceedings of a Symposium on Variations in Work–Sleep Schedules*, DHHS (NIOSH) Publication No. 81-127, U.S. Government Printing Office, Washington, D.C.

Kohlenberg, R., Phillips, T., and Proctor, W. A. (1976). Behavioral analyses of peaking in residential electrical-energy consumers, *Journal of Applied Behavioral Analysis*, **9**, 13–18.

Krausz, M., and Freibach, N. (1983). Effects of flexible working time for employed women upon satisfaction, strains, and absenteeism, *Journal of Occupational Psychology*, **56**, 155–159.

Lee, R. A. (1983). Flextime and conjugal roles, *Journal of Occupational Behavior*, **4**, 297–315.

Lee, R. A. (1984). *The Study of Flextime*, Department of Management Studies, Loughborough University of Technology.

Leib, Lefkowitz and Associates (1981). Alternative work schedules, Internal report prepared for the National Institute for Occupational Safety and Health.

McEwan Young, W. (1981). Innovations in work patterns, *Personnel Review*, **10**, 23–30.

Mahoney, T. A., Newman, J. M., and Frost, P. J. (1975). Workers' perceptions of the four-day week, *California Management Review*, **18**(1), 31–35.

Maklan, D. M. (1977). *The Four-Day Workweek: Blue-Collar Adjustment to a Non-*

conventional Arrangement of Work and Leisure Time, Praeger, New York.

Monk, T. H., and Embry, D. E. (1981). A field study of circadian rhythms in actual and interpolated task performances. In *Night and Shiftwork: Biological and Social Aspects* (Eds. A. Reinberg, N. Vieux and P. Andlauer), Pergamon, Oxford.

Mott, P. E., Mann, F. C., McLoughlin, Q., and Warwick, D. P. (1965). *Shiftwork: The Social, Psychological, and Physical Consequences*, University of Michigan Press, Ann Arbor, Mich.

Naitoh, P. (1981). Circadian cycles and the restorative power of naps. In *The Twenty-Four Hour Workday: Proceedings of a Symposium on Variations in Work–Sleep Schedules* (Eds. L. C. Johnson, D. I. Tepas,. W. P. Colquhoun, and M. J. Colligan), U.S. Department of Health and Human Services, Cincinnati, pp. 693–720.

Nollen, S. (1979). *New Patterns of Work: Highlights of the Literature*, Work in America Institutes, Scarsdale, N.Y.

Nollen, S. D., and Martin, V. H. (1978). *Alternative Work Schedules*, Part 3: *The Compressed Work Week*, AMACOM (Division of the American Management Association), New York.

Nord, W. R., and Costigan, R. (1973). Worker adjustment to the four-day week: a longitudinal study, *Journal of Applied Psychology*, **58**(1), 60–66.

Northrup, H. R., Wilson, J. T., and Rose, K. M. (1979). The twelve-hour shift in the petroleum and chemical industries, *Industrial and Labor Relations Review*, **32**(3), 1979.

Orpen, C. (1981). Effects of flexible working hours on employee satisfaction and performance: a field experiment, *Journal of Applied Psychology*, **66**, 113–115.

Ott, M., Slavin, H., and Ward, D. (1980). The behavioral impacts of flexible working hours, Report No. DOT UMTA-80-10, U.S. Department of Transportation, Urban Mass Transportation Administration, Washington, D.C.

Pierce, J. L., and Newstrom, J. W. (1983). The design of flexible work schedules and employee responses: relationships and processes, *Journal of Occupational Behavior*, **4**, 247–262.

Ronen, S. (1981). *Flexible Working Hours: An Innovation in the Quality of Work Life*, McGraw-Hill, New York.

Rutenfranz, J., Colquhoun, W. P., Knauth, P., and Ghatas, J. N. (1977). Biomedical and psychosocial aspects of shift work, *Scandinavian Journal of Work Environment and Health*, **3**, 165–182.

Schein, V., Maurer, E. H., and Novak, J. F. (1977). Impact of flexible working hours on productivity, *Journal of Applied Psychology*, **62**, 463–465.

Sharko, J. R., and Price, J. P. (1976). Impacts of energy conservation measures applied to commuter travel (Regional Environmental Studies Group, Mathmatica, Inc., Philadelphia), Report prepared for the Office of Planning and Evaluation, U.S. Environmental Protection Agency, Washington, D.C.

Swart, J. C. (1978). *A Flexible Approach to Working Hours*, AMACOM, New York.

Tepas, D. I., and Tepas, S. K. (1981). Alternative work schedules practice in the United States, Internal report prepared for the National Institute for Occupational Safety and Health.

Tepas, D., Walsh, J., and Armstrong, D. (1981). Comprehensive study of the sleep of shiftworkers. In *The Twenty-Four Hour Workday: Proceedings of a Symposium on Variations in Work–Sleep Schedules* (Eds. L. C. Johnson, D. I. Tepas, W. P. Colquhoun, and M. J. Colligan), DHHS (NIOSH) Publication No. 81-127, U.S. Government Printing Office, Washington, D. C.

U.S. Bureau of Labor Statistics (1980). *Current Population Survey*, U.S. Department of Labor, May supplement.

U.S. Bureau of Labor Statistics (1981). Ten million Americans work flexible schedules, 2 million work full-time in 3 to 4½ days, U.S. Department of Labor, Office of Information, News Release, 24 February 1981, Washington, D. C.
Volle, M., Brisson, G. R., Perusse, M., Tanaka, M., and Doyon, Y. (1979). Compressed work-week: psychophysiological and physiological repercussions, *Ergonomics*, **22**, 1001–1010.
Wade, M. (1974). *Flexible Working Hours in Practice*, John Wiley, New York.
Weiss, D. J., Dawis, R. V., England, G. W., and Lofquist, L. H. (1976). *Manual for the Minnesota Satisfaction Questionnaire*, University of Minnesota, Industrial Relations Center, Work Adjustment Project, Minneapolis.
Wever, R. A. (1981). On varying work–sleep schedules: the biological rhythm perspective. In *The Twenty-Four Hour Workday: Proceedings of a Symposium on Variations in Work–Sleep Schedules* (Eds. L. C. Johnson, D. I. Tepas, W. P. Colquhoun, and M. J. Colligan), DHHS (NIOSH) Publication No. 81-127, U.S. Government Printing Office, Washington, D.C.
Wheeler, K., Gurman, R., and Tarnowieski, D. (1972). *The Four-Day Week*, American Management Association, New York.
Winget, C. M., Hughes, L., and LaDou, J. (1978). Physiological effects of rotational work shifting: a review, *Journal of Occupational Medicine*, **20**, 204–210.
Winett, R. A., and Neale, M. S. (1980). Modifying settings as a strategy for permanent, preventive behavior change: flexible work schedules and family life as a case in point. In *Improving the Long-term Effects of Psychotherapy* (Eds. P. Karoly and J. J. Steffen), Gardner Press, New York.
Winett, R. A., and Neale, M. S. (1981). Flexible work schedules and family time allocation: assessment of a system change on individual behaviour using self-report logs, *Journal of Applied Behavioral Analyses*, **14**, 39–46.
Work in America Institute (1981). *New York Schedules for a Changing Society*, Work in America Institute, New York.

Job Stress and Blue Collar Work
Edited by C. L. Cooper and M. J. Smith
© 1985 John Wiley & Sons Ltd

Chapter 9

Emerging Technology and Stress

Olov Östberg

Swedish Telecommunications Administration,
Farsta, Sweden

and

Carina Nilsson

Swedish Confederation of Trade Unions,
Stockholm, Sweden

INTRODUCTION

'Freedom is slavery' read one of the signs displayed throughout Oceania, the capital of big brother society in George Orwell's book *1984*, written in 1948. 'Freedom is having a job' read one of the signs displayed throughout the capital of social-democratic Sweden in 1984. The latter statement was issued by the Swedish Confederation of Trade Unions (LO), and it can be traced back to 1938 and the historical Saltsjöbaden agreement on Work Peace signed by LO and its counterpart SAF (the Swedish Employers' Confederation).

In addition to their amusing symmetry, these parallel slogans convey a message about the forms and contents of jobs. For a job to symbolize freedom rather than slavery, one must not only live in an at large free and democratic society, one must also experience democracy in the workplace, with safe and healthy working conditions, meaningful tasks, and the potential and encouragement for personal growth. Conversely, any discussion of emerging technology and stress in the workplace is of limited relevance without reference to the structure of society. The Swedish Working Environment Act of 1977 reflects this fact in its central theses, which are that (1) the work shall be adapted to the physical and psychical makeup of the worker, (2) the worker shall have the possibility of influencing the form and content of his/her work, (3) the employer must notify employees of any planned changes that bear on their working conditions, and (4) the working conditions shall reflect the technical and social development in society at large.

149

THE SHIFT FROM PHYSICAL TO PSYCHOLOGICAL STRESS

'This job consists of 1 per cent. stress and 99 per cent. monotony.' Such statements are often encountered by 'working life' researchers probing into the human aspects of new technology being implemented in process production (Östberg, 1977). The speaker is referring to the problems encountered in staffing control rooms for production monitoring. The dilemma is to formulate a staffing policy that both avoids overload stress and underload/monotony stress, and at the same time employs a fixed-size control room crew. Achieving this goal is difficult or impossible because of the changing needs of the production line. Less than one worker is needed when all is running smoothly, but several workers are needed when difficulties arise. Such job design dilemmas are typical of those encountered as technology advances.

Production automation has gradually reshaped the work process, beginning with truly manual jobs and progressing to partly mechanized jobs, jobs supervising automation, and, finally, automated tasks that require no workers. Each of these stages is linked to specific task-related stresses, including the stress of 'fearing unemployment' and the stress of being unemployed. Emerging technology has gradually shifted the demands on workers from those of heavy physical labour in a hazardous environment to those of a solitary, sedentary job in a comfortable environment. The shift may appear to be advantageous, but in fact it has produced stressors that may be equally or more hazardous to worker health and well-being.

A recent development in Japan acknowledges the connection between emerging technology and stress—the development of a special curriculum known as robot medicine (Noro, 1984). This course of study is offered to industrial doctors by the University of Occupational and Environmental Health, Japan. Robot medicine is defined as the branch of medicine that studies stress and other mental and physical problems of workers in automated and roboticized production. Robot medicine addresses a general societal concern and concentrates on preventive measures such as the design of production equipment, work tasks, and systems.

There are several reasons for the general concern in Japan and elsewhere over the gradual shift from physical and physiological stress to mental and psychosocial stress. It is obviously disturbing that a technology claimed to be 'worker-friendly' is met with scepticism from the workers. It may actually be argued that the shift involves an increase in occupational stress. Physical and physiological stress is simply not perceived as such in the traditional working environment, whereas mental and psychosocial stress better fits the general notion of stress. This type of stress has also become more visible because the direct and obvious safety and health threats in the workplace have decreased.

Definitions of stress tend to reflect the bias of the researchers (Sharit and

Salvendy, 1982). In the present review, the authors will avoid that pitfall by declining to define stress explicitly. Our working assumptions are as follows:

1. Work stress combined with lack of job choice and social support has detrimental effects on worker health.
2. Work stress is a combination of quantitative overload and qualitative underload (Gardell, 1982). Thus stress involves excessive workloads, environmental pressure, repetitive work flow, and narrow job demands combined with lack of varied stimuli, creativity, problem-solving, and social interaction.
3. Work stress may also involve worries about the future, personal psycho-social problems on or off the job, shift work, etc.

Stress, then, is related to the physiological, psychological, and social aspects of the individual's working and living conditions and to the worker's coping behaviour when faced with a perceived imbalance between demands and ability to respond. Stress is therefore a concept that is nearly as individual as its opposite—comfort.

Lack of comfort on the job was used by Magnus (1970) in setting the priorities for a Swedish working environment laboratory. A representative sample of worksites was visited, and troublesome jobs were identified. These included jobs that experienced safety and health problems, high turnover rates, staffing difficulties, complaints from workers, uneven production output, etc. Next identified was a list of factors that were most likely to cause or contribute to the troublesome nature of these jobs. In order of importance, these factors were as follows:

1. Taxing static muscular workload.
2. High sensory demands.
3. Machine-paced muscular workload.
4. Taxing peak muscular workload.
5. Noise.
6. Gas, dust, fumes.
7. Taxing dynamic muscular workload.
8. Adverse temperature conditions.
9. Vibration.
10. Unsatisfactory lighting.

Perhaps it is surprising that traditional factors such as heavy physical labour and chemical hazards do not rank higher. What is also worthy of note is that many sedentary operator jobs clearly have the characteristics of stressing, troublesome jobs. For example, the above top three factors are those that best describe many office jobs with visual display terminals (NIOSH, 1981).

Table 1   Breakdown of the 1980 official Swedish statistics on
occupational diseases

Factors in occupational diseases and injuries	Incidence (%)
Ergonomic factors	52.9
Chemical factors	22.1
Noise	12.1
Biological hazards	3.2
Other causes	9.7

Source: Kilbom, 1983.

As to the manifestations of troublesome jobs, Table 1 presents a breakdown of the occupational diseases and injuries reported to the Swedish occupational safety and health authorities in 1980. Ergonomic factors cause by far the greatest incidence (52.9 per cent.). To this category belong all musculoskeletal disorders caused by unsuitable work posture, working movements, and workloads. Typically, these disorders result from the long-term wear and tear of short-cycle, one-sided, monotonous, machine-paced tasks. Again, such tasks involve the top three troublesome job factors listed earlier. These factors are believed to be the primary and secondary causes of stress-related ailments, but the current Swedish reporting system largely misses such disorders.

Are such stress-prone working environments linked to or synonymous with emerging production technologies and methods? Some observations may give a clue to the answer. The number of operator jobs has increased extensively in industry during the past decade. A study of 258,000 employees (including 61,000 assembly workers) in 43 industrial firms in the Federal Republic of Germany (Seitz, 1984a, 1984b) reported that, on the average, the cycle time was shorter than 90 seconds for 42 per cent. of the workshop sites and even shorter than 30 seconds for 26 per cent. These findings are of great concern because short cycle times produce psychological stress and determine the degree of monotony. The Union of Metal Workers in the Federal Republic of Germany reports continued increase in workloads despite extensive humanizing programmes financed with government funds during the 1970s (IGM, 1983).

WORKERS' VIEWS OF STRESS PROBLEMS

A survey published in 1970 was carried out by LO to obtain a more comprehensive picture of their members' working environments. This survey was confined to physical hazards in the working environment. The objective was to determine the extent and degree to which members experienced discomfort and physical difficulties from such aspects of the workplace as air pollution, the risk of eczema, and physical problems of a traditional ergonomic nature (e.g. heaving lifting, awkward working postures, etc.).

A few years later, a supplementary LO survey aimed to study the psycho-social aspects of the environment. This survey showed that 31 per cent. of the members experienced their work situation as stressful. The definition of stress here was very vague, but some 9 per cent. of LO's members could, with some certainty, be described as working in a situation with psychosocial risks (i.e. very stressful).

Such experiences of stress and mental strain were closely linked with working environments that were physically unsatisfactory. The factors involved included excessive pace of work, monotonous or uninteresting work, isolation, strict discipline, remuneration systems such as payment by results, etc.

To study how the 1970's working environment developed, LO replicated the survey 10 years later and consulted a representative sample of safety representatives as well. Under stature and agreement, these safety represen-tatives have the responsibility for trade union insight at plant level, and they must make sure that such questions are pursued along union lines. The purpose of the replication survey was to obtain representative replies about the working environment from both ordinary union members and safety representatives. The survey included about 4000 ordinary members and about 5000 safety representatives (LO, 1980b).

Stress and mental strain

In the 1980 survey, some 15 per cent. of the responding LO members felt that their work involved stress or mental strain to a high degree, and 37 per cent. reported this to some extent. In the 1970 survey, the corresponding figures were 9 and 22 per cent. respectively. The proportion of persons experiencing stress in their work seems to have increased between 1970 and 1980.

In the 1970 survey, the LO members were asked what factors they regarded as the causes of stress and mental strain. The most common answer was the pace of work. In 1980, pace of work was still the main cause of stress cited. In 1970, monotonous work ranked fifth among the stress-causing factors, but in 1980 it was cited as often as the pace of work. The results further showed that physical environment factors had become a more common cause of stress in the larger companies. Aside from these, there were no striking differences with regard to the causes of stress in the surveys.

When the LO members in the 1980 survey indicated changes during the preceding 5-year period, stress was the most usual feature cited among worsening conditions (14 per cent.). This factor was also the most stubborn · with regard to improvements: 71 per cent. said that no change had taken place, which means that 85 per cent. of those who experienced stress and mental strain in their working environment had not noted any change for the better.

The painters, electricians, and food workers were the main unions who commented that stress had worsened. Some unions indicated changes for the better: 30 per cent. of the forest workers and 22 per cent. of the mining workers commented that conditions had improved. This result can probably be correlated with change from piece-rate to monthly pay.

Psychosocial problems

In the 1980 LO survey, 35 per cent. of the safety representatives stated that psychosocial problems do arise, 58 per cent. said that such problems were not present, and 7 per cent. said that they could not judge this. A detailed account is given in Table 2. The results indicate that psychosocial health hazards increase with the size of the company.

Table 2   The judgement of safety representatives on the presence of health hazards resulting from psychosocial factors in the workplace

Psychosocial health hazards?	Number of employees in the respondent's company					
	1–10	11–50	51–250	251–1500	>1500	Total average
Yes	25	34	46	56	67	35
No	70	59	46	33	27	58
Don't know	5	7	8	11	5	7

Source: LO, 1980b.

Some 53 per cent. of the safety representatives listed in Table 2 cited shortage of staff as the primary cause of stress and mental strain at work. Nearly as many pointed to bad planning at work. Stress was blamed on piece-rate renumeration by 32 per cent. and on monotonous and one-sided work by 31 per cent. Work carried out in a regimented fashion at a high pace was cited by roughly as many. Reference were also made to working alone, working inconvenient hours, and risking accidents. Even though the answer alternatives provided for safety representatives and members were not exactly identical, the two groups cited about the same reasons for stress.

Of the safety representatives, 70 per cent. said that measures to combat such environmental problems had not been taken and 9 per cent. did not know whether measures had been taken. The measures that were taken were first and foremost those concerning work organization and procedures for introduction and training. Also mentioned were improved planning and a decreased workload through additions to the work force. Primarily the larger companies had attempted to address the psychosocial issues.

General trends

A strong reason for workers to cite a factor in their working environment as problematic or harmful to health is that they believe themselves to have suffered ill health as a result of it (see Table 3).

Table 3   Causes of occupational diseases cited by members of Swedish blue collar unions

Cause cited[a]	Percentage citing the cause	
	1970 survey	1980 survey
Physical strain	41	41
Draughts	31	20
Noise	27	30
Eczema	19	15
Temperature	10	10
Vibration	9	10
Gases	6	4
Solvents	3	7
Stress at work	_[b]	24

[a] Includes only those factors to which more than 5 per cent. of the sample responded positively.
[b] Stress at work was not covered by the 1970 survey.
Source: LO, 1980b.

Three features stand out in Table 3. Most marked is the great extent to which stress at work is cited in the 1980 survey (unfortunately, this item was not covered in the 1970 survey). Secondly, the fact that there is good correlation between the two surveys lends credibility to both. Thirdly, there seems to be no general improvement in the Swedish working environment.

The most widespread problems cited in the 1970 member survey and in the 1980 member and safety representative surveys were those of climate, work postures and working movements, and noise, Problems with air pollution and chemical–technical products are cited less frequently. What is striking, however, is that psychosocial environmental problems ranked so high in the 1980 member survey. According to the union members, the main cause of stress and mental strain at work is the escalated, rapid pace of work. The results here doubtless reflect the demands for efficiency, rationalization, and (to a certain extent) automation and computerization in working life. The safety representatives also cite, among other factors, shortage of staff and defective work planning as the cause of psychosocial problems.

Note that the results from the LO surveys correspond rather well with other Swedish surveys. The Swedish National Central Bureau of Statistics (SCB, 1982) has published 5 years of surveys on living conditions, indicating that many employees have increasing psychosocial problems at work, while many other working conditions are improving. The Swedish Institute for Social Research has arrived at the same conclusions. In a series of surveys (Erikson and Åberg, 1984), they have found a steady increase in the percentage of the population having stressful working conditions. Thus, three Swedish sources appear to support the hypothesis of increased stress and mental strain among the employees. Even if the technological development in many areas has contributed to improvements in the working environment, the findings nevertheless indicate that there has been an increase in reported stress and mental strain at work during the 1970s.

Recently, a further job-stress analysis based on the aforementioned surveys on living conditions has cast more light on the relationship between working conditions, experienced psychosocial problems, and ill health. Using three different Swedish registers, Alfredsson, Spetz, and Theorell (1985) undertook a cohort study to describe the relationship between type of occupation and hospitalization. A total of 985,096 persons aged 20 to 64 years were followed up for one year regarding inpatient care. Several significant associations were found between type of occupation and incidence of hospitalization. For example, a significantly elevated incidence of myocardial infarction was found for men in occupations where a high proportion reported a combination of hectic work and few possibilities to learn new things. Similarly for women, a combination of hectic and monotonous work was associated with a significantly elevated incidence of hospitalization for myocardial infarction.

Trade union action programmes

Based on the survey findings and the perceived general trends in society, LO initiated a series of measures to combat psychosocial problems in working life. These measures were formulated in an LO Action Programme (LO, 1980a). The major points are as follows:

1. Legislation and agreements must increasingly deal with mental and social health hazards in the working environment. Bargaining ought not to be burdened with demands that could be dealt with by other means (for instance, by referring particular questions to the factory inspectorate).
2. Information and education on mental and social health hazards must be developed. These activities must be directed not only to the exposed workers but also to those responsible for the exposure (employers, supervisors, production engineers, etc.).
3. Research and development programmes must be started on how to decrease the risk of mental and social health hazards of new technology, new working methods, new work organization, etc.
4. Local union organizations should draft action programmes of their own. It is important to coordinate working environment issues and co-deter-

mination issues. To prevent the risk of stress and mental strain at work, more emphasis should be given to shaping work organization, personnel and work planning, remuneration systems, training, and work time scheduling.
5. Physical and chemical problems in the work environment should also be dealt with in the light of their psychosocial effects.

The Central Organization of Salaried Employees in Sweden (TCO, the white collar equivalent of LO) has carried out a working environment survey similar to that of LO (Östberg, 1984). In the ensuing action programme (TCO, 1982), warnings were raised about the 'factory of the past' as a model for the office of the future.

These blue and white collar action programmes have many similarities, but an interesting point of departure is that TCO believes that actions to improve the psychological and social working environment have been suppressed by too much patience and humility vis-à-vis the psychosocial research community. The report states that we must not wait for the researchers to cast our problems in their scientific moulds; rather we must address the problems when they are recognized at the local level. For example, stress is usually the result of management style combined with existing overt or covert wage policy, staffing policy, employment policy, resource allocation policy, decision latitude policy, etc. Stress problems must be addressed accordingly, and low priority must be given to superficially and/or individually oriented programmes on stress awareness and relaxation, screening for optimal person environment fit, drugs and alcohol programmes, physical fitness programmes, and social support promotion.

TRENDS IN ROBOT-BASED PRODUCTION

Industrial robots have come to epitomize emerging production technology. Do robots also epitomize emerging stressful jobs? What is in fact known about workers stress in roboticized production systems?

An authoritative textbook from a robot manufacturer explains:

In the interest of production efficiency, work has been broken down into a series of simple, repetitive tasks that can be taught quickly. In fact, much factory work has been reduced to activities that are grossly subhuman. . . . The prime issue in justifying a robot is labor displacement. Industrialists are mildly interested in shielding workers from hazardous working conditions, but the key motivator is the saving of labor costs by supplanting a human worker with a robot (Engelberger, 1980).

Another authoritative source arrives at a similar conclusion from a safety and health perspective:

> The development of the robot was logical. The idea underlying mass production was that a job broken down into simple steps could be done more rapidly if each worker was confined to repeating one simple process. Later as most of the processes were taken over by machinery, the worker was left with the function of a loader, positioner, operator or unloader. Without going much further, it was possible to replace him in these functions, so the robot was born (ILO, 1983).

These two quotations indicate that industrial robots are used as traditional tools for boosting productivity. On the other hand, robotics may represent a completely new production philosophy and have potentials to 'free the human race from the regimentation and mechanization imposed by the requirement for manual labor' so that instead 'millions of exciting new jobs will be created' (Albus, 1982, 1983). Unfortunately, field surveys fail to provide supporting evidence that such will be the case. In some instances, it actually strongly challenges the idealistic claims:

> It is often asserted that industrial robot application results in improvement of working conditions, reduction of hard physical work as well as liberation of workers from monotonous and environmental stressful jobs. However, at least three different studies in the Federal Republic of Germany alone have been undertaken, which strongly challenges this conclusion (Kalmbach et al., 1982).

The expectation is that in some magic way robotics technology will result in improved conditions for the production workers. Similar expectations have been voiced with regard to the maintenance personnel; but here, too, contradictory experiences are reported. For example, in a study of the consequences of working on a complex, very expensive, highly integrated system (a body-welding line in the auto industry), Shaiken (1984) concluded that the pressure on many production workers, maintenance workers, and, in particular, repair foremen could create highly stressful conditions.

Robot-based production may appear to have had more definite positive effects in Japan, where robots were introduced early on a large scale and where today one out of every two of the world's robots are found. However, Japan's industrial production philosophy, methods, and tools are basically no different from those of other industrialized nations, and, accordingly, the same basic effects appear. Rather than lighten workloads, the increasing use of robots and other microelectronic technology is resulting in more overtime, less leave, and greater mental stress at factories and plants in Japan (Robots add stress in Japan, 1983). Whereas U.S. workers often have narrowly (union-) defined job trades within which they encounter the roboticization effects, the Japanese workers pledge loyalty to the employer and the chosen design of the production system. As a result, they may suffer repeatedly from being transferred between jobs like impersonal workunits. Kamata (1983) has given an insider's account of the work pressure Japanese workers may have to endure when this work ethic is combined with an absurd escalation of cost effectiveness.

Lynn (1983) pointed to the industrial unrest in Japan caused by the stress that occurred when robots were brought in and workers were transferred. The stress was especially severe for women and for the two-thirds of the work force *without* any form of employment security. Saga (1983) related the workers' distress about management's use of robots for undermining the traditional Japanese workplace harmony. For example, workers were repeatedly reassigned, thereby making their acquired job skills obsolete. With no external release for pent-up frustrations, older workers then tended to keep their feelings to themselves, withdraw from social contact with colleagues, and participate passively in quality control circles. Younger workers were more actively opposed to the prospect of never being promoted, let alone obtaining tenure. Unless they could infringe on the employer's prerogative of making decisions about working conditions, their lot in working life, according to Saga, seemed to be to endure the frequent job reassignments management imposed on them. Eventually, the Japanese workers' discontent with the aforementioned roboticization trend resulted in the first robotics agreement. Among other things, this document states that the introduction of new technology may not result in degraded working conditions or in transfer of workers without first providing proper education and training (Nissan Motor management pledges, 1983).

In the United States, the introduction of industrial robots has lagged, but it is now rapidly picking up speed. Without the partial employment security found, for example, in Japan (which has the greatest number of robots) and Sweden (which has the greatest number of robots per capita), a forceful U.S. roboticization holds the potential for stressed management–labour relations as well as stressed individuals. The situation is illustrated by Table 4, which outlines the developments and plans within the General Motors Corporation (GM), the giant U.S. auto manufacturer.

Table 4   Past, present, and projected applications of industrial robots within the General Motors Corporation

Type of application	Number of robots in use			Percentage of workers displaced by 1990
	1980	1985	1990	
Welding	138	1700	2,700	20
Painting	47	650	1,500	40
Assembly	17	1200	5,000	10
Machining	68	1200	4,000	20
Parts transfer	32	250	800	5
Total	302	5000	14,000	15–20

Source: GM documents disclose first specifics, 1984; adapted from Hunt and Hunt, 1983.

Table 4 shows the impressive robotization plans publicized by GM in 1982, when 1800 robots had been installed. However, 2 years and twice as many robots later, GM announced that the previous estimate of 14,000 robots installed by 1990 had been updated to nearly 20,000 (Mittelstadt, 1984). This escalation may be related to the statement by Roger B. Smith, the chairman of GM, that 'Every time cost of labor goes up $1 an hour, 1000 more robots become economical' (Foulkes and Hirsch, 1984). Since then it has been revealed that the true GM plans actually beat all earlier official announcements. According to the new plans, GM will cut as many as 12,000 hourly jobs as early as late 1986 through productivity gains involving new uses of robots, production-monitoring systems, and other forms of computer-based technology (GM documents disclose first specifics, 1984).

TRENDS IN THE SWEDISH AUTO INDUSTRY

The world over, the automobile production industry is a forerunner in the large-scale use of advanced production technology. Sweden is no exception, but she probably departs from the norm because of the Swedish auto industry's traditionally progressive work environment. Figure 1 shows the earliest—1926—line for assembling gasoline engines for Volvo autos, as well as the latest—1983—line for gasoline engines for Saab autos. Both illustrations indicate that some real effort has gone into providing ergonomically sound workstations. This section elaborates on this development by outlining the four development steps discerned by Östberg and Enqvist (1984).

Volvo's biotechnology (1961)

Ergonomics on a large scale was introduced in Sweden through the 'biotechnology concept' implemented at the Volvo Penta plant for engine assembly in 1961. The harsh moving-belt production, based on piecework and MTM-designed jobs, was modified according to man's biological functions. The driving force for biotechnology was the plant's safety and health unit, which came to serve as a model for industrial ergonomics in Sweden. In a very ambitious training programme, production engineers were taught biotechnology principles and were encouraged to bring in outside experts in ergonomics and biotechnology during major development projects. The basic goals were to aim for an optimal area between the risk zone and the luxury zone, and to create physically safe and healthy workplaces. Thus to cushion unrest and possible ill health, researchers were encouraged to aim at enhancing the human values in the paced-work environment without hindering productivity (Salvendy and Smith, 1981).

Figure 1   Ergonomic considerations in the design of gasoline engine assembly workstations. The Volvo 'string line'
(*top*) was photographed in Skövde in 1926. Reproduced by
permission of Volvo Components Corporation, Skövde,
Sweden the Saab-Scania robot carrier and handtools
carousel line (*bottom*) was photographed in Södertälje in
1983. Reproduced by permission of Saab-Scania AB

Saab's sociotechnology (1972)

Volvo's biotechnology was very successful, but during the 1960s it was realized that physically safe and healthy workplaces were not enough. These alone could not prevent worker monotony, stress, and alienation, which in turn resulted in high turnover, absenteeism, and low productivity. The labour movement argued that it was not enough to have shorter working hours, longer annual leave, more sick compensation, and higher pay; the empty working time could not be compensated by a full leisure time. In fact, it became generally accepted that 'empty work' *resulted* in 'empty leisure' (Johansson, 1970).

The Saab-Scania assembly plant in Södertälje pioneered a sociotechnical approach as a means of enriching the working conditions. 'Socio' refers to a work organization that makes room for job enlargement, job rotation, social contact, and (to some degree) self-determination within smaller production units. 'Technical' refers to bringing in new technology to boost productivity and develop the new work organization to uncouple the workers from the line speed.

At Saab-Scania, sociotechnology meant that sections of the production were highly mechanized in traditional line fashion, and thus, as a counter-measure, the manual assembly line for building engines was broken up into parallel flow lines in the shape of loops on the main line (Goldmann, 1979; Agurén and Edgren, 1980). This arrangement was achieved by means of ergo-nomically designed assembly trolleys that could be individually pulled into the loops and assigned to one of the workers within the loop unit. With these trolleys, an engine block could easily be positioned at the correct working height for the worker, who could then carry out a complete assembly cycle. Most of the workers were women, and thanks to the loop system (which also served as an 'in and out' buffer), they could help each other during difficult or heavy work tasks.

This system was highly productive and met some of the desires for quality in working life. However,shortcomings existed with regard to both the social and the technical subsystems. Though no salary penalties were imposed if the production quota could not be met, the workers were asked to discuss and find solutions to the problems. This approach resulted in group pressure on workers who fell behind in production; it also caused the workers in a loop to voluntarily speed up the production to obtain a period of non-work of up to 2 hours at the end of the shift. In turn, even greater group pressure was exerted for greater production demands than required by management. Another shortcoming of this approach was that social interaction was prohibited by language barriers between the workers, who represented a great many nationalities. A serious technical drawback was that the loops were still lines within which it was not possible to change positions between individual assembly trolleys.

Volvo's teamwork (1974)

The Volvo Skövde plant for engine assembly, which opened in 1974, amplified both the concepts of biotechnology and sociotechnology. The production design held potentials for vertical job enlargement, self-propelled assembly carts, ergonomically designed workstations and handtools, and a flow layout and plant architecture that supported the teamwork concept. The Volvo Kalmar plant for final car assembly is internationally better known, but it is based on the same principles. Union and management representatives from all over the world have made study visits to this plant during the last decade. Gyllenhammar (1977), the Volvo chief executive officer, was rightly proud of the Kalmar plant and its embodiment of the 'New Factories' ideas voiced by the Swedish Employers' Confederation (see Augurén and Edgren, 1980). In connection with the tenth anniversary of building the Kalmar plant, Gyllenhammar (Gyllenhammar has landed at his vision, 1984) declared that he was still proud of the plant, especially as it was the most productive within the Volvo family. Though the workers are still positive about the basic ideas embodied there, they maintain that the plant has received more praise than it deserves. Young, strong men are needed to perform the main assembly-line work, and the absentee rate (24 per cent.) and personnel turnover (7 per cent.) are equal to those of traditional Volvo production units (The everyday story of the Gyllenhammar dream plant, 1984). Table 5 shows how the Kalmar workers' views of their working environment have changed over the years.

Table 5 Percentage of blue collar workers satisfied with the working environment in the Swedish Volvo Kalmar plant in 1976 and 1983

Feature of the working environment	Percentage of satisfied workers	
	1976[a] (N=69)	1983[b] (N=70)
Physical workload	83	67
Work postures	55	57
Noise	80	64
Lighting	86	79
Windows, outlook	71	74
Climate, air pollution	49	39
Chemical labelling, etc.	58	58
Personnel areas	71	63
Safety hazards	81	77
Company health services	96	67
Safety and health precautions	86	84
Workplace and environment	83	–
Working pace	–	54

[a] Interview investigation reported by Gyllenhammar (1977).
[b] Questionnaire investigation reported by Agurén et al. (1984).

Table 5 makes it appear that deterioration has occurred in the Volvo Kalmar working environment. The key factor is the workers' dissatisfaction with the working pace, a factor that unfortunately was explored only in the most recent investigation. As reported by Agurén *et al.* (1984), the following alterations have taken place over the years to improve the productivity:

1. The dock assembly with its job organization freedom for the workers has been abolished.
2. The possibility of working ahead for breaks has been limited to ensure a steady work flow throughout the entire plant, but as a result the traditional and stressful habit of running upstreams with materials and tools has come back as an unauthorized method of extending breaks.
3. Functional assembly and the practice of having a worker always responsible for particular work tasks (to encourage identification with the product) has had to be abandoned because it entailed worker specialization and generated some ergonomic problems and balancing difficulties.
4. A result-linked wage system has been introduced, but with very limited possibilities for individuals to influence the result.
5. The labour time per car has dropped by about 40 per cent., the uptime has increased by 45 per cent. , and the number of assembled cars has increased by 45 per cent. without adding a second shift.

Many of the innovative original solutions have had to be abolished or become eroded in the course of gradually improving productivity. However, in spite of these retreats, and compared with many traditional auto assembly plants, Volvo Kalmar still provides a good working environment.

Saab's self-paced work (1983)

While the world is still admiring the teamwork in the Swedish auto industry, the Saab-Scania plant for engine assembly in Södertälje has gone further and has actually abandoned the moving-belt and teamwork concepts. The work design principles of biotechnology and ergonomics are further amplified here, as is the drive towards truly parallel production flow lines. A computer-aided assembly carrier has been developed that surpasses Volvo's pioneering robot cart.

In this system, a number of heavy and/or short-cycle operations have been assigned to industrial robots. Their tasks include mounting valve springs, sealing valves, mounting flywheels, and treading and torquing bolts. Great care is taken to separate the robot and the manual assembly operations. The manual assembly is carried out in individual, ergonomically well-designed workstations (Figure 1). As the workers complete their tasks, they send away completed products and order new assembly carriers according to their individual work paces.

Purely ergonomic considerations aside, the new assembly system was launched to boost output capacity. In particular, it was designed to handle custom-order production. Thus about 30 different engine versions are being assembled at any given time. For the workers, this self-paced work is an improvement over the previous group-paced work, with its concomitant, self-inflicted high workload. Even if the overall production is not lower in the new system, self-paced work is obviously less stressful than that set by the group of workers.

The workload under the group-paced assembly production, during the Saab sociotechnology era, was witnessed by a group of U.S. auto workers testing the previous Saab-Scania system. As reported by Goldmann (1979), the U.S. workers found the plant superior to U.S. counterparts with regard to ergonomics and environmental factors, but they were troubled because the women they worked with 'worked harder than anyone in Detroit'. This hard work showed up as increased sick leave. The visiting U.S. workers' concern was well founded, as demonstrated in a Saab-Scania management report on the technological merits of the *new* systm:

> With the passage of time, this system did not prove entirely satis-factory—factors such as stress began to appear when operators were working at different rates and there was a mutual feeling of harassment. Some of the work postures and lifts imposed too much strain on operators, most of whom were women. Again, some of the tools used in assembly work, especially nutrunners, gave rise to physical discomfort in the form of back-ache and pains in the neck (Ericsson, 1984).

A team of stress researchers followed the engine assembly work for the two years before the introduction of robots and setting up of individual manual assembly workstations (Edgren, 1984). The researchers reluctantly confirmed that, for medical reasons, the sociotechnology concept of group work had to be abandoned. The individuals did not feel harassed or pressured to work hard; rather they set the working pace too high without being aware of it. Individuals who were lazy but physically strong were not overworked, but those who were ambitious and physically weak ended up with musculo-skeletal ailments in the neck and shoulders. Though it is still too early to draw firm conclusions from the new individual workstations with self-paced work, the prevailing impression has been that though it prevents stress and load injuries, it makes for a less interesting job (Östberg and Enqvist, 1984).

CONCLUDING REMARKS

In the absence of solid empirical data on the relationship between emerging technology and worker stress, the present review can be seen as a compilation of documented observations and piecemeal research findings. Accordingly, no firm cause-and-effect conclusions can be made, especially as neither emerging technology nor worker stress has been defined. A holistic approach is sufficient and even necessary.

When negative effects on health and welfare begin to make themselves felt, workloads will often be experienced as heavier, the speed requirements as tougher, and the shift system as more inconvenient. As a result, the negative effects on health are reinforced, and we are confronted with a highly complex network of circular processes that intermingle causes and effects. No single factor in the working environment can be singled out as the cause. To bring about a change in the workplace, the traditional method has been to prove that a particular environmental factor has a negative effect. However, as pointed out by Gustavsen and Hunnius (1981), proof is very difficult to secure because of the great complexity of many workplace situations and the rapid emergence of new technology. Gustavsen and Hunnius therefore believe that the burden of proof must be shifted—i.e. that there must be proof that no negative effects exist. Such a stance would allow more development activity on work environment problems and quicker adaptation to new conditions.

In the Scandinavian countries, such development activities are called for and promoted by legislation. For example, the general criteria of Section 12 in the Norwegian Work Environment Act of 1977 outline how technology, work organization, work time, and payment systems are to be viewed holistically (see Sharit and Salvendy, 1982). The resulting jobs are not only to be safe and free from undue physical and mental workloads, but they are also to provide for self-determination and growth opportunities in terms of personal development and job skills. In the ensuing bargaining process, the Employers' Confederation and the Confederation of Trade Unions reached an agreement on the practical handling of new technology issues. This national contract for the period 1982–1985 agrees that technical development and computerization is to be evaluated with regard to technical and economic criteria, and social aspects as well. If a local trade union is faced with a major proposal from the employer, and if the union resources are insufficient for coming to grips with the proposal, then the union may consult with outside experts at the expense of the employer.

We conclude that work stress in many cases has been caused by the *application* of new production technology. This conclusion is supported by the Volvo management (Jöhnsson, 1983) who agrees that before its socio-technology phase, Volvo had an industrial engineering phase characterized by the (1) introduction of time-study engineering, (2) productivity programmes, (3) increasing numbers of monotonous jobs, and (4) increased competition. As witnessed from Toyota's industrial engineering phase (Kamata, 1983), this phase clearly resulted in increased worker stress. Even though Volvo long ago moved ahead and now claims to use new technology with a more human and holistic approach, the present review indicates that Volvo's workers continue to be pressured by the omnipresent pursuit of productivity. Consider also all the world's workplaces that are still in the industrial engineering phase or perhaps even in the preceding primitive phase.

To speak positively about new technology and new approaches—which the present authors do—is to speak negatively about old technology and old approaches. Our challenge is to ensure that future judgement of present efforts will not be as harsh as those we have made of our predecessors.

REFERENCES

Agurén, S., Bredbacka, C., Hansson, R., Ihregren, K., and Karlsson, K. G. (1984). *Volvo Kalmar Revisted*, Efficiency and Participation Council SAF-LO-PTK, Stockholm.

Agurén, S., and Edgren, J. (1980). *New Factories: Job Design through Factory Planning*, Swedish Employers' Confederation, Stockholm.

Albus, J. S. (1982). Industrial robot technology and productivity improvement. In *Exploratory Workshop on the Social Impact of Robotics*. Office of Technology Assessment, U.S. Congress, Washington, D. C.

Albus, J. S. (1983). Socio-economic implications of robotics. *Proceedings of the 1983 SME World Congress on the Human Aspects of Automation*, MM83-479.

Alfredsson, L., Spetz, C. L., and Theorell, T. (1985). Type of occupation and near-future hospitalization for myocardial infarction and some other diagnoses, *International Journal of Epidemiology*, **13**, No. 3.

Edgren, B. (1984). Results from the research on ailments in neck/shoulders among female assembly workers in the Saab-Scania gasoline engine assembly plant, Personal communication, KTH, Stockholm, October 1984.

Engelberger, J. F. (1980). *Robotics in Practice*, American Management Association, New York.

Ericsson, S. (1984). Automated engine assembly with industrial robots at Saab-Scania, *Proceedings of the 14th International Symposium on Industrial Robots*, pp. 251–260.

Erikson, R., and Åberg, R. (Eds.) (1984). *Welfare in Transformation. Level of Living in Sweden 1968–1981* (in Swedish), Prisma, Stockholm.

Foulkes, F. K., and Hirsch, J. L. (1984). People make robots work, *Harvard Business Review*, **63**, No. 1.

Gardell, B. (1982). Scandinavian research on stress in working life, *International Journal of Health Services*, **12**, 31–41.

Goldmann, R. (1979). Six automobile workers in Sweden. In *American Workers Abroad* (Ed. R. Schrank), MIT Press, Cambridge, Mass., pp. 15–55.

GM documents disclose first specifics of plans to cut jobs through automation, *Wall Street Journal*, 6 September 1984, p. 4.

Gustavsen, B., and Hunnius, G. (1981). *New Patterns of Work Reform. The Case of Norway*, Universitetsforlaget, Oslo.

Gyllenhammar, P. G. (1977). *People at Work*, Addison-Wesley, Reading, Mass.

Gyllenhammar has landed at his vision (in Swedish), *Ny Teknik*, No. 7, 1984, 26–27.

Hunt, H. A., and Hunt, T. L. (1983). *Human Resource Implications of Robotics*, Upjohn Institute, Kalamazoo, Mich.

IGM (1983). *'You want machines—but not us humans.'* Rationalization in the Metal *Working Industry* (in German). Industriegewerkschaft Metall, Frankfurt am Main, FRG.

ILO (1983). *Encyclopaedia of Occupational Health and Safety* (on 'Robots and automatic production machinery'), 3rd and rev. ed., International Labour Office, Geneva.

Johansson, S. (1970). *On the Level of Living Survey* (in Swedish), Allmänna Förlaget, Stockholm.

Jönsson, B. (1983). Productivity and survival—key words in industry, Paper presented to the Management Centre Europe conference on 'Productivity—The Key to Survival in the 80s', London, 14–15 November 1983.

Kalmbach, P., Kasiske, R., Manske,. F., Mickler, O., Pelull, W., and Wobbe-Ohlenburg, W. (1982). Robots' effect on production, work and employment, *Industrial Robot*, **9**, No. 1, 42–45.

Kamata, S. (1983). *Japan in the Passing Lane. An Insider's Account of Life in a Japanese Auto Factory*, George Allen and Unwin, London.

Kilbom, Å. (1983). Occupational disorders of the musculoskeletal system, Newsletter of the Swedish National Board of Occupational Safety and Health, No. 1, pp. 6–7.

LO (1980a). *LO's Action Programme on Mental and Social Hazards to Health in the Working Environment*, LO, Stockholm.

LO (1980b). *What's Happening with the Working Environment?* (in Swedish), LO-Tiden, Stockholm.

Lynn, L. (1983). Japanese robotics: challenge and—limited—exemplar, *Annals of the American Academy of Political and Social Science*, **470**, 16–27.

Magnus, P. (1970). *Investigation of Troublesome Jobs* (in Swedish), The Swedish Board for Technical Development, Stockholm.

Mittelstadt, E. (1984). Robotics—thoughts about the future. *Proceedings of the Robots 8 Conference*, 2:12–2:21.

NIOSH (1981). *Potential Health Hazards of Video Display Terminals*, National Institute for Occupational Safety and Health, Cincinnati, Ohio.

Nissan Motor management pledges not to sacrifice workers to robots, *Japan Economic Journal*, 8 March 1983, **21**.

Noro, K. (1984). Education and training in relationship between man and robot. In *Human Factors in Organizational Design and Management* (Eds. H. W. Hendrick and O. Brown), Elsevier Science, Amsterdam, pp. 441–445.

Östberg, O. (1977). From worker to operator (in Swedish), University of Luleå Reports, No. 50T.

Östberg, O. (1984). Work environment issues of Swedish office workers: a union perspective. In *Human Aspects in Office Automation* (Ed. B. G. F. Cohen), Elsevier Science, Amsterdam, pp. 127–141.

Östberg, O., and Enqvist, J. (1984). Robotics in the workplace: robot factors, human factors, and humane factors. In *Human Factors in Organizational Design and Management* (Eds. H. W. Hendrick and O. Brown, Jr.), Elsevier Science, Amsterdam, pp. 447–460.

Robots add stress in Japan (translated from *Tokyo Shimbun), Washington Post*, 6 September 1983.

Saga, I. (1983). Japan's robots produce problems for workers, *Wall Street Journal*, 28 February 1983, **19**.

Salvendy, G., and Smith, M. J. (Eds.) (1981). *Machine Pacing and Occupational Stress*, Taylor and Francis, London.

SCB (1982). *Living Conditions* (in Swedish), The Swedish National Central Bureau of Statistics, Stockholm.

Seitz, D. (1984a). Automation, employment and qualification in future assembly work—some results of a representative survey, *Proceedings of the 1984 SME World Congress on the Human Aspects of Automation*, MM 84-641.

Seitz, D. (1984b). Developments in assembly work, *Proceedings of the 1st International Conference on Human Factors in Manufacturing*, pp. 137–148.

Shaiken, H. (1984). The effects of programmable automation on the work environment. A case study of an auto assembly plant. In *Computerized Manufacturing Automation: Employment, Education, and the Workplace. II. Working Papers (A)*. Office of Technology Assessment, U.S. Congress, Washington, D. C.

Sharit, J., and Salvendy, G. (1982). Occupational stress: review and reappraisal, *Human Factors*, **24**, 129–162.

Swedish National Central Bureau of Statistics (1982). Living conditions, Report No. 32, Working environment 1979 (in Swedish), Central Bureau of Statistics, Stockholm.

TCO (1982). *The Elusive Working Environment: On the Psychological and Social Consequences of the Working Environment* (in Swedish), TCO, Stockholm.

The everyday story of the Gyllenhammar dream plant (in Swedish), *Ny Teknik*, No. 6, 1984, pp. 16–17.

Job Stress and Blue Collar Work
Edited by C. L. Cooper and M. J. Smith
© 1985 John Wiley & Sons Ltd

Chapter 10

An Apparent Case of Mass Psychogenic Illness in an Aluminium Furniture Assembly Plant

Michael J. Colligan

National Institute for Occupational Safety and Health,
U.S. Department of Health and Human Services,
Cincinnati, Ohio, USA

Outbreaks of industrial mass psychogenic illness have been the subject of several recent reports (e.g. Colligan and Stockton, 1978; Colligan and Murphy, 1979). These investigations were conducted by the National Institute for Occupational Safety and Health (NIOSH) in response to the sudden and simultaneous expression of symptoms by groups of workers in the workplace. Preliminiary results of these investigations suggest that the illness affects primarily (though not exclusively) females engaged in boring, repetitive work performed against a background of considerable psychological stress arising from occupational, organizational, and personal life sources. The symptoms may vary from incident to incident but typically involve subjective physical complaints (e.g. headache, muscle weakness, nausea, lightheadedness) which spread rapidly throughout the workplace. The outbreak is usually triggered by an ambiguous stimulus such as an identifiable odour or a new dye process although repeated environmental testing by industrial hygienists fails to identify a probable causal agent.

The present chapter describes one such investigation of apparent mass psychogenic illness conducted by NIOSH at a Midwestern plant engaged in the assembly of aluminium lawn furniture.

Assembly of the furniture from fabricated aluminium tubing and plastic webbing was the primary activity at the plant. No manufacturing was performed, nor were any chemicals used in the assembly process. Work began in the spinning and fabrication department located at the west end of the building. Here aluminium tubing was received at the loading dock, contoured (ends spin-tapered) and cut into various lengths for the different models. The aluminium tubes were then punch-pressed to form molds for

171

attaching the plastic webbing. Plastic and redwood arm rests were drilled and attached to the aluminium tubes and plastic caps were put onto the end pieces. From here, the aluminium tubes were sent to one of four assembly lines.

Immediately adjacent to the spinning and fabrication department was the webbing department. Here long rolls of plastic webbing were received, cut to specification for the various models, and eyeletted for attachment to the aluminium frames. The webbing moved from this department to the four assembly lines.

The four model assembly lines were located adjacent to the webbing department and ran parallel to each other. The pre-cut aluminium tubes were shaped and assembled to form the various model frames (e.g. chair, lounge, or rocker model). Webbing was then attached (riveted) to the frames as the product moved down the assembly line towards the packers located at the end of each model line.

CHRONOLOGY OF EVENTS

On a Wednesday morning in November 1977, at approximately 8.30, a female employee in the webbing department became ill with symptoms of headache, nausea, dizziness, burning throat, and general weakness. She complained of a strange odour prior to the onset of her illness, which she felt was due to exhaust fumes from diesel trucks idling at the loading dock at the west end of the building. Within minutes, three other female employees of the department became ill with similar symptoms. All four women were taken to the first aid room where they rested for 5 to 10 minutes before returning to work.

Within a half an hour of the first incident, six more women from the same department reported to first aid with the same subjective, non-specific symptoms. The company's carbon monoxide monitor, located just north of the webbing department to measure exhaust fumes from lift trucks indicated only 3 to 5 ppm CO (the permissible OSHA Standard is 50 ppm, NIOSH recommended standard is 35 ppm). Nevertheless, the dock doors at opposing ends of the building were opened and exhaust fans were turned on.

Despite these precautions, individuals in the plant continued to develop symptoms. By 9.30 a.m., 29 women had expressed symptoms and were taken to the local hospital. Meanwhile, the plant was closed. Twenty-two of these workers were treated for anxiety and hyperventilation and then released. Seven others were admitted. One of those was released after five days. Individual medical examinations revealed no abnormalities in chest X-rays, haematology, serology, urinanalyis or blood gases in any of those individuals.

Environmental testing within the plant was conducted by state OSHA representatives and an industrial hygienist from a local Navy installation.

Sampling on the day of the outbreak from locations throughout the plant indicated no detectable CO, 20 to 22 per cent. oxygen, and 0.1 per cent. carbon dioxide all within acceptable limits. The plant remained closed for the Thanksgiving weekend with operations resuming on Monday. By approximately 8.45 a.m., a female worker on the lounge assembly line became ill with symptoms of nausea, dizziness and headache. She was seen by a local physician (specifically in attendance for the resumption of plant operations), treated in the first aid room, and sent home at her request. Between 9.15 a.m. and 10.15 a.m., nine additional workers from various areas of the plant sought treatment in the first aid room for similar symptoms. All affected workers and some non-affected workers complained of gas fumes; however, environmental sampling by a consulting industrial hygienist failed to identify any toxic agents. All exhaust fans were in operation and the dock doors had been kept open for the entire day.

Workers from scattered areas of the plant filtered into the first aid room throughout the day and a total of 27 employees (5 males and 22 females, including 8 who had previously been affected on Wednesday) were treated in the first aid room. On Tuesday, operations were normal and no dramatic outbreaks of illness occurred in the plant. There were isolated complaints of headache and nausea, but environmental sampling during the day did not find sufficient concentrations of toxic agents capable of producing the observed symptoms.

In addition to the previously mentioned industrial hygienists, a representative of the Bureau of Mines was on-site to sample for methane gas possibly arising from coal deposits under the plant. No traces of methane were found.

Water for the plant was supplied by the same wells which furnished the nearby city and local public health officials found no indications of townspeople developing symptoms similar to those of the plant employees. In addition, the plant did not provide cafeteria services and employees brought their own lunches or ate out. Candy and soft drink machines were present in the plant but the examining physician found no consistent relationship between usage of these machines and illness.

The NIOSH investigation was conducted by a team of medical specialists, industrial hygienists, and psychologists approximately 60 days after the initial illness occurrence. Although there were no dramatic outbreaks of collective illness during the intervening period, there were daily complaints of odours and isolated cases of first aid visits by employees with symptoms of nausea, headaches, burning throat, etc. Symptom reporting gradually diminished over the ensuing months, returning to baseline levels approximately 4 months after the initial outbreak.

The results of the medical, industrial hygiene, and psychosocial components of the NIOSH investigation were eventually described in a detailed report which was summarized as follows:

'A combined environmental, medical and behavioural Health Hazard Evaluation was conducted by NIOSH at a midwestern aluminum furniture assembly plant on January 31 and February 2 and 7, 1977. The environmental and medical studies discovered no definite evidence that toxic substances caused the outbreaks of illness on November 19, 24 and 29, 1976.

Numerous environmental conditions (e.g., ventilation, noise, dry air, diesel exhaust, etc.) were identified which could have contributed to the outbreaks of illness. Also, a natural gas leak was discovered that may have been the source of the "gas odor" complaints. Whatever the precipitating cause of the outbreak, no environmental toxins were discovered that could totally account for the continuing outbreaks of illness.

Behavioral factors may have been involved in propagating the outbreaks. NIOSH investigators from the Division of Biomedical and Behavioral Science found some significant psychological differences between affected and non-affected workers.'

The present discussion focuses only on the psychosocial aspect of that investigation.*

SAMPLING PLAN

At the time of the investigation the plant employed approximately 350 people, 78 per cent. of whom were female. A total of 48 people had been identified by company records as receiving treatment on at least one of the two occasions involving mass illness at the plant. Of these, approximately 40 were available on the day of the NIOSH investigation to receive the questionnaire developed by NIOSH psychologists and epidemiologists for previous investigations of this nature. In addition, a random sample of 140 workers who had not received medical treatment on either of these two occasions received questionnaires. Thus, of the 358 workers, 180 received a questionnaire. Workers were requested to take the questionnaires home, fill them out, and return them the following day. Participation was voluntary. A total of 94 completed questionnaires (13 males and 81 females) were obtained for statistical analysis. The male/female ratio in the sample was 13.8/86.2 per cent. as compared to the male/female ratio of 22/78 per cent. in the plant population.

The survey instrument had been specifically developed for investigations of apparent mass psychogenic illness. In addition to sociodemographic (age, sex, level of education, marital and parental status, etc.), and epidemiological information (date and time of illness, symptomatology, location of workplace at time of illness onset, etc.), the questionnaire contained individual items designed to measure sources of perceived job stress (unwanted overtime, role ambiguity, boredom, etc.) using a Likert-type response format. Five

*NIOSH HHE Report No. 77-27-437 available from the National Technical Information Service (NTIS), 52185 Port Royal Rd., Springfield, Va. 22161.

standardized personality/psychodiagnostic instruments were also included in the study protocol and are listed below. (For details on these tests, see Smith, Colligan, and Hurrell, 1978).

1. *The Work Environment Scale.* This scale measures 10 dimensions of the social structure operating in the workplace which are believed to be predictive of worker satisfaction or adjustment (Moos, Insel, and Humphrey, 1974).

2. *Internal–External Control Scale (Valecha, 1973).* This is an 11-item scale designed to measure the extent to which an individual attributes causation for his experiences to internal versus external sources. For example, it was felt that individuals experiencing vague, psychosomatic symptoms might attribute them either to internal factors (stress, anxiety, fatigue) or to external factors (a gas leak, a virus, etc.). This attribution, in turn, would affect individual susceptibility to the expression and contagion of symptoms.

3. *The Eysenck Personality Inventory.* This scale measures personality in terms of two pervasive, independent dimensions: extroversion–introversion and neuroticism–stability. There is some evidence to indicate that hysteria-prone personalities score lower on the extroversion scale than normals (Eysenck and Eysenck, 1968).

4. *The Mini-Mult of the MMPI (Kincannon, 1968).* This is a factor analytically derived scale of the Minnesota Multiphasic Personality Inventory (MMPI). Three subscales from this instrument were included in the present survey protocol. These were:

    (a) The Hysteria Scale. This measures the extent to which the individual exhibits behavioural patterns characteristic of the hysteria-prone personality: excitability, emotional instability, self dramatization.
    (b) The Hypochondriasis Scale. This measures the extent to which the individual somaticizes emotional or psychogenic strain or tension.
    (c) The Depression Scale. This measures the extent to which the individual experiences feelings of dejection, hopelessness, worthlessness, etc.

5. *The Holmes–Rahe Recent Life Scale (1967).* This is a 43-item scale which measures the number of stress-inducing events which the individual has experienced in the recent past. This scale has been shown to be predictive of psychosomatic illness.

STATISTICAL PROCEDURES

An initial problem in analysing data collected in incidents of this nature is that of defining who was, and was not, affected by the outbreak of illness.

From interview and survey responses obtained from plant employees, it was apparent that receiving medical treatment for expressed symptomatology was not a valid criterion for identifying those affected in the outbreak. As a result of the general confusion present in the plant on the days of the outbreak, medical treatment was administered on a first-come, first-served basis. Thus, individuals with pre-existing, unrelated complaints may have been included among those receiving treatment for symptoms directly associated with the outbreak. Conversely, other workers experiencing a greater range of symptoms (e.g. headache, nausea, weakness, etc.), as determined by interview and questionnaire responses, did not overtly display illness and therefore did not appear on any official list of affected employees. Consequently, affected workers were defined in terms of the number of self-reported symptoms obtained via the questionnaire. For the purposes of this report, individuals reporting two or less symptoms were presumed to represent 'baseline' and were defined as 'non-affected', while those reporting three or more symptoms were defined as 'affected'. Using this criterion, the sample consisted of 42 affected (4 male, 38 female) and 52 non-affected (9 male, 43 female) workers.

Point biserial correlations were then computed to ascertain the relationship between 'affectedness' and the various demographic, organizational, and psychosocial variables measured by the questionnaire.

RESULTS

Twenty-four physical symptoms, identified from the literature as characteristic of contagious psychogenic illness, were contained on the questionnaire. Each respondent was requested to check which, if any, of the listed symptoms was experienced during the outbreak. Table 1 presents the 24 symptoms rank-ordered in terms of incidence rate for the entire sample. The seven principal symptoms were: (1) headache (37.2 per cent.), (2) bad taste in mouth (33 per cent.), (3) dry mouth (31.9 per cent.), (4) dizziness (28.77 per cent.), (5) lightheadedness (26.6 per cent.), (6) tightness in chest (26.6 per cent.), and (7) nausea (21.3 per cent.).

Sociodemographic factors

The average respondent was 34.6 years old (s.d. = 12.9), had an 11th grade education (s.d. = 1.0), and had worked for the company for 43.3 months (s.d. = 34.6). Affected status was not related to age, sex, level of education, employment, seniority, or marital/parental state.

Table 1   Symptoms rank-ordered in terms of frequency of occurrence for the entire sample ($n = 94$)

Symptom	Number affected	Percentage of total sample having symptom
1. Headache	35	37.1
2. Bad taste in mouth	31	33.0
3. Dry mouth	30	31.9
4. Dizziness	27	28.7
5. Lightheadedness	25	26.6
6. Tightness in chest	25	26.6
7. Nausea	20	21.3
8. Abdominal pain	17	18.1
9. Ringing in ears	17	18.1
10. Watery eyes	17	18.1
11. Sleepiness	15	16.0
12. Blurred vision	13	13.8
13. Racing heart	10	10.6
14. Difficulty swallowing	10	10.6
15. Passed out	9	9.6
16. Numbness	9	9.6
17. Tingling feeling	7	7.4
18. Vomiting	7	7.4
19. Chest pain	5	5.3
20. Fever	4	4.3
21. Muscle soreness	4	4.3
22. Weakness	4	4.3
23. Diarrhoea	2	2.1
24. Couldn't catch breath	2	2.1

Psychosocial/Organizational factors

The affected workers indicated a higher overall level of stress than the non-affected workers. This could be attributed to a combination of job and life conditions. With respect to specific sources of stress, the affected individuals:

1. Reported being dissatisfied with the lack of security which their jobs offered them ($r = 0.20, p < 0.05$).
2. Reported experiencing a sharp increase in their workload ($r = 0.19$, $p < 0.05$).
3. Reported frequently being bothered by unwanted overtime ($r = 0.20$, $p < 0.05$).
4. Reported frequently being bothered by noise ($r = 0.37, p < 0.05$) and temperature variations ($r = 0.33, p < 0.05$) in the workplace.

Strained and ambiguous supervisory relations were implicated as a potential source of stress as indicated by the fact that affected persons:

1. Reported frequently receiving conflicting orders from their supervisors ($r = 0.19, p < 0.05$).
2. Reported feeling unable to influence the decisions of their supervisors ($r = 0.19, p < 0.05$).
3. Reported less uncertainty about their job performance and supervisor expectations as measured by the clarity subscale of the Work Environment Scale ($r = 0.25, p < 0.05$).

Finally, a correlation of $r = 0.20$ ($p < 0.05$) was obtained between affected status and general life stress as measured by the Holmes–Rahe Recent Life Events Scale.

General health factors

In response to an item asking the respondents to rate their general health, affected persons reported poorer overall health from non-affected persons ($r = 0.19$, $p < 0.05$), and indicated more frequently feeling tired or sleepy ($r = 0.18, p < 0.05$) and more frequently experiencing sneezing spells ($r = 0.21$, $p < 0.05$).

Personality measures

The only standardized personality measures to correlate with affected status were the hysteria ($r = 0.20$, $p < 0.05$) and hypochondriasis ($r = 0.29, p < 0.05$) scales of the MMPI Mini-Mult.

DISCUSSION

The results suggest that the reporting of symptoms in the present investigation was related to a variety of stresses and dissatisfactions associated with the job. Unwanted overtime, role ambiguity, production pressures, and bothersome physical stressors (e.g. noise, temperature variations, etc.) were specifically identified as sources of tension by the affected workers. These findings must be interpreted cautiously, however. It is conceivable that the job dissatisfaction reported by the affected workers may have been a consequence, rather than a cause, of symptoms they experienced.

The dramatic outbreak of mass illness in the workplace is a traumatic and threatening event. Consequently, the workers might be expected to reinterpret their feelings about various aspects of their job in the light of their experienced fear and resentment. This negative bias could be expected to vary as a function of symptom severity or frequency such that those workers experiencing the greatest discomfort would report the greatest job dissatisfaction.

The present data do not permit any causal inferences to be drawn regarding the direction of the job stress–affectedness relationship. Supplementary interviews and anecdotal information gathered in the conduct of this investigation suggest that the level of work-related tension was high prior to the illness outbreak.

The plant, located in a rural Midwestern area, was a major source of employment for the local community. The company was owned and operated by a corporation located in a distant state. All decisions regarding plant functions were made at corporate headquarters and transmitted daily to the local plant supervisor for implementation. Corporate control was so rigid that the local plant manager called corporate headquarters to request permission to send for an ambulance and emergency health personnel on the day of the initial outbreak. Although generally well liked by the workers, the plant manager was perceived as being unable to respond to their work-related grievances. In addition, corporate headquarters, in response to a purported decline in production, had put the plant on probation with the threat that the entire operation might be closed down if there were not substantial increases in output.

Based on information provided by the workers during informal interviews, the psychosocial climate of the plant prior to the illness outbreak was highly strained. Workers resented the autocratic and unilateral style of the absentee management and felt anxious and threatened by the possible loss of their jobs if they didn't meet demands for higher production standards. Furthermore, the scarcity of employment alternatives in the surrounding region meant that the workers were effectively locked into their present job. Given this set of circumstances, it seems quite probable that the strain arising from combined psychological (e.g. production pressure, role ambiguity, managerial discord, job insecurity) and physical (e.g. noise, temperature variations) workplace stresssors may have resulted in some transient physical symptoms (headache, fatigue, muscle tension, etc.) among a subset of workers. The sudden and dramatic display of symptoms by the index case may have triggered illness displays by similarly predisposed workers in the immediate surroundings. Attempts to determine the sociometric dispersion of symptoms were unsuccessful because of the confusion in the plant at the time of the illness outbreaks and the workers' inability to recall the specific spatial and temporal characteristics of the epidemic. It is accurate to say, however, that the vast majority of workers knew one another (in fact many of them were related) and frequently interacted off the job. This cohesion would be expected to facilitate the social comparison process (e.g. Festinger, 1954; Collins and Raven, 1969) such that aroused workers, feeling a need to evaluate their ambiguous reactions, depended on their peers for an explanation of their experienced strain (Schachter and Singer, 1962). The suggestion that a toxic gas in the workplace was responsible for the illness explained the symptoms and sanctioned their expression. In addition, the outbreak of illness, regardless of the presumed cause, provided the distressed workers with a legitimate mechanism for voicing concerns about a variety of work-related stressors. This does not imply that the symptoms were not real, or that their expression was a contrivance on the part of the workers to protest unsatisfactory working conditions. Rather the dramatic outbreak of illness and the resultant search for a cause may represent an attempt on the part of the workers to 'make sense' out of the job-related distress they experience and to rectify the perceived problem.

While this explanation has a certain face validity, it begs the question regarding the observed limits of contagion in the focal plant. As Milgram and Toch (1969) have noted, it is important to understand not only why a behaviour becomes contagious among certain individuals, but also why it does not become contagious among others. The present data indicate a relationship between affectedness and self-reported job stress, suggesting that susceptibility may vary as a function of pre-existing job dissatisfaction and consequent strain. As previously discussed, this relationship must be interpreted cautiously due to possible reactance effects in completing the questionnaires.

A second potential limiting factor in the spread of symptoms may have involved the workers' interpretation of the illness. Interviews with a sample of workers indicated that many of those not affected simply did not believe that a toxic agent was responsible for the illness outbreak. They tended to attribute the epidemic to 'nervousness' or 'overwork'. This view was reinforced by local newspaper reports of the incident which ridiculed the seriousness of the illness, suggesting in one article that 'spirits' might be possessing the plant. Consequently, even the affected workers reevaluated the incident. Some of them, in retrospect, reported during the interviews that they may have been overly anxious, while others became more firmly convinced than ever that the plant was hazardous. The result of this alternate interpretation was to further factionalize the work force, adding to the overall strain and confusion surrounding the event. In the future, investigators might wish to collect more intensive information regarding the coping strategies and attribution processes of affected and non-affected workers.

Finally, in contrast to previous reports of mass illness episodes having a psychogenic component (e.g. Kerckhoff and Back, 1968; Stahl and Lebedun, 1974; Colligan et al., 1979), suggesting that only females were involved in the epidemic, the present report found no relationship between gender and affectedness. Although the sample of males was small ($n = 13$), the male respondents in the present study were performing the same job as the females. This suggests that the preponderance of females involved in previous episodes (see Colligan and Murphy, 1979) may have been a function more of the job conditions under which entry-level females work than of gender or sex-role characteristics. Women may simply be more frequently assigned to the boring, repetitive, 'dead-end' types of job than males. Coupling this situation with an authoritarian, patronizing management style could predispose them to express their experienced stress through physical symptoms. This hypothesis has interesting implications not only for preventing mass illness outbreaks, as in the present case, but also for programmes aimed at job enrichment, worker satisfaction, and upward mobility.

REFERENCES

Colligan, M. J., and Murphy, L. R. (1979). Mass psychogenic illness in organizations: an overview, *Journal of Occupational Psychology*, **52**, 77–90.

Colligan, M. J., and Stockton, W. (1978). The mystery of assembly-line hysteria, *Psychology Today*, **12**, 93–94, 97–99, 114, 116.

Colligan, M. J., Urtes, M. A., Wisseman, C., Rosensteel, R. E., Anania, T. L., and Hornung, R. W. (1979). An investigation of apparent mass psychogenic illness in an electronics plant, *Journal of Behaviour Medicine*, **2**, 297–309.

Collins, B. W., and Raven, B. H. (1969). Group structure: attraction, coalitions, communication and power. In *Handbook of Social Psychology* (Eds. G. Linzey and E. Aronson), Vol. 4, Addison-Wesley, Reading, Mass.

Eysenck, H. J., and Eysenck, S. B. G. (1968). Eysenck Personality Inventory. Educational and Industrial Testing Service, San Diego, Calif.

Festinger, L. (1954). Theory of social comparison processes, *Human Relations*, **7**, 117–140.

Holmes, T. H., and Rahe, R. H. (1967). The social readjustment rating scale, *Journal of Psychosomatic Research*, **11**, 213–218.

Kerckhoff, A. C., and Back, K. W. (1968). *The June Bug: A Study of Hysterical Contagion*, Appleton-Century-Crofts, New York.

Kincannon, J. C. (1968). Prediction of the standard MMPI scale scores from 71 items, *Journal of Consulting and Clinical Psychology*, **32**, 319–335.

Milgram, S., and Toch, H. (1969). Collective behavior: crowds and social behavior. In *Handbook of Social Psychology* (Eds. G. Lindzey and E. Aronson), Vol. 4, Addison-Wesley, Reading, Mass.

Moos, R. H., Insel, P. M., and Humphrey, B. (1974). *Work Environment Scale*, Consulting Psychologists Press, Palo Alto, Calif.

Schachter, S., and Singer, J. E. (1962). Cognitive, social, and physiological determinants of emotional state, *Psychological Review*, **69**, 379–399.

Smith, M. J., Colligan, M. J., and Hurrell, J. J., Jr. (1978). Three incidents of industrial mass psychogenic illness: a preliminary report, *Journal of Occupational Medicine*, **20**, 399–400.

Stahl, S. M., and Lebedun, M. (1974). Mystery gas: an analysis of mass hysteria, *Journal of Health and Social Behavior*, **15**, 44–50.

Valecha, G. K. (1973). Abbreviated 11-item Rotter I–E scale. In *Measures of Social Psychological Attitudes* (Eds. J. P. Robinson and P. R. Shaver), Institute for Social Research, Ann Arbor, Mich.

PART THREE
Controlling Blue Collar Stress

Job Stress and Blue Collar Work
Edited by C. L. Cooper and M. J. Smith
© 1985 John Wiley & Sons Ltd

Chapter 11

EAPs and Blue Collar Stress

Angus G. S. MacLeod

Institute of Industrial Relations,
University of California, Los Angeles, USA

It has long been recognized that workers at all levels are subject to stresses on and off the job, which can interfere with effective and efficient job production as well as job satisfaction. For instance, as early as 1932, Hersey (1932) pointed out that 'In any plant, at any time, some workers or executives, or both, are confronted with major crises, which upset digestion, lower efficiency and disturb emotional health.' The purpose of this chapter is to explore the relationship of employee assistance programmes (EAPs) to blue collar stress and the use of EAPs for the reduction or elimination of such stress.

It is now recognized that there are numerous causes of occupational stress, which may affect job efficiency. Among these are problems which result from a poor fit between a person and his/her work environment, as well as major crises and/or conditions outside of work. Any or all of these pose physical or psychological threats to the individual, which bring about feelings of insecurity, inadequacy, and non-productive use of energy as the individual tries to cope with them.

To assist such individuals on a humanitarian basis as well as in an effort to keep their problems from affecting production efficiency and, consequently, the profits of their business, many managements have turned to the development and use of EAPs.

An EAP is a programme which uses a set of company policies and procedures for identifying or responding to employees' personal or emotional problems which interfere directly or indirectly with job performance. It provides counselling, information, and/or referral to appropriate counselling treatment and support services for which the company may pay in whole or in part. Continuing contact and follow-up on an individual's progress are also an integral part of this activity (Walsh, 1982).

DEVELOPMENT OF EMPLOYEE COUNSELLING

Although for many years a number of companies have provided a counselling service for executives and upper level management on an individual basis, it has been rare for a company to provide a similar service to blue collar and/or lower white collar workers prior to the 1960s. A few innovative companies and certain landmark research studies contributed significantly to the premise that blue collar or factory workers are subject to both psychological and physical distress, due in part to the demands of the job and the work environment.

In 1919, Marian Brockway, a prominent New York City registered nurse at the time, was hired by the Metropolitan Insurance Company to counsel the firm's many female employees on coping with the problems of being both housewife and full-time worker. (Daily Labor Report, 1984). A major non-psychiatric industrial counselling programme was put into operation in 1936 at the Hawthorne, Illinois, plant of the Western Electric Company as a result of the experiments of Elton Mayo, whom many regard as the father of industrial sociology. This programme resulted from a series of studies which showed the impact of worker attitudes and worker participation on pro-ductivity and which contributed greatly to the growth of the 'human relations' movement in American industry (Mayo, 1945). A few other companies followed this example. In 1949, Prudential Life Insurance company estab-lished a counselling programme in its Newark, New Jersey, Home Office and the Polaroid Corporation started a similar programme in 1958 (Staples, Kelsey, and Thomas, 1980). In the early 1950s, Walker and Guest (1952) showed the detrimental effects socially and psychologically on automobile assembly-line workers on repetitive machine-paced operations. Kornhauser (1965) pointed out the effects of factory operations on the mental health of industrial workers, such as anxiety and threats to the security and adequacy of individuals.

However, progress in establishing counselling programmes was slow until the establishment in the 1960s of an increasing number of occupational alcoholism programmes. Eastman Kodak and Consolidated Edison of New York were among numerous companies which set up counselling programmes designed primarily to assist employees who were alcoholics.

The last 20 years have seen a steady accumulation of evidence from research and from work statistics to show a link between stress and impaired physical and mental health, on the one hand, and decreased performance at work and individual quality of life on the other (Cooper, 1983). In a major study of occupational differences in psychological stress and reported illness, Caplan et al (1975) showed that assemblers and relief workers on machine-paced assembly lines had the highest level of stress and strain of any of the 23 occupations.

In a recent book, Marshall and Cooper (1981) pointed out that an employee counselling service contributes to helping employees cope with job stress. It provides a mechanism capable of reducing a person's anxiety level and a heightened perception of self-control necessary for mental well-being and effective job performance. Since the counselling process is at the heart of an effective EAP, there is a direct relationship between EAPs and alleviation of blue collar stress.

GROWTH OF EAPs

The extensive literature on occupational stress and increased interest in occupational health and employee welfare in general over the last 20 years have been accompanied and accelerated by the growth of EAPs, many of which were focused initially on alcohol and/or drug abuse. Interest in EAPs has been greatly increased by the activities of the National Institute on Alcohol Abuse and Alcoholism (NIAAA), which has done an outstanding job in promoting knowledge about the impact of alcoholism both on and off the job.

Since 1939, when the first alcoholic assistance programme was started by Dr. Daniel Lynch at the New England Telephone Company (Trice and Schonbrunn, 1981), there has been a steady rise in occupational alcoholism programmes. A US Government report (US Department of Health and Human Services, 1981) showed the growth of such programmes from 50 in 1950, to 500 in 1973, to 4400 in 1979–1980.

A recent estimate by Tom Delaney, executive director of the Association of Labor-Management Administrators and Consultants on Alcoholism (ALMACA), a nation-wide organization of EAPs, puts the number of EAPs at about 8000. However, a precise number is hard to come by, because EAPs are loosely defined and few state or federal laws have been enacted which govern them or require them to be registered.

Many EAPs have expanded well beyond the substance abuse area and now cover a wide variety of personal problems, including marital, financial, parent–child difficulties, and other psychological problems. Such activities are referred to as 'broad-brush' EAPs (Wrich, 1980).

Pelletier (1984) notes that many EAPs have become involved in corporate health promotion and 'wellness' programmes, clearly an appropriate activity for collaboration with corporate medical departments. This growth in EAPs indicates a willingness for many corporations to take responsibility for helping employees (and in some cases, dependents also) to cope with job stress, as well as a wide variety of personal and family problems.

ESSENTIAL ELEMENTS OF AN EFFECTIVE EAP

Although EAPs vary greatly from one to another in mission, scope, and in aspects of their operation, certain concepts and elements are generally regarded as essential ingredients of an effective EAP (Wrich, 1980; Walsh, 1982). They are as follows:

(1) Top management support and a written policy statement.
(2) A policy statement to the effect that the company wants to help employees to relieve anxiety and to improve job performance, and that the company will not discriminate against any person seeking professional help with emotional or psychological problems.
(3) Supervisors able to recognize job performance problems and the skills to help an employee to recognize such a problem.
(4) If the plant is organized, efforts should be made to gain the support and cooperation from the union.
(5) A professionally competent diagnostic component to assist the employee in assessing a problem.
(6) A continuum of care, including referral to competent professional resources.
(7) A follow-up on each case.
(8) A system of records for measuring various definitions of success (evaluating the programme).
(9) A focus on voluntarism and not solely on supervisory referral.
(10) A high degree of confidentiality. Information should be released only with the written permission of the client.
(11) An appropriate package of employee benefits, especially health insurance coverage.
(12) A service available to all employees. Many companies offer the same service to dependents of employees.

Along with these elements, management should remember that some EAPs have failed entirely, and some have failed to gain acceptance of employees for the following reasons (among others):

(1) Lack of top management support.
(2) Inadequate health insurance coverage.
(3) The stigma attached to those who have emotional problems.
(4) Placement of the programme office so that it is perceived by employees as a completely management-oriented activity.
(5) Use of the facility perceived by employees as a threat to one's job.
(6) Management's failure to involve the union (in a union-organized operation).
(7) Resistance from a union and from employees if they perceive management as disciplining employees in an arbitrary manner.

FACTORS INFLUENCING MANAGEMENT TO BE MORE AWARE OF BLUE COLLAR STRESS

Recently management has become more concerned about blue collar stress for a number of reasons. There is a need for improving productivity in a highly competitive economy. Another reason is the growing recognition that stress has a direct bearing on job performance. The loss or potential loss of some highly skilled employees due, particularly, to 'substance abuse' has often caused major personnel problems. A third reason is the sharply rising costs related to occupational health.

The last point is by far the most important factor and is due primarily to substantial increases in the costs of worker compensation, disability retirements, and health insurance. Worker compensation costs increased from $1.8 billion in 1965 to $13.4 billion in 1980. As one example of the increase in retirement disability costs, a California public official was recently granted a disability retirement for a heart attack, which he claimed was caused primarily by harassment from another public official.

Private health expenditures paid for by insurance have increased more than fivefold over the last 15 years (MacLeod, 1984). For example, since 1962 the average daily cost of hospitalization in California has risen more than 700 per cent. to an average of $714 in 1982.

A substantial part of increased costs in worker compensation (WC) is due to the phenomenon of 'cumulative trauma', or cumulative injury cases which are stress-related. A cumulative injury case is one in which an individual has incurred a succession of slight injuries or traumas, none of which are disabling, but the cumulative effect of which has become disabling. A typical example would be a blue collar worker who eventually suffers a low back disability resulting from years of repeated bending and lifting.

A generation ago, interpretation and administration of the WC laws was much simpler than today. An injury or trauma (for example, a cut resulting from touching moving machinery) which could be traced to a particular incident and point of time was clearly compensable. However, compensability was highly questionable in the event of a disability that could not be traced to one given event.

Today, interpretation of WC statutes is much more complex and thousands of WC awards are made annually on the basis of a disability that could not be traced directly to one given event.

Disabilities due to back injuries, cardiovascular problems, hearing difficulties, and even neuroses and psychiatric claims are some examples of stress-related cases. In a recent 2-year period in California, cumulative injury cases increased 22 per cent. for each of the two years, and today the average cost of a cumulative injury case is more than four times the cost of an average WC claim (MacLeod, 1984). The increasing costs of job stress and occupational health are indeed a major motivation of management interest in these fields.

STRESS REDUCTION AND EVALUATION OF EAPs

The increased interest on the part of management in EAPs over the years is clearly due to the success of numerous industrial occupational alcoholism programmes, many of which evolved into broad-brush EAPs, and the need to reduce occupational health costs.

A few examples will help to illustrate the effectiveness of some of these programmes. The Illinois Bell Telephone Company has had an alcohol rehabilitation programme since 1950 and made an extensive evaluation of the period between 1968 and 1978, using 752 participants who had at least 5 years of employment experience prior to and at least 5 years of service subsequent to referral to the medical department. The job rehabilitation rate was 77 per cent.. Job efficiency ratings of 'good' rose from 10 to 60 per cent., off-duty accidents were reduced by 42 per cent., on-the-job accidents were reduced by 61 per cent., and there was an estimated savings to the company of over $1,270,000 from reduction of absences alone (Asma et al., 1980).

Another example of a successful EAP is exemplified by a study made by the Insight programme of the Kennecott Copper Company of Ogden, Utah. Using a sample of 150 clients in 1971–1972, they focused on (1) a period of 6 months prior to participation, (2) approximately 1 year during participation, and (3) 6 months after participation. Although a primary focus was on job dysfunctions due to alcoholism, approximately 80 per cent. of these 'troubled employees' served by this broad-brush EAP suffered from a wide variety of problems. The study showed a 52 per cent. attendance improvement, a 75 per cent. decrease in weekly indemnity (state disability) costs, and a 55 per cent. decrease in health, medical, and surgical costs after participation in the Insight programme. A comparison with 150 non-participants in the same period showed an increase in absenteeism, and in health, medical, and surgical costs, and a much smaller decrease in weekly indemnity costs. The programme director estimated that the return on investment was $6 for every $1 expended (Wrich, 1984).

In a more recent study, EAP programme director, James Wrich (1984), of United Air Lines, said that for every dollar spent, the company gets $16.35 back in the form of reduced absenteeism alone. The figure is based on the troubled employee's absenteeism during the 12 months just before entering the programme versus absenteeism during the first 12 months after completing the counselling or treatment, extended over the employee's expected career life. Although the method used in arriving at these figures might be questionable, it is only fair to point out that the use of sick leave among participants in two major United locations dropped by between 74 and 80 per cent. after use of EAP services.

An independent study of cost-effectiveness in four EAPs in the Detroit area (Foote et al., 1978), funded by the Michigan Department of Public Health and the Office of Substance Abuse Services, used the following measures (where available): (1) absenteeism, (2) on-the-job accidents, (3) visits to the medical unit, (4) disciplinary actions, (5) grievances, (6) worker compensation, and (7) sickness and accident benefits. The study showed an estimated cost savings of $198,397 in one company in one year and of $154,178 in the second company in one year. This study was particularly important in that it showed a number of difficulties in evaluating the cost-effectiveness of EAPs as a factor in stress reduction in an organization. For example, the authors indicated that (1) programmes dealing with chronic health problems must expect slow recoveries; (2) a 2 to 5-year period is necessary to evaluate the impact on sickness and accident benefits; (3) expectations about programme impact on work performance should take into account the degree to which programme clients deviate from the average employee in work performance; and (4) expectations about programme impact on sicknesss and accident benefits must be geared to the liberality of the company's policy on the use of sick leave. Their most important point was that company norms vary greatly and often data critical to an objective analysis are either unavailable or not readily accessible.

In a comprehensive review of 22 EAPs, Jones and Vischi (1979) found that all but one equated reductions in use of hospital and physicians' offices services with treatment for emotional stress. The decline in use of general medical services ranged from 5 to 85 per cent., with a mean of 34 per cent. for mental health intervention, and from 26 to 68 per cent., with a mean of 45 per cent. for alcoholism programmes. They also caution that many studies have methodological limitations, such as small study groups, inadequate comparison groups, short-term spans, and questionable measures of medical utilization. If these studies are indicative of the impact a well-designed EAP can have on the use of insured medical services by employees and their families, then such a programme could indeed result in substantial savings and have a substantial impact on stress reduction in an organization (Foote *et al.*, 1978).

FUTURE ROLE OF EAPs

Although the continuing use and growth of EAPs is evidence of management's belief in their value, it is important to recognize that most EAPs are conceived primarily as *rehabilitation* efforts whereas 'in the long run our aim is to find ways of *preventing* job stresses from impacting upon the worker rather than ways of developing a better tranquilizer for the resulting strains' (Caplan *et al.*, 1975).

It is obvious that the present rehabilitation thrust should continue but that EAP administrators, or other parts of the organization in collaboration with the EAP, should be encouraged to take a broader view of stress reduction. The following are some steps that EAPs should consider:

(1) EAPs should increase their activity on health promotion and health education.
(2) EAPs should be involved in identifying stress centres; e.g. areas with high turnover and high absenteeism, areas of high interpersonal conflict, areas with rising trends on medical costs, etc., and should be prepared to recommend action designed to diminish the impact of stressors. Although this may appear to be in conflict with the necessary high degree of confidentiality, it is conceivable that some information could be utilized to accomplish important remedial changes.
(3) EAPs should recognize that each individual has his/her own way of coping with stress and that the EAP should offer alternatives to a one-on-one counselling approach; e.g. a support group composed of individuals who share a common problem.
(4) Improve and refine methods of evaluating EAP activity.
(5) Consider involving the union towards gaining greater employee acceptance. Former Chairman Murphy of the General Motors Corporation recently spoke about a fruitful experience in an EAP programme enhanced by joint labour–management cooperation.
   Trice and Roman (1978) have reported at length on those features which discourage or encourage union participation in management-based EAPs.
(6) Increase the trend towards professionalization among EAP administrators.
(7) Increase the dialogue between independent researchers and those companies interested in innovation and experimentation.
(8) EAP administrators should collaborate fully with other parts of the organization which are concerned primarily with the development and utilization of human resources, especially in the field of preventive health care.

CONCLUSION

The industrial EAP, as a mechanism for rehabilitation of substance abusers or as a programme for troubled employees with a wide variety of emotional and/or physical problems, has enjoyed substantial growth and management acceptance in contributing to increased productivity, lower medical costs, and the reduction of blue collar stress. Although the present thrust of rehabilitation and/or helping employees to cope with stress should continue, in the long run EAPs should be involved in *preventing* job stresses from impacting on workers. Managements should consider expanding the scope of EAPs to cover health education and health promotion and other preventive activities with a view to diminishing the impact of stress on blue collar workers.

REFERENCES

Asma, F., Hilker, R., Shevlin, J., and Golden, R. (1980). Twenty-five years of rehabilitation of employees with drinking problems, *Journal of Occupational Medicine*, **22**, 4.

Caplan, R., Cobb, S., French, J., Jr., Harrison, R., and Pinneau, S. (1975). *Job Demands and Worker Health—Main Effects and Occupational Differences*, National Institute for Occupational Safety and Health, U.S. Department of Health, Education, and Welfare.

Cooper, C. L. (1983). *Stress Research: Issues for the 80s*, John Wiley and Sons, Chichester.

Daily Labor Report (1984). Bureau of National Affairs, Washington, D. C.

Foote, A., Erfurt, J., Strauch, P., and Guzzardo, T. (1978). *Cost Effectiveness of Occupational EAPs—Test of an Evaluation Method*, Published by the Worker Health Program, Institute of Labor and Industrial Relations, University of Michigan–Wayne State University, Ann Arbor, Michigan.

Hersey, R. (1932). *Workers' Emotions in Shop and Home: A Study of Individual Workers from the Psychological and Physiological Standpoint*, University of Pennsylvania Press, Philadelphia, Pa.

Jones, J., and Vischi, T. (1979). *Summary of Impact of Alcoholism Treatment on Medical Care Utilisation and Cost*, U.S. Department of Health, Education and Welfare, Public Health Service—Alcohol, Drug Abuse and Mental Health Administration.

Kornhauser, A. (1965). *Mental Health of the Industrial worker*, John Wiley and Sons, New York.

MacLeod, A. (1984). In *Human Aspects in Office Automation* (Ed. B. Cohen), Elsevier Science Publishers, Amsterdam.

Marshall, J., and Cooper, C. L. (1981). *Coping with Stress at Work*, Gower Publishing Co. Ltd., Aldershot, Hants.

Mayo, E. (1945). *Social Problems of an Industrial Civilisation*, Harvard University Press, Boston, Mass.

Pelletier, K. (1984). *Healthy People in Unhealthy Places*, Delacorte Press, New York.

Staples, L., Kelsey, J., and Thomas, R. (1980). An in-house industrial counselling program: the Northwestern Bell Telephone Company experience, *Journal of Occupational Medicine*, **22**, 1.

Trice, H., and Roman, P. (1978). *Spirits and Demons at Work*, New York State School of Industrial and Labor Relations, Cornell University, New York.

Trice, H., and Schonbrunn, M. (1981). A History of Job-based Alcoholism Programs—1900–1955, *Journal of Drug Issues*,

US Department of Health and Human Services (1981). Fourth Special Report to the U.S. Congress on Alcohol and Health, US Department of Health and Human Services, Washington, D.C.

Walker, C., and Guest, R. (1952). *The Man on the Assembly Line*, Harvard University Press, Boston, Mass.

Walsh, D. (1982). Employee Assistance Programs, *Milbank Memorial Fund Quarterly/Health and Society*, **60**, No. 3.

Wrich, J. (1980). *The Employee Assistance Program: Updated for the 1980s*, Hazelden Educational Foundation, Minnesota.

Wrich, J. (1984). *The Employee Assistance Program*, Hazelden Educational Foundation, Minnesota.

Job Stress and Blue Collar Work
Edited by C. L. Cooper and M. J. Smith
© 1985 John Wiley & Sons Ltd

Chapter 12

Union Efforts to Relieve Blue Collar Stress

Arthur B. Shostak

Department of Psychology and Sociology,
Drexel University, Philadelphia, Pa., USA

What does labor want? We want more schoolhouses and less jails; more books and less arsenals; more learning and less vice; more constant work and less crime; more leisure and less greed; more justice and less revenge (Samuel Gompers, President, AFL, 1893).

America's labour unions have a substantial record of accomplishment in alleviating negative stress in blue collar lives. Since their start on these shores in the 1700s they have sought to curb supervisory excesses, enlarge employee input into the setting of compensation terms, and enhance worker empowerment and self-esteem:

> Most importantly, unions have given dignity to the individual worker. No longer does he have to grovel before management to maintain his rights and privileges. Freeing workers from an arbitrary punitive atmosphere may be the single most important factor in making life in the workplace more palatable (Schrank, 1978, p. 127).

Five related efforts are currently made by unions to prevent, alleviate, and eliminate blue-collar stress: labour acts as an *advocate*, a *buffer*, a *critic*, an *initiator*, and a *provider*. Each of these functions is explained and illustrated below, the better to highlight the strategic responsibility here of unions to their members, to stress relief campaigners outside labour's ranks (concerned MD's, industrial hygienists, quality circle proponents, etc.), to progressive elements in the business community, and to society at large.

UNIONS AS ADVOCATES

Typical of labour's contribution as a promoter of stress-relieving advances is the path-breaking use of applied futuristics being made by the Communication Workers of America (CWA), and the controversial advocacy of 'comparable worth' gains by the American Federation of State, County, and Municipal Employees (AFSCME).

Stress-relieving futuristics

Few unions can match CWA in its attempt to anticipate negative stressors and move out boldly to counter them before they become unmanageable.

In 1981 the CWA created labour's first 'Committee on the Future', and the union asked its blue-ribbon group of rank-and-filers and staff members to rigorously study CWA options in responding to telecommunication break-throughs. The unique Committee was also asked to research the impending AT&T divestiture, and to advise CWA about union 'survival skills' after the breakup of the 'Ma Bell' system.

Two eventful years later, at the CWA convention in 1983, the Committee had delegates listen to the first-ever keynote address given by a world-famous futurist (Alvin Toffler) to a labour union gathering. With Toffler's compli-ments for their pro-active research ringing in their ears, the delegates heard the CWA Committee on the Future report on the completion of its assignment.

To help relieve the considerable negative stress expected from mind-boggling technological change, the Committee offered delegates a thorough-going blueprint for the next 10 years of union–management negotiations. Influenced by blueprint reasoning and details, the CWA proceeded thereafter to negotiate a $36 million retaining programme. It also won generous financial incentives for workers choosing early retirement and new severance pay agreements for workers displaced by new technology. So valuable did the Committee's blueprint prove in these negotiations that its existence has since been copied by other unions ranging from the bricklayers to the postal workers (Keller, 1984).

Typical is the 1984 report prepared for the Steelworkers Union by its 'Future Directions of the Union' Committee, an influential 38-page document that capped 13 months of study. The Committee urged several controversial adaptations to changing stressful circumstances; e.g. new organizing campaigns should be undertaken in the Carribbean Islands and anywhere in the Western Hemisphere, rather than just in North America, as at present. The union should maintain a state-of-the-art computer data bank on the voting records of members of Congress, and should systematically poll its members on political issues. As well, the union should mount a major effort to mobilize its 300,000 retirees, and get them to help with political and organ-izing efforts.

Controversial and invigorating ideas of this sort help reduce stress and galvanize welcomed reforms in progressive labour organizations.

'Comparable worth' as a stress-relieving aid

Women workers are often distressed by low wages in female blue collar occupations they judge comparable to male-dominated posts that pay much more. Such women now have a major advocate in the American Federation of State, County, and Municipal Employees (AFSCME), the nation's leading proponent of an idea hailed by certain feminists as '*the* civil rights issue of the 1980s' (Goodman, 1984).

First brought to prominence in 1983 by a successful AFSCME suit against the State of Washington, the comparable-worth thesis argues that different jobs can be compared in such a way that 'equal pay for equal work' can become 'equal pay for comparable work' (Freeman, 1984). Proponents like AFSCME want employers to be required by law to use job-evaluation techniques to compare dissimilar jobs and adjust wage levels, especially in the case of underpaid female workers (the 80 per cent. of all women workers concentrated in only 20 of the Labor Department's 427 job categories) (Gold, 1983; Remick, 1984).

A related tactic focuses on the use of a joint labour–management committee to study this complex topic and negotiate voluntary gains. Representative of this approach is the 1983 AT&T/CWQ collaborative model.

Following years of bitter labour relations, the parties resolved in 1980 to begin a new era of cooperation and joint problem-solving. One result was the formation of a joint national Occupations Job Evaluation Committee to research, develop, and make 'comparable worth' recommendations concerning the design and implementation of an improved job evaluation plan. The Committee agreed no wages would be reduced as a result of its work, and all employees would have training opportunities to improve their skills. The psychological and emotional effects of technological change would be considered in any job evaluation, and all employees would have the right to appeal any scoring of the relative worth of their jobs. The key to the entire process, Committee members agreed, was holding interviews with AT&T workers, who are 'the only real experts on the jobs being studied'. While fully aware of the enormity of their undertaking, the joint labour–management committee maintains that with the mutual backing of both CWA and the new Bell companies 'the task is not insurmountable' (Straw and Foged, 1982).

UNIONS AS BUFFERS

Typical of labour's contribution as an intervening agent, an intermediary between negative stress and blue collarites, is the recent effort of unions to force the government to investigate alleged corporate misuse of genetic screening techniques. Also relevant here is labour's buffer role where corporate misuse of industrial psychology is concerned.

Genetic screening as a stressor

In 1982 various unions and AFL–CIO asked Congress to consider protective legislation as a safeguard against a new form of unreasonable discrimination in hiring practices. Colourful media attention had many blue collarites alarmed that certain major corporations, particularly leaders in the chemical industry, were secretly 'screening' job applicants: blood test results were allegedly being used to see if the genes of an unsuspecting subject revealed potential health danger if the subject worked with certain workplace substances.

The Oil, Chemical and Atomic Workers Union, in particular, worried that such screening techniques could 'create an army of untouchables who couldn't find work'. The ensuing flurry of congressional and media attention to labour charges and company rebuttal helped correct serious misimpressions on both sides, and seems to have significantly reduced the stress here of union leaders and rank-and file blue collarites alike (Greenberger, 1982).

Industrial psychology as a stressor

Especially vexing for manual workers is their long-standing suspicion that industrial psychology uses at work are seldom in their best interest. Many believe their need for an effective buffer between themselves and mind-moulding manipulators could not be greater.

Organized labour has always been leery of psychologists-for-hire, especially when corporate enthusiasm for such allies seemed to patronize and otherwise trifle with the adulthood and hard-earned prerogatives of rank-and-filers (Shostak, 1964). Unions naturally resent efforts by company psychologists to discourage resorting to collective action (such as local union militancy), and to urge, instead, individual adaptation (the use of meditation, relaxation techniques, vigorous exercise, etc.).

Many workers join labour in rejecting the notion that only their poor attitudes explain their workplace grievances, and that they themselves are somehow at fault ('if the worker is unhappy at work, the best thing would be a change in attitude about work'). Unions move in to help buffer members against this sort of 'blame the victim' manipulation (Gordon, 1980). They especially resent corporate stress-reduction programmes that minimize deep-set sources of negative stress—such as worker powerlessness, workplace, tedium, or job-loss jitters.

Labour helps its membership stay focused on power inequities in the workplace, a focus that clarifies and fortifies, even as it buffers against the self-blame and passivity invited by corporate misuses of industrial psychology.

UNIONS AS CRITICS

Going beyond its relatively restrained role as a skeptical buffer, labour helps reduce negative stress by adopting an unequivocably hostile role on occasion.

Labour versus NLRB

Typical of unions serving as *critics* is the heated campaign labour is leading to force the national Labor Relations Board (NLRB) to regain its impartiality and steer a middle course.

Dominated by Reagan appointees, the Board has sharply raised the stress level of unionists with a series of recent anti-union rulings of unprecedented severity; e.g. the NLRB held in 1983 that employers will not be compelled to bargain even if they have committed massive unfair labour practices—threatening to close the plant, cutting pay of union backers, firing workers who serve as organizers—to prevent a union from signing up a majority of workers. In the past, the NLRB would and did issue a bargaining order when a union drive was derailed by such employer conduct.

Using its political influence the AFL–CIO struggles to prevent the Reagan Board from getting even more right-wing members, even as it explains and castigates Board rulings to its anxious and disappointed membership.

Labour versus right to work legisation

Another front on which labour fights as a major critic involves its opposition to 'right to work' laws that forbid mandatory union membership of all workers covered by a freely won labour contract.

Founded in 1955, a 1.5 million member National Right to Work Committee (NRWC) employs over 125 staffers in a concerted effort to win a national right to work law via a constitutional amendment. Successful in getting 20 states to pass such a law, the NRWC has been blocked by the AFL–CIO since 1976 in achieving any new statehouse victories. Labour won 13 such contests in 1979, and another one more recently in 1981, all of which required labour to win over the (non-union) public and labour's own membership in hard-fought ballot contests.

Labour's ongoing efforts here necessitate a higher quality adult education effort, one that helps 'organize the organized', and generates labour support outside its ranks—both valuable stress-relieving gains (Howard, 1982).

UNIONS AS INITIATORS

Much less well known, and far more worthy of attention from all concerned with blue collar stress relief, is the union role as an inventive, imaginative agent.

Health cost containment

Typical of labour's contribution here is an ongoing effort to relieve stress on blue collar incomes caused by rising health costs. Intent on protecting the hard-won gains of workers in negotiated health benefits, even while adapting new cost-cutting measures, unions are joining labour–management campaigns to invent cost-containment advances worth rank-and-file utilization (Klett, 1984). Local unions are sponsoring novel health fairs, unprecedented labour conferences to boost enrollment in HMOs, and clever programmes to win anti-smoking, weight-reducing types of health promotion gains. As research has established the workplace as a *very* effective prevention and treatment site, labour's inventiveness translates into significant dollar savings for all concerned (Rosen, 1984).

'Right-to-know' gains

Another type of initiation is clear in labour's 'deal-cutting' on behalf of controversial 'Worker and Community Right-to-Know' legislation.

Typical was the situation in Pennsylvania in 1984 when an 18-month state AFL–CIO campaign for passage of a 'right-to-know' bill ironically secured House approval of one so uncompromising that the Governor pledged to veto it. Eager to keep the bill's slim chances alive, the state AFL–CIO and Philaposh (an activist group with much labour support) signalled a willingness to 'horse trade' on bill provisions with its business opponents.

In short order the labour people met and negotiated with representatives of the state's largest chemical companies and the Pennsylvania Chamber of Commerce. They produced an inventive compromise bill that kept intact most worker protections, but also offered the companies more safeguards for proprietary information construed as trade secrets. Estimates of enforcement costs came down from $215 million to $100 million after labour agreed to the elimination both of on-site testing and requirements for immediate labelling. Instead, with a new 2½-year enactment schedule, the compromise bill earned both the state legislature and the Governor's approval.

When fully implemented in 1987 the bill will require about 25,000 companies to provide specific information on over 2,500 hazardous chemicals to their employees, and be more specific than ever in labelling chemicals with generic names, rather than trade or blank labels. It also establishes a procedure whereby anxious employees can challenge their employer's right to deny information on grounds it is proprietary or a trade secret. Not surprisingly, the state AFL–CIO characterized the final version as 'the most comprehensible and workable right-to-know bill in existence', a standout among the 20 state laws now covering this area of stress (Mykrantz, 1984).

UNIONS AS PROVIDER

The last of the contributions labour makes to stress relief is the most obvious, but no less significant for all of that.

Stress reduction campaigner

Labour experiments continuously with its own version of formal stress-reduction programmes. A pioneering effort in 1979 by the Communication Workers Union, for example, had locals across the country draw 500,000 members into a national Job Stress Day. Rallies, speeches, and informational picketing were used to remind the Bell System and the public of the workers' wish to relieve negative stressors (such as the infamous 'potty break policy', whereby workers were forced to wait as much as half an hour before they were allowed by supervisors to go to the lavatory).

Another union tact has focused on winning stress-relieving government intervention, a strategy pursued, for example, by the Office and Professional Employees International Union (OPEIU). Preoccupied with VDT stressors, including eye, neck, and back pains, the OPEIU has sought to negotiate better seating and lighting standards, more frequent breaks, and more reasonable production standards. Frustrated by the results of contract settlements, OPEIU joined with the Newspaper Guild, the Typographical Union, and several others to form a coalition that continues (unsuccessfully) to pressure OSHA—on both the national and state levels—to regulate VDT use and set stress-reducing production standards for the machine.

Although preoccupied with large-scale causes of workplace discontent, labours' stress-reduction efforts do not ignore the individual and his/her intimate, personal, and immediate problems. Certain key union leaders urge their locals to teach rank-and-filers how to profit from down-to-earth stress-relief aids, such as referrals to AA, biofeedback, gamblers anonymous, narcotics anonymous, spouse abuse therapies, pastoral counselling, physical exercise, or the valuable like. As well, local union safety and health committees help evaluate and publicize relevant community mental health resources, even while focusing on *the* most effective tool available, or the language of the union contract, to reduce work-related causes of stress, e.g. extensive or unwanted overtime, improper or erroneous information entered in personnel files, improper work assignments, etc. (Arndt, 1981).

Reciprocal bargainer

Labour can help set contract terms that lower stress levels by enabling a troubled business to regain financial security and remain a viable employer of rank-and-filers.

Widely hailed in this connection is an ongoing experimental effort to keep Eastern Airlines aloft, a situation made all the more interesting by the fact that earlier labour–management relations here were among the worst in the airlines industry. In late 1983, however, the near-bankrupt company negotiated for about $370 million in wage concessions and anticipated productivity gains. In return, Eastern agreed to seat four union representatives on its 19-member board, share power in other ways, and give its employees a 25 per cent. equity share (with the stock held in trust until 1986).

Every level of the organization now has 'employee involvement' committees, and labour proposals have led to everything from the elimination of a time clock at one airport to retention of considerable work at all sites previously contracted out (at a new savings of $2 million a year). In Detroit, labour relations were so bad that certain managers were thought by unionists to use binoculars to spy on workers, and retaliation took the form of intentionally smashing equipment. Now, among other cost-cutting reforms generated by a Detroit joint labour–management committee, the workers devised a new system for employee parking that should save Eastern about $20,000 a year.

Eastern's unions also won full access to the company's books, plus the right to review its business plans and major capital-spending proposals before they were sent to the Board. In this way the unions were involved in nearly 5 months of quiet consultations prior to the company's 1984 reduction of half the work force at its loss-ridden Houston operation. These talks enabled labour to persuade management to assign some new repair work to Houston, thereby saving nearly a score of jobs for union mechanics. Similarly, months of quiet consultation before the opening of Eastern's new hub in Kansas City enabled management to persuade labour to accept more flexible job definitions than used elsewhere. Partly as a result, the hub has become one of Eastern's most successful operations.

When asked to sum it all up, especially as regards negative stress, supporters point proudly to the grievance-filing record of the traditionally militant Machinists' Union (IAM): in 1982, the union filed 1068 grievances against Eastern; in 1983, 1010; and to 1 November 1984, only 356. The Eastern local IAM president insists the new system is 'not just tokenism', even as Frank Borman, company President (and a previous opponent of workers on the Board) boasts that: 'The process works. It's often frustrating. It requires more time. but the effort is well worth it.' The leading academician here, Cornell's Professor William F. Whyte, predicts that 'Eastern has set a pattern in the airline industry that will probably be widely imitated' (Cohn, 1984; Kuttner, 1984, p. 23).

Busisness provider

While still very small in numbers and recognition, a third tactic here is so promising as to warrant inclusion in even a brief consideration of labour's provider options. Specifically, more and more locals are addressing the fears members have of job loss by financing new businesses that create payrolls for the rank-and-file.

Typical of the imaginative possibilities here is the 1984 investment in a building project of $17 million dollars in pension funds by three Philadelphia building trade locals. Union officials hailed the project, the first of its kind in the city, as both 'an investment opportunity to benefit our pension-fund members and as an opportunity to provide work for our contractors'. During construction, local union members got 2000 well-paying jobs through a $12 million payroll, and the union pension fund expected to earn 15 per cent. thereafter on its investment. City Hall officials were especially enthusiastic, one of them explaining: 'The unions are, for the first time in our region, putting their pension money where their workers are. It is bringing union and management together, and enhancing the economic development of the city.'

Pennsylvania state government officials joined in the cheering, and cited the expanding role of their Milrite Council, a state agency that promotes the use of union–management pension funds to add jobs to the state's economy. The Council is putting together a $100 million investment pool capitalized with public and private pension funds. Earmarked for Pennsylvania firms that want to expand or modernize to remain competitive, the Milrite Council project enables unions to use their $40 billion in pension funds to protect and promote the job-holding status of their members.

In the past, union pension funds, jointly overseen by both labour and management trustees, were typically invested in government securities, stocks, and bonds. While the funds may have come from Philadelphia or Pennsylvania blue collarites, they often ended up financing construction in the Sun Belt. Recently, however, labour has financed 70 union-built construction projects across the nation, with another 23 under construction in 1984. Union leaders remain very enthusiastic, for as a Philadelphia local officer explains: 'We get it at both ends. We get a good investment and a guarantee that our people will be working' (Collins, 1984).

Contract change agent

No discussion of union efforts to relieve blue collar stress, however constrained by space restrictions, is complete without even brief consideration of the first thing manual workers themselves refer to when this matter of stress relief is raised, or the bottom-line impact of labour on their well-being. Academic research released in 1984 brings fresh and overdue clarity to this complex and contentious topic.

According to two leading university economists, blue collarites might experience increased stress from at least three aspects of labour's impact: unions are not especially successful in getting Congress to pass pro-labour legislation. They cause slightly more unemployment because high union wages force management to lay off employees more frequently. Unlike non-unionists, the members of locals openly acknowledge considerable dissatisfaction with their work (but neither intend to, nor do, leave it). They voice their complaints loudly to enable the local union to convince the firm that its workers are unhappy and warrant a better contract, albeit the entire situation aggravates the negative stress level of everyone involved.

In contrast to these drawbacks, the two economists also found unions so improve the work environment that organized workplaces have a quit rate 30 to 65 per cent. lower than the average for all workers. Labour creates, at no extra cost to management, workplace practices and compensation packages of clear-cut value to both sides (more effective and fairer compensation practices, increased productivity, and better morale). Overall, unions are given credit for securing 20 to 30 per cent. more in wages and fringes for members than is true in non-union settings. They raise blue collar earnings relative to white collar earnings. They also compel management to operate in more professional, less paternalistic, and far less authoritarian ways—all of these being stress-relieving gains of the greatest significance (Freeman and Medoff, 1984, pp. 20–21, 2248).

SUMMARY

As more than 50 per cent. of the US work force is employed by companies that deal with unions, the nation's nearly 170 international unions influence the lives of many more employees than is implied by the rate of unionization (20 per cent. of the labour force) (Freeman and Medoff, 1984, pp. 34–35). Serving variously as *advocate, buffer, critic, initiator*, and *provider*, the unions do many things that relieve job stress but are not specifically stress programmes. Their 65,000 locals continue to make a diverse and meaningful contribution to the effort to reduce the toll that negative stress takes in blue collar lives.

REFERENCES

Arndt, R. (1981). Coping with job stress—the role of the Union Safety and Health Committee, *Labour Studies Journal*, 6(1), Spring, 53–61.
Cohn, G. (1984). Uncharted paths, *Wall Street Journal*, 31 October 1984, p. 1-A.
Collins, H. (1984). Unions put their money where the work is, *The Philadelphia Inquirer*, 10 December 1984, pp. 1-B, 5-B.
Freeman, J. (1984). Unions push pay equity fight, *In These Times*, 12–18 September 1984, p. 11.
Freeman, R. B., and Medoff, J. L. (1984). *What Do Unions Do?*, Basic Books, New York.
Gold, M. E. (1983). *A Dialogue on Comparable Worth*, ILR Press, Cornell University, Ithaca, N.Y.
Goodman, W. (1984). Equal pay for 'comparable worth' growing as job-discrimination issue, *New York Times*, 4 September 1984, p. B-9.
Gordon, S. (1980). Workplace fantasies, *Working Powers*, September/October 1980, pp. 36–41.

Greenberger, R. S. (1982). Labor letter, *Wall Street Journal*, 30 March 1982, p. 1.
Howard, R. (1982). Solidarity begins at home, *Working Papers for a New Society*, January/February 1982, pp. 18–27.
Keller, B. (1984). A union copes with deregulation, *New York Times*, 18 November 1984, p. 4-F.
Klett, S. V. (1984). The labor factor, *Business and Health*, September 1984, pp. 31–35.
Kuttner, (1984.
Mykrantz, C. (1984). Right-to-know passes Senate, *Philadelphia Business Journal*, 8–14 October 1984, p. 16.
Remick, H. (1984). *Comparable Worth and Wage Discrimination*, Temple University Press, Philadelphia, Pa.
Rosen, R. (1984). Worksite health promotion, *Corporate Community*, 1(1), June 1984, 1–8.
Schrank. R. (1978). *Ten Thousand Working Days*, MIT Press, Cambridge, Mass.
Shostak, A. B. (1964). Industrial psychology and the trade unions: a matter of mutual indifference. In *The Frontiers of Management Psychology* (Ed. G. Fish), Harper and Row, New York, pp. 144–155.
Straw, R. J., and Foged, L. E. (1982). Job evaluation: one union's experience, ILR Report, Spring 1982, pp. 24–26.

Job Stress and Blue Collar Work
Edited by C. L. Cooper and M. J. Smith
© 1985 John Wiley & Sons Ltd

Chapter 13

Social Support and Stress Reduction*

David R. Williams and James S. House
Survey Research Center and Department of Sociology,
University of Michigan, Ann Arbor, Michigan, USA

The topic of social support has emerged, seemingly out of nowhere, in the last decade to become a central focus of basic and applied research on social and occupational stress. In the course of a recent review of methodological issues in the study of social support (House and Kahn, 1985) we discovered that published research on social support has increased at a geometric rate over the past decade, from a few entries annually in the Social Science Citation Index in the period 1972–1975 to almost 100 entries in the last year (1983) for which complete data are available.

The growth in research interest is matched by growing popular and applied interest. The reasons for this interest lie not in the novelty of the concept of social support, since the idea of social support and its potential for enhancing health and well-being has been around for centuries, albeit under different labels from love to social integration (Cobb, 1976; House, 1981). Indeed, there is not complete agreement as to what constitutes social support, though most would agree that it involves a flow between people of emotional concern and caring, information, and instrumental help, with emotional concern being most central (cf. House, 1981). What has made social support such a hot topic is the particularly potent role it may be able to play in reducing the prevalence and health impact of one of the major emerging health hazards of the modern industrial world—stress at work and outside of work. For these same reasons, social support must be central in any comprehensive effort to control stress (or its adverse effects) in blue collar work.

More specifically, a number of factors make social support a promising avenue for efforts at reducing or alleviating the effects of occupational stress. First, social support is a 'triple threat' in such efforts (House, 1981, chap. 1).

*Preparation of this chapter has been supported by an American Sociological Association pre-doctoral award to the first author and by Grants 5 T32 MH16806 and 5 P50 MH38330-02 from the National Institute of Mental Health, US Public Health Service. We are indebted to Linda Bronfmen for comments on a previous draft and to Marie Klatt for preparation of the manuscript.

That is, supportive social relationships have been conceptualized as operating in three possible ways to alleviate the problem of work stress (House, 1981). Two of these mechanisms can be termed main effects. Firstly, support can directly enhance health by supplying human needs for affection, approval, social contact, and security. Secondly, by reducing interpersonal tensions and generally having other positive effects in the work environment, support can directly reduce levels of stress and indirectly improve health. In either case, higher levels of support would enhance health irrespective of the level of stress. The third effect of support is a buffering or interactive one. According to the buffering hypothesis, instead of having direct effects on stress or health, social support modifies the relationship between stress and health and protects the individual from the negative consequences of stress. Thus, when exposed to stress, health risks would decline as support levels increase. Conversely, as support levels decline, stress would have an increasingly adverse impact on health. This third mechanism means that social support can be helpful not only in directly reducing stress and improving health, but also in alleviating the adverse health effects of work stresses that cannot be reduced for whatever reason at a given point in time.

Not only is social support a potential triple threat, it has proved empirically potent and robust in all three of these ways—reducing stress, improving health, and buffering the impact of stress on health. We review and assess this empirical evidence below, focusing especially on studies of blue colar workers. Finally, social support is an appealing approach to controlling work stress because it appears to have beneficial effects on other aspects of organizational functioning, and to be closely related, though in ways we do not yet fully understand, to other factors—such as worker participation and control and patterns of coping with stress—which are central to actual or proposed efforts to reduce blue collar stress and improve individual and organizational well-being. Thus, efforts to enhance social support at work and hence to alleviate problems of blue collar stress are likely to be congruent with, and even constitute, parts of other efforts to enhance individual and organizational well-being.

This chapter will review evidence on the relationships among social support, work stress, and health from a variety of sources—general population or community surveys, studies of job loss and unemployment, and studies of particular organizational or occupational groups. We focus wherever possible on studies of blue collar populations. Though the relevant stresses may differ by occupation or by types and sources of support which are most salient and significant, existing evidence provides little basis for concluding that the nature and operation of social support differs for blue collar workers versus others. From this review we seek to draw conclusions regarding unresolved theoretical and empirical issues and implications of existing evidence for efforts to control or alleviate blue collar stress or its adverse effects on individual or organizational well-being.

WORK STRESS, SOCIAL SUPPORT AND HEALTH: EMPIRICAL EVIDENCE FOCUSING ON BLUE COLLAR POPULATIONS

General population surveys

Brown and his associates (e.g. Brown and Harris, 1978) have studied psychiatric disturbance among women in South London. They have accumulated impressive evidence that severe life events provoke the onset of depression and that social support operates as a mediator between life events and the onset of depression. Severe events were those that involved the loss of a person, a role, or an idea and included job loss and job transitions. However, women who had experienced one of these events but who also had an intimate confiding relationship with a husband or boyfriend did not have an increased risk of depression.

In a study of 1003 adults in Los Angeles county, Aneshensel and Stone (1982) reported a negative relationship between social support and depressive symptomatology. Both of their measures of stress included occupational stressors. Employment losses were included in the life event losses and financial, marital, and work-related sources of strain were combined into a perceived strain index. This study found that while both life events and perceived strain were positively related to depressive symptomatology, the number of close relatives and friends as well as perceived social support were negatively related to these symptoms. Brownell (1982) also explored the relationship between social support, occupational stress, and health in a large community sample of 4034 adults. In this study, emotional and tangible support from family, friends, or coworkers buffered the association between occupational stress and psychological and physiological symptoms (Brownell, 1982).

Two large prospective studies highlight the role that work and non-work sources of support can play in reducing the negative effects of job stress. The Israel Ischemic Heart Disease Project followed 10,000 men aged 40 years and older for 5 years. Men who reported lack of appreciation and felt hurt by their superiors and coworkers had a higher incidence of angina pectoris than those who were well supported (Medalie et al., 1973). Also, even at high levels of anxiety, having a loving and supportive wife significantly reduced the risk of angina (Medalie and Goldbourt, 1976). Haynes and Feinleib (1980) report from the Framingham Heart Study that female clerical workers with a non-supportive boss have an elevated incidence of coronary heart disease when compared to other working women and housewives.

Job loss

Interest in the role that social relationships can play in helping people cope with the stress of unemployment dates back to the Great Depression (see

Liem and Liem, 1979, for a review). Much of our recent knowledge comes from a longitudinal study of a cohort of 100 married blue collar workers whose jobs were terminated by the permanent shut-down of the two plants where they worked (Cobb and Kasl, 1977; Gore, 1978; Kasl and Cobb, 1979). Public health nurses obtained measures on the men at five points in time: 6 weeks before the scheduled shut-down, within a month of termination, and at 6, 12, and 24 months after the plant closure. Seventy-four men who were stably employed at comparable jobs were used as a control group.

This study found that the longer one's period of unemployment, the higher his level of stress and ill health. However, high levels of support shielded the workers from the deleterious effects of unemployment. This protective effect of support was impressive since it was evident for several indicators of workrole deprivation, mental health, and physical health. The measure of social support was an index of 13 questions which most effectively tapped emotional support from wives.

Vinokur, Caplan, and Williams (1984) have recently reported similar findings from a one-year study of unemployed Vietnam veterans. This study utilized a control group of employed men and also obtained data from wives or other close friends. Unlike most studies of social support, this study measured both social support and social conflict. Social support and social conflict had independent effects. While support improved mental health, social conflict undermined it. An index of net social support was constructed in which conflict was subtracted from support. In addition to its positive effects on mental health, support also motivated the unemployed to participate in job search activities. Support further served as an 'emotional safety net' when frustration was encountered in the process of finding employment.

These two studies of social support and unemployment are particularly noteworthy in the social support literature, for, despite their limitations, they contain certain desirable features that are often lacking. They were both prospective, included controls, and focused on a well-defined occupational stressor.

Employee populations

There have been many reviews of the literature on the role of social support in the occupational environment (e.g. Payne, 1980; House, 1981; Kasl and Wells, 1985). Researchers are generally agreed that social support reduces at least some of the deleterious effects of job stress. At issue are the processes through which support operates.

The question of buffering has been hotly debated from the inception of the recent research interest in social support. In one of the earliest studies to investigate the effects of social support in the work environment, French (1973) presented evidence in support of buffering. In this study of 165 men at the Kennedy Space Center, good supportive relations with one's supervisor, peers, and subordinates conditioned the impact of a stressful workload on physiological but not psychological strain. In a similar vein, Cobb's influential 1976 paper cautioned against the expectation of dramatic main effects of support and offered buffering as the primary way in which support affects health. Since that time, the question of buffering has been central to the research and writing on support (House, 1981).

The study of over 2000 male workers in 23 white and blue collar occupations that culminated in the publication of *Job Demands and Worker Health* (Caplan *et al.*, 1975) has played a central role in the developing literature on social support and occupational stress. Firstly, it provided convincing evidence that in a large population representing diverse occupational categories, social support was consistently negatively related to stress and a variety of strains. Secondly, subsequent research has often utilized the same or similar items to measure work and non-work sources of support. Thirdly, it provided an adequate data set for the test of the buffering hypothesis.

Pinneau (1976) utilized a random subsample of about 28 workers from each of the 23 occupations to study the effects of support. While he found strong main effects for support on both stress and health, the number of buffering effects did not exceed what might be expected by chance. After criticial re-examination of earlier studies that had reported buffering effects, Pinneau concluded that these studies had serious defects and that there was little clear evidence in support of the buffering hypothesis.

LaRocco, House, and French (1980) reanalysed the Pinneau data. They noted that Pinneau had incorrectly assumed that a buffering effect could occur only if a main effect of stress on health was present. Thus, they tested for buffering effects on a wide range of stress–health relationships, regardless of the nature of the stress–health relationship that they obtained when support was not in the analysis. They found that while support did not buffer the effect of job stress on job strain (job dissatisfaction, boredom, dissatisfaction with workload), it did buffer the association between stress and mental and physical health outcomes (anxiety, irritation, initiation, somatic symptoms).

These findings were similar to those that had been earlier reported by House and Wells (1978) in a study of over 1800 white male blue collar workers in a large tire, rubber, chemicals, and plastic manufacturing plant. Using similar measures and the same analytic technique, House and Wells found that over half of the 35 stress–health relationships studied were buffered in the predicted way by at least one form of support. Social support conditioned the effects of job stress on ulcers and neurosis more than on other health problems (skin rash, cough, and phlegm). Utilizing this same data set, Wells (1982) investigated the potential for social support to mediate the relationship between objective job conditions and perceived occupational stress. For five of the nine indicators of perceived stress, Wells found a buffering effect for social support.

Several other reports have provided positive findings for the buffering model. In one of the more comprehensive studies, Winnubst, Marcilssen, and Kleber (1982) investigated the effects of coworker and supervisor support in a Dutch sample of 1246 employees from 13 industrial organizations. The measures included five indices of stress (role conflict, role ambiguity, overload, future uncertainty, and responsibility), four indices of psychological strain (irritation, depression, anxiety, and threat), five indices of health problems (heart complaints, general somatic complaints, systolic and diastolic blood pressure, and cholesterol), and two measures of behavioural strain (smoking and alochol use). They found important main effects. Social support was negatively correlated with job stressors, psychological strains, and heart and somatic complaints. In addition, although support did not buffer the impact of stress on most of the physiological strains, conditioning effects were found for psychological and behavioural strains and blood pressure. Support also buffered the relationship of psychological and behavioural strains to health strains.

Karasek, Triantis, and Chaudhry (1982) have also reported evidence that supports the buffering hypothesis. They studied 1016 male workers from a national sample of the US work force. Stress was measured as high job demands and low decision latitude. The psychological strains assessed included depressed mood, life satisfaction, job dissatisfaction, job-related depressed mood, and absenteeism. In 18 of 35 tests support was found for the buffering hypothesis. Seers et al (1983) have also found that interaction effects were as common as direct effects in a study of 104 predominantly female employees in a government agency. Similarly, in a study of 89 managerial personnel, Abdel-Halim (1982) reported that work group and supervisor support moderated job strains in the presence of role conflict and role ambiguity.

Evidence against buffering effects has also been noted in some studies. In a study of 3725 enlisted Navy men (LaRocco and Jones, 1978), stress was measured as a component score reflecting perceived conflict and ambiguity, and the measures of strain included job satisfaction, satisfaction with the Navy, intent to reenlist, and number of medical visits. The potential conditioning effects of supervisor and coworker support were measured by both moderated regression and subgrouping analysis. While main effects were evident for both sources of support, neither analytic technique yielded evidence for buffering effects. LaRocco, House and French (1980) suggested that this lack of buffering effects could have been due to the failure to measure general affective and physiological strains. This criticism would also apply to Blau's (1981) study of 166 bus operators that detected additive but not moderating effects for social support.

A recent study by Jayaratne and Chess (1984) addressed this criticism. In a national sample of 553 social workers, they used moderated regression to examine the relationship between work stress (role conflict and ambiguity), work-related strains (job satisfaction, emotional exhaustion, and depersonalization), health-related strains (anxiety, depression, irritability, and somatic complaints), and emotional support. While ample evidence was found for main effects of support, neither coworker nor supervisor support conditioned the effects of stress and strain.

Conclusions: past research and future prospects

There is not perfect consensus at this point regarding the nature and extent of the relationships of social support to occupation stress (or stress more generally) and health. Because the pattern of results, especially regarding buffering effects, is not uniformly consistent, some have argued that the overall evidence does not support the existence of such effects (Wallston *et al.*, 1983; Kasl and Wells, 1985). Because much of the data came from cross-sectional studies in which all variables are measured by self-report, others have questioned whether support really has a causal impact on stress or health, suggesting that the apparent main and buffering effects of support may actually reflect effects of stress and health on support or methodological problems confounding the measures of support and measures of stress or health (Gore, 1981; Thoits, 1982).

While we are concerned with the need for better research designs—especially more independent assessment of support, stress, and health and greater use of prospective, experimental, or quasi-experimental designs—we feel the overall body of evidence supports the existence of major and important main and buffering effects of support on occupational stress and health (LaRocco, House, and French, 1980; House, 1981; House *et al.*, 1984). Other careful reviews of the broader literature on social support (non-occupational) stress, and health reach similar conclusions (Cohen and Wills, 1985; Kessler and McLeod, 1985). The issue at this point is not whether or not social support has main or buffering effects, but rather *under what conditions* do we tend to observe main effects versus buffering effects versus combinations of main and buffering effects.

Kessler and McLeod (1985) have demonstrated the usefulnesss of such an approach in their recent review of the relationship between social support and mental health in community studies. They report that different aspects of support are consistently associated with mental health and that the nature of the relationship varies from one aspect to another. They discovered, for example, that while membership in affiliative networks does not buffer the impact of stressful life events on mental health, it has small main effects on mental health. In contrast, emotional support and perceived availability of support have pervasive buffer effects but tend not to have general effects on mental health when high stress is not present. Cohen and Wills (1985) reach similar conclusions in an even more thorough, review of studies of occupational as well as more general stress.

Buffering versus main effects

What conclusions can we draw about effects of social support on occupational stress and health? As noted earlier (House, 1981), social support tends to have main but not buffering effects on job-related strains such as job satisfaction. This pattern of results is clearly evident in the reasonably comparable LaRocco, House, and French (1980) and Winnubst, Marcelissen, and Kleber (1982) studies. This insight also indicates that some apparently negative findings for the buffer hypothesis can be viewed as confirmatory evidence for the specificity of buffering effects. For example, LaRocco and Jones (1978) and Blau (1981) failed to detect buffering effects in their studies. Since job-related strains were the primary outcome measures in both studies, conditioning effects should not have been expected.

Another clear trend in the literature is that buffering effects are more limited than main effects but they appear to be particularly evident for mental health symptoms such as depression, irritation, and anxiety (LaRocco, House, and French, 1980; Karasek, Triantis, and Chaudhry, 1982; Winnubst, Marcelissen, and Kleber, 1982). In terms of physiological symptoms, the pattern of findings is less clear, although buffering effects appear to be limited to those outcomes that are generally regarded as sensitive to interpersonal processes (cf. House, 1981). Thus House and Wells (1978) found a clear buffering effect for ulcers and Winnubst, Marcelissen, and Kleber (1982) reported buffering effects for blood pressure. Overall, the results suggest that buffering effects are likely to be found when support is measured in terms of the perceived willingness of others to be helpful and responsive in the face of stress and when the health outcome is one which suggests a manifest need for support (e.g. depression and anxiety versus physiological measures), elevations of which may not be evident to the person experiencing them and even less so to others (LaRocco, House, and French, 1980).

Sources of support

Several studies have noted that social support from different sources co-vary only slightly—suggesting that different effects might be expected (e.g. Karasek, Triantis, and Chaudhry, 1982; Wells, 1982). Not surprisingly, then, different sources have emerged as consequential in different studies, and on the surface the results appear to be bewildering. For example, House and Wells (1978) found strong effects for supervisor and wife support with coworker and friend support being relatively weak. LaRocco, House, and French (1980) found the strongest effects for coworker support while Wells (1982) found supervisor and friend/relative support to be most important. Karasek, Triantis, and Chaudhry (1982) found an equal number of buffering effects for supervisor as for coworker support.

On balance, both work and non-work sources appear important, with the effects varying depending on the stressor and strain under consideration. In general, support from work sources seems to be most relevant for work-associated strains, while support from non-work sources appears to be important for the more general strains (LaRocco, House, and French, 1980). This helps to explain otherwise puzzling findings. For example, Blau (1981) noted that, contrary to Caplan *et al.* (1975), he found significant main effects for coworker and supervisor but not for non-work sources of support. However, since Blau only measured work-related strains, it is consistent that only coworker and supervisory support was important. On the other hand, while Jayaratne and Chess (1984) measured general strains they failed to assess non-work sources of support—the relevant support for the more general indications of health. This omission may be partly responsible for their failure to detect buffering effects.

We do not have clear and consistent evidence for the determinants of the salience of coworker versus supervisor support. However, the work environment appears to be a critical determinant of the relative importance of coworker versus supervisory sources of support. In contrast to Winnubst, Marcelissen, and Kleber (1982) and LaRocco, House, and French (1980), House and Wells (1978) did not find coworker support important. They suggested that the organization of work in the factory setting (e.g. machine-bound jobs, high noise levels) discouraged communication among coworkers.

Further evidence for the part played by non-work sources of social support comes from a study of 769 married men in an unnamed occupational group (Clark, 1983). Participation in family activities (which presumably involved the giving and receiving of support) was significantly related to health problems. The higher the level of family participation, the lower the indicators of ill health. The indicators of ill health included mild aches and pains, feelings of exhaustion, mild headaches, irritability, sleeplessness, indigestion, heartburn, and sweating.

SOME NEGLECTED ISSUES

Negative social exchanges

Although the overwhelming majority of social support measures attempt to assess the positive contributions of social relationships, researchers are becoming increasingly aware that the impact of social relationships can also be negative. Available descriptive data indicate that interpersonal contact in the occupational setting does not always have positive results. Burke and Belcourt (1974), for example, studied the strategies used by 137 managers and managerial trainees to cope with stress. 'Talking to others' emerged as the most frequently mentioned effective technique for handling tensions on the job. At the same time, it was also the second most frequently mentioned ineffective coping strategy.

Kiev and Kohn (1979) reported similar findings from their study of 2685 managers. Over 70 per cent. of the managers talked with coworkers and/or relied on chats with a spouse or friend to relieve tension. While 20 per cent. claimed that they profited from spouse and friend support, only a meagre 13 per cent. found coworker support helpful. Burke and Belcourt (1974) suggest that the restraints placed on open communication by the competitive nature of the managerial setting may be responsible for this pattern of findings. While this may be partly responsible for the findings with respect to coworker support, we are not persuaded that this accounts for the low report of helpfulness for spouse and friend support. More generally, the actual supportive exchanges may appear less beneficial than the perceived availability of support because people only need to seek support explicitly in the face of their most severe problems.

A number of 'aggravation effects' (buffering effects in the reverse direction) were evident in some of the studies we reviewed earlier. In the face of role conflict, for example, high levels of support were positively associated with heightened anxiety, while the the reverse was true for persons with low levels of support (Abdel-Halim, 1982). Winnubst, Marcelissen, and Kleber (1982) also reported aggravation effects when responsibility was used as the stressor. Well-supported people with high responsibility had more depression and smoked more cigarettes than similarly stressed persons with less support. As was also true in the Abdel-Halim (1982) study, aggravation effects here were not uniform for a given stressor across different outcomes. For example, the high responsibility group showed positive buffering effects for threat and irritation.

The study by Karasek, Triantis, and Chaudhry (1982) raises more questions about negative social exchange than it answers. Firstly, instrumental support from coworkers increased depressed mood in the presence of task strain. Secondly, demanding authoritarian supervision failed to display clearly the expected aggravation effects. Surprisingly, a U-shaped pattern was found for four of the five dependent variables. Aggravation was evident when moving from medium to high levels on demanding authoritarian supervision, while buffering occurred when proceeding from low to medium levels. Thirdly, in 12 of 35 tests, the results supported a stress-transfer buffering model. This model predicts that at low levels of stress, people with high support would experience *more* strain than those with low support. This stress-transfer theory holds that social support assists group members in coping with stress by equalizing stress among group members. While adding stress to some persons, this process ensures that no individual would have to cope with excessively high levels of stress. In a multiple regression framework, this model is evaluated by testing for significant slope *and* intercept differences.

While it is difficult to make sense out of these results, it is clear that social interaction can and does have deleterious effects on health. Nonetheless, the conditions under which social support is ineffective and/or aggravation effects are most likely are yet to be clearly delineated. Achieving this specificity should be made a priority in future research on blue collar stress, since major potential sources of support (coworkers, supervisors) are also major potential sources of aggravation. Researchers should begin by adding measures of social conflict and unpleasant social interactions to social support scales. It is also evident that a better understanding of these processes can be gained by moving from more global measures of support to the assessment of specific support transactions in different environments (cf. Gottlieb, 1978). The importance of this issue may be strengthened by recent studies indicating that there is a stronger relationship between negative social exchanges and psychiatric morbidity than between social support and mental health (Fiore, Becker, and Coppel, 1983; Rook, 1984).

Sociocultural variations

Most major studies of stress at work have utilized samples of the white male labour force. We know little of how the effects of social support varies by sex or race. However, there are some preliminary indications of intriguing differences by gender and race.

Burke and Belcourt (1974) noted that female managers are more likely to use social support to deal with job-related problems than their male counterparts. Women are also more likely to be the providers of support (Belle, 1982) and to become more emotionally affected by the problems of others and thus incur higher psychological costs (Kessler, McLeod, and Wethington, 1985).

Orpen (1982) examined the relationship between occupational stress, health, and social support among 90 black and 93 white clerical employees in nine government agencies in South Africa. Building on earlier studies that had documented that blacks place greater value on the support available in the occupational context than their white counterparts, Orpen (1982) investigated racial differences in the moderating effects of support. The study found that social support reduces the negative effects of job stress among blacks but not among whites.

These findings hint at important sociocultural variations and suggest the possibility that social support processes may vary from one group to another. Since women and minorities may both experience unique and perhaps greater stress and also have greater needs for social support, future studies of occupational stress must adequately sample blacks and women so that these possibilities can be explored. Since women and minorities are also likely to be 'token' members of many work settings, means of enhancing support at work, to which we now turn, may be especially problematic for this group.

ENHANCING SOCIAL SUPPORT FOR BLUE COLLAR WORKERS

As one of us has argued elsewhere (House, 1981), although we do not know everything we would like to about the effects of support on occupational stress and health, we know enough to suggest that efforts to enhance levels of social support at work should be an important component of efforts to reduce work stress and its deleterious effects among blue collar workers, and workers more generally. Such efforts are likely to be cost-effective and not highly controversial, since enhancing support is consistent with other efforts to improve individual organizational functioning and not economically costly.

The literature on social support does not yet really address the issues of how and why support has the effects it does, or what conditions are likely to enhance the level of supportive behaviours or the perceived availability of support. One of us has discussed many of these issues at greater length elsewhere (House, 1981). Here we would like to address three issues which we feel are particularly important in efforts to enhance the perceived availability of support and the flow of supportive behaviour among blue collar workers: (1) creating structural arrangements that facilitate support among workers; (2) using other organizational change processes to enhance social support and in turn having support enhance the efficacy of these processes; and (3) facilitating supportive supervisory behaviour.

Structural factors

Matsumoto (1970) has proposed a theory of social stress to account, at least partially, for the lower incidence of coronary heart disease in Japan compared to the United States. He argues that a diet lower in fat and a less stressful life style are health-enhancing features of Japanese life. His theory of social stress contends that there are institutionalized mechanisms in Japanese society which operate to reduce stress. One of these primary mechanisms is the in-group work community.

Japanese companies usually hire workers once per year. Thus, each new worker joins the company with a large number of other men. Strong feelings of in-group solidarity develop within this 'entering cohort'. Individual interests tend to be merged into that of this larger group and this work group 'offers satisfying emotional support and social attachment in a group relation of human feelings and intimacy' (Matsumoto, 1970, p. 18). The high level of employment security in Japan results in the continuity of this group member-ship over one's entire career. Matsumoto (1970) provides detailed descriptions of several group-based, non-work social activities that serve as stress-reducing mechanisms for the Japanese worker.

This persuasive theory emphasizes the role that structural mechanisms can play in providing and enhancing social support. Alcalay and Pasick (1983) argue that these prevention strategies must be built into the overall structure of the work environment. They suggest, for example, that the organization of the work environment should facilitate stable interaction in the performance of job tasks and allow for the maintenance of social ties. Empirical evidence underscores the importance of taking these suggestions seriously. As we noted earlier, the expected positive effects of coworker support were absent in an industrial environment that discouraged social interactions (House and Wells, 1978). Similarly, Cassel (1963) reports that people who had a constant set of coworkers had lower cholesterol levels than those whose coworkers changed frequently. Thus, one critical component of a stress-reducing work environment is the provision of mechanisms that foster social interaction among workers.

Social support and other organizational changes

It is also possible to capitalize on existing developments in industry that offer the possibility of providing additional social support. Participative manage-ment schemes such as Quality Circles (QCs), for example, have potential not only to improve quality and increase production but also to increase support, reduce stress, and thus enhance health and well-being (cf. Cobb, 1976).

Amsden (1983) defines a QC as a problem-solving group of 8 to 10 people from the same work area who meet voluntarily on a regular basis (usually one hour each week). The groups usually meet on paid time and the regularity of meeting fosters the development of cohesiveness such that QC members begin to think and work as a team.

Quality Circles began in Japan in 1961 (Amsden and Amsden, 1983a) and have spread to several Western countries. Over 100 US companies are exper-imenting with QCs and American industry is 'on the verge of an explosion of interest' (Cole, 1983). The QC movement is also well established in Brazil and in several European firms, most notably Volvo of Sweden (Dewar, 1983).

The group process and the promotion of effective teamwork are central components of the QC and can readily include the provision of social support. Amsden and Amsden (1983a, 1983b) reveal that in QC meetings social needs are met, an outlet is provided for grievances and irritations, and immediate recognition is provided for members' abilities and achievements. Not surprisingly, then, QCs provide workers with a new sense of dignity

(Cole, 1983) and a higher level of employee morale (Dewar, 1983). Further, the cohesiveness developed on the job spreads to non-work activities as Circle members engage in social activities outside the workplace (Amsden and Amsden, 1983b).

Crouter's (1984) recent review of the emerging literature on the impact of participative work reinforces the view that QCs can increase the ability of workers to give support. The review indicated that participative work 'enhances employees' psychological and social functioning in ways that make them more effective as spouses, parents, and members of the community' (Crouter, 1984, p. 74). This is realized because participative work teaches employees new skills and attitudes—skills and attitudes that should enhance the giving and receiving of support. In an exploratory study at one factory, Crouter (1984) reveals that 36 per cent. of the sample reported learning new interpersonal skills, 27 per cent. communication skills, 27 per cent. listening skills, and 8 per cent. decision-making skills. Reported attitude change included new self-confidence (24 per cent.), learning the value of trust (16 per cent.), and responsibility (9 per cent.).

Crouter (1984) also cautions that participative work can have un-anticipated negative effects. Employees may feel more responsible for problems on the job, worry about these problems, and take this new stress into their non-work life. There is also some suggestive evidence that marriage relationships can be hurt when wives transfer the new independence and competence learned at work into their home life.

Workplace-based health promotion and employee assistance programmes are potential delivery systems for the provision of social support. Pelletier (1984) has documented the increasing visibility of these programmes in corporate America and he correctly argues that we must concentrate on developing ways to enhance social support within these programmes. Many of the health promotion programmes explicitly deal with the management of stress. However, to the extent that all health promotion programmes are group-based instead of being person-oriented, they can constitute social support interventions and thus serve as powerful stress-reducing strategies. Cooper (1981) also suggests ways in which employee assistance programmes can provide emotional social support. He described, for example, a chemical company in Britain that developed a stress counselling programme with a trained counsellor. Annually, almost 10 per cent. of the employees contacted the counsellor for advice or help for a wide range of personal and behavioural problems.

The importance of supervisory support

For several reasons, enhancing supportive behaviour by supervisors, and the perception of the availability of supervisory support among subordinates, is a particularly appealing mechanism for enhancing support in organizations, especially with regard to blue collar workers. Firstly, this is a means of ensuring that a large number of workers have at least one supportive relationship at work, when the absence of any supportive relationships has been shown to be especially damaging (House, 1981). As House (1981, p. 121) has argued:

> ... enhancing the ability of supervisors or managers to provide social support, especially toward subordinates but also toward colleagues and superiors, allows an organization to enhance the amount of support available to many workers by interventions involving a smaller number.

Secondly, 'because supervisors are involved in established channels of organizational communication and authority, they are accessible to influence through those channels' (House, 1981, p. 121). Thirdly, supportive supervisory behaviour is likely not only to reduce stress and improve health but is also likely to improve organizational effectiveness. Organizational theory and empirical evidence are consistent in showing that supportive supervision improves individual and organizational performance (Likert, 1961; Jablin, 1979; see House, 1981, pp. 94–98 and 126–127).

Support as a systemic issue

Supervisors and managers, however, are not just supporters of others, they must also be supported. Pelz (1951) showed that supportive supervisors were more effective if they themselves are supported by their superiors, and Seers *et al.* (1983) found that second-level supervisory support could buffer the impact of stress on lower level employees. Efforts at enhancing support must be systemic and natural, as we have argued elsewhere (House, 1981, p. 122):

> Although efforts to enhance social support can be targeted on certain types of organizational roles, these efforts must occur in the context of a broader organization-wide effort and commitment. Workers will not support each other to the extent they could if the power and reward structures of the organization do not encourage (much less discourage) such efforts. Management can ask first-line supervisors to provide support to their subordinates, and give them training in doing so, but if the first-line supervisors receive little or no support from their superiors, of if they are evaluated and rewarded solely on the basis of the instrumental activity or productivity of their subordinates (especially viewed in the short run), they will have little motivation to support their subordinates. Similarly, if workers are not supported by their first-line supervisors, are constantly placed in competition with their peers, and are rewarded only for productive activity for which they are clearly personally responsible, they will have little motivation to provide coworker support. Thus, higher levels of an organization should constitute models and positive sanctions for the efforts of lower levels to be more supportive.

REFERENCES

Abdel-Halim, A. A. (1982). Social support and managerial affective responses to job stress, *Journal of Occupational Behavior*, **3**, 281–295.

Alcalay, R., and Pasick, R. J. (1983). Psychosocial factors and the technologies of work, *Social Science and Medicine*, **17**, 1075–1084.

Amsden, D. M. (1983). Introduction to quality circles. In *Quality Circles Papers: A Compilation*, American Society for Quality Control, Milwaukee, Wis., pp. ix–xi.

Amsden, R. T., and Amsden, D. M. (1983a). Results of research on Q Circles. In *Quality Circles Papers: A Compilation*, American Society for Quality Control, Milwaukee, Wis., pp. 98–101.

Amsden, D. M., and Amsden, R. T. (1983b). Do Q Circles Capitalize on the Hawthorn effect. In *Quality Circles Papers: A Compilation*, American Society for Quality Control, Milwaukee, Wis., pp. 98–101.

Aneshensel, C. S., and Stone, J. D. (1982). Stress and depression, *Archives of General Psychiatry*, **39**, 1392–1396.

Belle, D. (1982). The stress of caring: women as providers of social support. In *Handbook of Stress* (Eds. L. Goldberger and S. Breznitz), Free Press, New York, pp. 496–505.

Blau, G. (1981). An empirical investigation of job stress, social support, service length, and job strain, *Organizational Behavior and Human Performance*, **27**, 279–302.

Brown, G. W., and Harris, T. (1978). *Social Origins of Depression: A Study of Psychiatric Disorder in Women*, Free Press, New York.

Brownell, A. (1982). Emotional and tangible social support as moderators of occupational stressors, Paper presented at the meeting of the American Psychological Association, Washington, D. C.

Burke, R. J., and Belcourt, M. L. (1974). Managerial role stress and coping responses, *Journal of Business Administration*, **5**, 55–68.

Caplan, R. D., Cobb, S., French, J. R. P., Harrison, R. V., and Pinneau, S. R. (1975). *Job Demands and Worker Health*, U.S. Department of Health, Education and Welfare, HEW Publication No. (NIOSH) 75-160.

Cassel, J. (1963). The use of medical records: opportunity for epidemiological studies, *Journal of Occupational Medicine*, **5**, 185–190.

Clark, A. W. (1983). The relationship between family participation and health, *Journal of Occupational Behavior*, **4**, 237–239.

Cobb, S. (1976). Social support as a moderator of life stress, *Psychosomatic Medicine*, **38**, 300–314.

Cobb, S., and Kasl, S. V. (1977). *Termination: The Consequences of Job Loss*, U.S. Department of Health, Education, and Welfare, Publication No. (NIOSH) 77-224.

Cohen, S., and Wills, T. A. (1985). Stress, social support, and the buffering hypothesis, *Psychological Bulletin*, 98.

Cole, R. E. (1983). Will QC Circles Work in the U.S.? In *Quality Circles Papers: A Compilation*, American Society for Quality Control, Milwaukee, Wis., pp. 53–56.

Cooper, C. (1981). Social support at work and stress management, *Small Group Behavior*, **12**, 285–297.

Crouter, A. C. (1984). Participative work as an influence on human development, *Journal of Applied Developmental Psychology*, **5**, 71–90.

Dewar, D. L. (1983). Can quality circles make it in the Western world? In *Quality Circles Papers: A Compilation*, American Society for Quality Control, Milwaukee, Wis., pp. 49–52.

Fiore, J., Becker, J., and Coppel, D. (1983). Social network interactions: a buffer or a stress?, *American Journal of Community Psychology*, **11**, 423–440.

French, J. R. P. (1973). Person role fit, *Occupational Mental Health*, **3**, 15–20.

Gore, S. (1978). The effect of social support in moderating the health consequences of unemployment, *Journal of Health and Social Behavior*, **19**, 157–165.

Gore, S. (1981). Stress-buffering functions of social supports: an appraisal and clarification of research models. In *Stressful Life Events and Their Contexts* (Eds. B. S. Dohrenwend and B. P. Dohrenwend), Prodist, New York, pp. 202–222.

Gottleib, B. H. (1978). The development and application of a classification scheme of informal helping behaviors, *Canadian Journal of Science/Rev. Canad. Sci. Comp.*, **10**, 105–115.

Haynes, S. G., and Feinleib, M. (1980). Women, work and coronary heart disease: prospective findings from the Farmington Heart Study, *American Journal of Public Health*, **70**, 133–141.

House, J. S. (1981). *Work, Stress, and Social Support*, Addison-Wesley, Reading, Mass.

House, J. S., and Kahn, R. L. (1985). Measures and concepts of social support. In *Social Support and Health* (Eds. S. Cohen and L. Syme), Academic Press, New York, pp. 83–108.

House, J. S., Strecher, V., Metzner, H. L., and Robbins, C. (1984). Occupational stress and health mong men and women in the Tecumseh community study, Unpublished paper, Survey Research Center, University of Michigan.

House, J. S., and Wells, J. A. (1978). Occupational stress, social support, and health. In *Reducing Occupational Stress: Proceedings of a Conference* (Eds. A. McLean, G. Black, and M. Colligan), U.S. Department of Health, Education and Welfare, HEW Publication No. (NIOSH) 78-140, pp. 8–29.

Jablin, F. M. (1979). Superior-subordinate communication: the state of the art, *Psychological Bulletin*, **86**, 1201–1222.

Jayaratne, S., and Chess, W. A. (1984). The effects of emotional support on perceived job stress and strain, *Journal of Applied Behavioral Science*, **20**, 141–153.

Karasek, R. A., Triantis, K. P., and Chaudhry, S. S. (1982). Coworker and supervisor support as moderators of associations between task characteristics and mental strain, *Journal of Occupational Behavior*, **3**, 181–200.

Kasl, S. V., and Cobb, S. (1979). Some mental health consequences of plant closing and job loss. In *Mental Health and the Economy* (Eds. L. A. Ferman and J. P. Gordus), W. E. Upjohn Institute, Kalamazoo, Mich., pp. 255–299.

Kasl, S. V., and Wells, J. A. (1985). Work and the family: social support and health in the middle years. In *Social Support and Health* (Eds. S. Cohen and L. Syme), Academic Press, New York, pp. 175–198

Kessler, R. C., and McLeod, J. D. (1985). Social support and psychological distress in community surveys. In *Social Support and Health* (Eds. S. Cohen and L. Syme), Academic Press, New York, pp. 219–240.

Kessler, R. C., McLeod, J. D., and Wethington, E. (1985). The cost of caring: a perspective on sex differences in psychological distress. In *Social Support: Theory, Research and Applications* (Eds. I. G. Sarason and B. R. Sarason), Mertin Nijhof, The Hague, pp. 491–506.

Kiev, A., and Kohn, V. (1979). *Executive Stress: An AMA Survey Report*, American Management Association, New York.

LaRocco, J. M., House, J. S., and French, J. R. P. (1980). Social support, occupational stress, and health, *Journal of Health and Social Behavior*, **21**, 202–218.

LaRocco, J. M., and Jones, A. P. (1978). Coworker and leader support as moderators of stress strain relationships in work situations, *Journal of Applied Psychology*, **63**, 629–634.

Liem, G. R., and Liem, J. H. (1979). Social support and stress: some general issues and their application to the problem of unemployment. In *Mental Health and the Economy* (Eds. L. A. Ferman and J. P. Gordus), W. E. Upjohn Institute, Kalamazoo, Mich., pp. 347–379.

Likert, R. (1961). *New Patterns of Management*, McGraw-Hill, New York.

Matsumoto, Y. S. (1970). Social stress and coronary heart disease in Japan: a hypothesis, *Milbank Memorial Fund Quarterly*, **48**, 9–36.

Medalie, J. H., and Goldbourt, U. (1976). Angina pectoris among 10,000 men, *American Journal of Medicine*, **60**, 910–921.

Medalie, J. H., Snyder, M., Groen, J. J., Neufeld, H. N., Goldbourt, U., and Riss, E. (1973). Angina pectoris among 10,000 men: 5 year incidence and univariate analysis, *American Journal of Medicine*, **55**, 583–594.

Orpen, C. (1982). The effect of social support on reactions to role ambiguity and conflict; a study of white and black clerks in South Africa, *Journal of Cross-Cultural Psychology*, **13**, 375–384.

Payne, R. (1980). Organizational stress and social support. In *Current Concerns in Occupational Stress* (Eds. C. L. Cooper and R. Payne), Wiley, London, pp. 269–298.

Pelletier, K.R. (1984). *Healthy People in Unhealthy Places: Stress and Fitness at Work*, Delacorte Press/Seymour Lawrence, New York.

Pelz, D. C. (1951). Leadership within a hierarchical organization, *Journal of Social Issues*, **7**, 49–55.

Pinneau, S. R. Jr. (1976). Effects of social support on occupational stresses and strains, Paper presented at the meeting of the American Psychological Association, Washington, D.C.

Rook, K. S. (1984). The negative side of social interaction: impact on psychological well-being, *Journal of Personality and Social Psychology*, **46**, 1097–1108.

Seers, A., McGee, G. W., Serey, T. T., and Graen, G. B. (1983). The interaction of job stress and social support: a strong inference investigation, *Academy of Management Journal*, **26**, 273–284.

Thoits, P. A. (1982). conceptual, methodological and theoretical problems in studying social support as a buffer against life stress, *Journal of Health and Social Behavior*, **23**, 145–159.

Vinokur, A., Caplan, R. D., and Williams, C. C. (1984). Coping with unemployment: a comparative longitudinal study of stress and coping among Vietnam veterans and nonveterans, Unpublished paper, Institute for Social Research, University of Michigan.

Wallston, B. S., Alagna, S. W., DeVellis, B. M., and DeVellis, R. F. (1983). Social support and physical health, *Health Psychology*, **2**, 367–391.

Wells,. J. A. (1982). Objective job conditions, social support and perceived stress among blue collar workers, *Journal of Occupational Behavior*, **3**, 79–94.

Winnubst, J. A. M., Marcelissen, F. H. G., and Kleber, R. J. (1982). Effects of social support in the stressor-strain relationship: a Dutch sample, *Social Science and Medicine*, **16**, 475–482.

Job Stress and Blue Collar Work
Edited by C. L. Cooper and M. J. Smith
© 1985 John Wiley & Sons Ltd

Chapter 14

Individual Coping Strategies

Lawrence R. Murphy

National Institute of Occupational Safety and Health,
US Department of Health and Human Services,
Cincinnati, Ohio, USA

In its broadest sense, coping refers to the things people do to avoid being harmed by stress (Pearlin and Schooler, 1978). These 'things' include cognitive, behavioural, and somatic responses which are aimed at (1) eliminating or reducing the source of discomfort, (2) altering one's appraisal of the stressor, or (3) managing or reducing the feelings of discomfort within the individual.

Coping research to be reviewed in this chapter focuses attention on psychosocial stressors; therefore self-protective behaviours directed towards physical or chemical agents (e.g. wearing safety apparel where indicated, adhering to established safe work practices, etc.), although clearly representing useful individual coping strategies, will not be detailed here. A rationale for individual coping strategies is presented first followed by a discussion of the coping process. Coping in work settings is reviewed next with special emphasis on stress management research. By and large, blue collar work groups have been underrepresented in coping research, particularly in the stress management area. Thus, while findings from community-based coping studies can be applied to blue collar workers, generalization of results of many studies which focus on white collar and 'carpeted floor' work groups cannot be made easily.

Coping implies the existence of stressors to be coped with and negative health consequences associated with failures to cope. The health consequences of stress have been described in a large and growing literature describing cardiovascular, mental, cerebrovascular, gastrointestinal, musculoskeletal, respiratory, and neoplastic disorders (Selye, 1976; Weiner, 1977; Kasl, 1984). The effects of stress reflected in psychosocial factors and adaptation requirements are evident in discussion of overall health (Dohrenwend and Dohrenwend, 1974) and general susceptibility to disease (Syme, 1974; Cassel, 1976), the latter being an explanation for the findings that a variety of diseases can be associated with stress, possibly acting via the immunologic system (Jemmott and Locke, 1984).

A rationale for the conceptual viability of individual coping strategies emerges from the pioneering work of Lazarus (1966), who suggested that one's appraisal of an event or situation determines the response. In this way, an objective event can be perceived as stressful and threatening by one individual, yet neutral or positive by another (one man's meat is another man's poison). Individual differences are also evident regarding the psychological, behavioural, and somatic reactions (strains) to perceived stressors. The importance of individual differences in both the perception of, and reactions to, stress suggests the potential efficacy of individual coping strategies.

THE COPING PROCESS

It has become apparent that coping is not an individual trait or a disposition which is stable over time and across types of stressful situations. Rather, coping is a continuous, transactional *process* which is modified by experience within and between stressful episodes (Cohen and Lazarus, 1979; Folkman and Lazarus, 1980). Moreover, any particular coping strategy (e.g. information-seeking) can alleviate stress in one situation yet be remarkably maladaptive in another (Cohen and Lazarus, 1973).

This view implies a leading role for individual differences in coping strategies, discrete elements of which a researcher may tap with any specific study. Indeed, this opens up a knowledge gap in terms of the things people *actually* do on a day-to-day basis to cope with stress. Much as the term stress connotes negative images, coping is commonly associated with positive, health-enhancing activities. Yet it is evident that the coping behaviours which people actually use (whether they call them coping or not) do include patently maladaptive behaviours such as smoking cigarettes, drinking alcohol to excess, or becoming ill (whether done consciously or, at some point in development, habitually).

A few attempts to develop a taxonomy or inventory of coping behaviours have been made (e.g. Dewe, Guest, and Williams, 1979; Folkman and Lazarus, 1980; Billings and Moos, 1981) and should provide necessary and instructive data on the range of coping activities (at and between the adaptive extremes). To be sure, some methodological problems associated with the study of coping as a process and with work on a coping inventory will need to be considered. Examples here included (1) the degree to which people recognize an activity as coping so as to report it as such when questioned and (2) the relative salience of effective and ineffective strategies used in past experiences (Cohen *et al.*, 1982). Regarding the latter, it has been suggested that people recall ineffective strategies more accurately than effective ones (Horowitz and Wilver, 1980).

Pearlin and Schooler (1978) make a useful distinction between the social and psychological *resources* at one's disposal and the coping *responses* people use in stressful encounters. Social (supports) and psychological (mastery, self-esteem) resources are what people draw upon in developing coping responses and they vary by sex, educational level, and income. For example, men appear to have more psychological resources than women and use them to develop and use more effective coping responses. Likewise, the better educated and more affluent appear to possess more resources and a wider range of coping alternatives (Pearlin and Schooler, 1978)

What is more important, aside from what people actually do to cope with stress, is the relative effectiveness of coping responses. Pearlin and Schooler (1978) considered a coping response effective if it reduced (buffered) the relationship between stressors and strains. The authors concluded that no single coping response was strikingly protective across life and work areas but that having a larger and more varied coping repertoire was effective in reducing stressor/strain relationships. In this regard, the effectiveness of problem-focused versus emotion-focused coping for buffering ill health seems to be a function of the controllability of the stressor, coping of any type being relatively ineffective in situations beyond the individual's control (Caplan, Naidu, and Tripathi, 1984; Felton, Revenson, and Hinrichsen, 1984; Fleishman, 1984; Krause and Stryker, 1984).

COPING WITH WORK STRESS

Turning attention to work settings, three types of studies are encountered: (1) those attempting to identify and categorize the coping activities people actually used in work settings, (2) those which additionally evaluate the degree to which coping reduces the association between stressors and strains or distress, and (3) studies of prescriptive strategies focused on helping workers manage or control the experience of stress and maintain good health (i.e. stress management).

The first two categories of study will be reviewed together, given their sparseness and homogeneity of results. Stress management studies will be covered in a larger section because of the popularity of such approaches in work settings and the significant number of evaluative studies which have recently appeared in the published literature. Furthermore, there is a need to catalogue what is known, future research needs, and what place such approaches should occupy in occupational stress-reduction efforts.

Pearlin and Schooler (1978) identified 17 coping responses through scheduled interviews with 2300 households representative of urban Chicago, Illinois. Coping responses reported to be used were grouped into three categories: (1) responses that changed the source of stress, (2) responses that changed the meaning or perception of the stressor, or (3) responses that controlled or managed the feelings of discomfort produced by the stressor.

Various coping behaviours were effective in minimizing the effects of stressors on strains or distress in the areas of marriage, child-rearing, and household finances. In the occupational sphere, coping was singularly ineffective as assessed by its ability to reduce stressor/strain relationships. For comparison purposes, in the area of marriage, the stepwise addition of specific coping behaviours to the regression of stressors on strains resulted in a progressive lowering of the regression coefficient (i.e. the impact of stressors on reported distress) by about 50 per cent. In the occupational area, the comparable reduction was 0 per cent. The authors suggested that the resistance of occupation to coping efforts may be due to the impersonal organization of work and the operation of forces beyond the worker's control. Pearlin and Schooler (1978) further suggest that coping in occupational settings '...may be best accomplished through worker collectivities' because individual workers alone cannot alter the social structure of work.

Another study examined the effects of adaptive and maladaptive coping responses on felt distress and job satisfaction among managers (Parasuraman and Cleek, 1984). Adaptive response included planning, organizing, prioritizing assignments, and enlisting the support of others. Maladaptive responses included working harder but making more mistakes, making unrealistic promises, and avoiding supervision. The authors found that adaptive coping had no effects on felt stress or job satisfaction but was associated with increased trait anxiety. Maladaptive coping, on the other hand, contributed independently to felt stress and job stressors. Both adaptive and maladaptive coping were inversely associated with organizational tenure. The authors conclude that a more significant reduction in felt stress and job dissatisfaction would result if workers learned to avoid maladaptive behaviours in coping with work stressors.

Using open-ended interviews, Burke (1971) and Burke and Belcourt (1974) identified and categorized behaviours used by managerial workers to cope with work tensions and anxiety. The latter study found that 65 per cent. of all reported coping behaviours could be grouped into five categories: talking to others, working harder and longer, changing to a non-work or leisure activity, adopting a problem-solving approach, and physically withdrawing from the stressful situation. Regarding the effectiveness of these types of coping behaviours, the authors noted that the same coping strategy was often reported to be effective in one situation yet ineffective in another. Which properties of the stressful situation(s) were related to the effectiveness of the coping behaviour(s) used could not be isolated in this study (Burke and Belcourt, 1974).

Howard, Rechnitzer, and Cunningham (1975) used the 10 coping categories developed in Burke's studies along with selected health indices to examine the frequency and relative effectiveness of coping in 300 managerial workers from 12 Canadian companies. Health indicators included blood pressure, blood levels of cholesterol, triglycerides and uric acid (after a 12-hour fast), and a stress symptom checklist. No relationships were found among reported coping behaviours and any of the physiological indicators. Also, the coping behaviours used more frequently by workers were not the ones associated with a reduction in stress symptoms. Indeed, coping behaviours which were directed towards the source of stress (e.g. changing one's strategy of attack towards the problem, working harder) were associated with *higher* levels of reported stress symptoms. Coping behaviours associated with *lower* levels of stress symptoms were those focused on detachment from work and maintaining good health habits to increase resistance to stress.

Multiplying the ranks of frequency of use of coping behaviours and number of stress symptoms reported, Howard, Rechnitzer, and Cunningham (1975) created the following rank-ordered list of the most effective coping behaviours: (1) change to an engrossing, non-work activity, (2) build better resistance through regular sleep and good health habits, (3) compartmentalize work and non-work life, (4) talk with coworkers, and (5) engage in physical exercise. The authors additionally noted that workers classified as type A (i.e. being hard-driving, competitive, hurried, and impatient) tended to use coping behaviours which were the *least* effective strategies for reducing stress symptoms (e.g. changing to a different work activity). In agreement with other studies reviewed here, there was no association of age with particular coping behaviours or relative frequency of use.

Also building upon Burke's categories of coping, Dewe, Guest, and Williams (1979) used factor analysis to group the coping behaviours reported to be used by administrative and clerical workers in three different studies. Four basic modes (factors) of coping were identified, only one of which involved actions to deal with the source of stress (i.e. sensible task-oriented behaviours).

The remaining three identified factors were: (1) expressions of feelings and search for support at work, (2) use of non-work activities, and (3) passive attempts to 'ride-out' the situation, all described as 'palliative' coping behaviours. Interestingly, when asked about specific work stressors via concrete examples, workers reported using task-oriented coping strategies, but when asked about what they did when they *felt* anxious or tense at work, they reported using 'palliative' strategies more frequently. Dewe, Guest, and Williams (1979) concluded that if workers do not (or cannot) attribute feelings of distress to specific stressors, they will employ emotion-focused coping strategies. However, the question posed to workers about what they did when feeling tense was, 'If, like most people, you occasionally get particularly fed up with your job and feel tense and frustrated, how do you cope?' As stated, this question seems to be tapping a more general attitude about overall satisfaction with work rather than eliciting responses to focal instances of distress. The reported use of palliative strategies, therefore, may reflect a failure on the part of workers to alter the way work is organized and structured and, thus, individual efforts to improve satisfaction and the quality of work life. In this sense, the results align well with those of Pearlin and Schooler (1978), Parasuraman and Cleek (1984), and Howard, Rechnitzer, and Cunningham (1975).

The following conclusions are supported by the above evidence: (1) occupational stressors are impervious to individual coping behaviours, (2) coping behaviours directed towards the source of stress at work may actually *increase* symptoms of stress, (3) length of time in an organization (or experience with stressors assessed crudely by age) is not associated with the use of more (or less) efficient coping behaviours, (4) personality traits (like type A behaviour and mastery) may influence type of coping strategy used, (5) the resistance of occupation to individual coping may result from the impersonal nature of work stress and lack of individual control over the way work is organized, and (6) the most efficient strategies for reducing the experience of work stress are preventive, health promotion type activities and those which increase the distance between the worker and the problem.

STRESS MANAGEMENT STRATEGIES

Distinct from the types of coping studies reviewed up to this point are those evaluating a set of prescriptive, relaxation-based techniques collectively labelled *stress management*. These include biofeedback, muscle relaxation, meditation, and cognition-focused methods, many of which were borrowed from traditional clinical practice where they have documented success in treating stress-related mental and physical complaints (e.g. Pomerleau and Brady, 1979).

As applied in work settings, stress management strategies generally have a distinctive, preventive flavour with an emphasis on imparting training skills to 'normal', healthy workers as opposed to treatment of evident stress-related problems. As such, these approaches are more properly viewed as health promotion/disease prevention efforts rather than as strategies to assist workers to cope with stressors on the job. Stress management strategies focus on reducing experience of stress and its attendant psychological, physiological, and behavioural symptoms and seek to short-circuit cumulative effects of unresolved stress on health and well-being (Cooper and Crump, 1978).

Stress management training, offered alone or within more general health promotion programmes, has become popular in occupational settings. In a survey of company health promotion programmes in California, 13 per cent. reported offering stress management training compared to 12 per cent. physical fitness, 10 per cent. hypertension screening, and 8 per cent. smoking cessation programmes. The most common programmes reported in the survey were accident prevention (65 per cent.), cardiopulmonary resuscitation (53 per cent.), and substance abuse/mental health counselling (18 per cent.). More companies reported plans to estabish stress management programmes in the near future than any other health promotion activity (Fielding and Breslow, 1983).

Evaluation of stress management studies

Studies evaluating the merits of worksite stress management training (SMT) have been reviewed elsewhere (Murphy, 1984b), so a restatement here is unnecessary. Rather, the salient points from the previous review (with a few recent studies added) shall be presented as a context for discussing research needs and some larger issues surrounding the use of SMT in blue collar work settings.

The difficulty in summarizing worksite SMT studies is the diversity in terms of design, techniques, work groups, length of training period, outcome measures, and duration of follow-up period. Thirteen studies, many of which were unpublished accounts, were reviewed previously (Murphy, 1984b) and an additional eight studies can be included here for review. Of these 21 studies, 11 used an experimental-level design involving a trained group(s) and a comparison or control group of some type (e.g. wait-list, self-relaxation). Given the findings in many studies of significant effects in comparison groups, as well as in trained groups, on both physiological and self-report measures, interpretation of studies employing pre- and quasi-experimental designs is made difficult.

The approach in this section will be to select those experimental-level studies and compare results immediately post-training and after a follow-up period on (1) individual-centred measures and (2) organization-centred measures. While the SMT techniques used in these studies differ in important characteristics, especially the cognitive strategies relative to the relaxation ones, they are considered as a single entity (SMT) in this review because: (1) too few studies have assessed the relative efficacy of different techniques, (2) relaxation has been used in *all* studies either as a major technique or as a component of cognitive and meditation techniques, and (3) most SMT programmes provided participants with educational information about stress, emphasizing the importance of cognitive mechanisms in the experience of stress. Each of these mitigates against summary-type statements of technique-specific effects.

Individual-centred effects

All worksite SMT studies evaluated the effects of training on individual-oriented variables via self-report and/or psychophysiological measures.

Among self-report indicators, prevalent indicators used (with the number of experimental studies in parentheses) were anxiety, usually trait anxiety (9), depression (5), and somatic symptoms of stress (5). Psychophysiological indicators used included blood pressure (5) and muscle tension (EMG) levels (4).

Anxiety reductions represent the most consistent outcome in SMT studies. Two-thirds of the studies found larger post-training decreases in anxiety among trained versus control groups, and some durability of anxiety reductions appear in follow-up evaluations. While post-training reduction in depression have been reported, follow-up assessments more often than not show no long-term reductions. Similarly, somatic stress symptoms may be reduced immediately after SMT training, but long-term gains specific to trained groups are the exception, not the rule.

Regarding psychophysiological indicators, three of the four studies which measured forehead EMG reported larger reductions in trained versus control groups, the remaining study finding within-session, but not between-session, EMG decreases. Blood pressure reductions after SMT have been reported in all five studies, although in two studies similar decreases were also observed in control groups and in one study the trained groups showed reductions on diastolic blood pressure while both trained and comparison groups showed decreases in systolic blood pressure. For both EMG and blood pressure, the reductions observed immediately after training were not completely maintained in follow-up evaluations. Although savings in post-training reductions were not optimal, relative to original baseline levels, long-term reductions on these measures were evident.

Organization-centred effects

Few SMT studies have focused on organization-relevant outcome variables such as job satisfaction, absenteeism, productivity, performance ratings, accidents, or injuries. SMT appears to have inconsistent effects on job satisfaction, most studies (3) reporting no change due to training, and one study each reporting an increase or decrease in satisfaction.

Two recent (and as yet unpublished) studies have examined the variables noted above before and after SMT. Riley, Friedman, and Winnett (1984) used multimodal SMT with hourly employees of a health insurance company and found a significant *decrease* in job satisfaction in trained, but not control, groups. Both trained and control groups evidenced lower absenteeism rates and improved productivity after SMT training, but these effects probably reflected known organizational events (e.g. moving to a new location, loss of a major contract, and consequent transfer and termination of some employees) which occurred during the course of the SMT study.

A second study examined organization records for absenteeism, work performance ratings, equipment accidents, and work injuries among highway maintenance employees who participated in a stress management programme previously (Murphy, 1984a). Data on these variables was collected for $2\frac{1}{4}$ years before the training programme and $1\frac{1}{2}$ years post-programme for (1) the 37 trained workers, (2) a group who volunteered for the original study but did not complete 50 per cent. of the sessions or did not pass the physical exam ($n = 22$), and (3) 80 employees drawn randomly from personnel rosters who could have volunteered for the programme.

Preliminary analyses of covariance revealed significant group time interactions for hours absent, Monday or Friday absence frequency, attendance ratings, and work injuries ($p \leq 0.05$). These interactions generally reflected significant changes for the muscle relaxation group relative to controls with biofeedback-trained workers evidencing intermediate changes. A multiple regression analysis revealed that the best predictor of post-training absence frequency was pre-programme absence frequency, which accounted for 24 per cent. of the variance. For worker performance ratings (by supervisors), pre-programme ratings accounted for 43 per cent. of the variance in post-programme ratings.

The group factor (trained versus control) did account for a unique 2 per cent. of the variance ($p \leq 0.03$) in instances absent on Monday or Friday and 4 per cent. of the variance ($p \leq 0.01$) in supervisory attendance ratings post-programme. Group did not account for significant variance among measures of absence frequency, hours absent, performance ratings, accidents, or injuries on the job ($p > 0.10$).

SMT in blue collar settings

Of the 21 SMT studies available to this author, only one involved a blue collar work group (Murphy, 1984a). SMT is more commonly offered to managers and, to a lesser extent, service and clerical workers. This bias may reflect obvious differences in aspects of the work environment and physical demands of jobs or it might be a function of some sociopolitical factors evident to a greater degree in blue collar environments.

Regarding the former, relative to 'carpeted floor' settings, blue collar work environments contain potential hazards from chemical and physical agents, involve more physically demanding jobs, and present more safety hazards to workers. Given the salience of these exposures, job stress concerns may not be considered a high priority area. Accordingly, accident prevention and hazard communication programmes, relative to SMT, would be preferred programme offerings. The repetitive and boring nature of many blue collar jobs, coupled with an emphasis on physical rather than mental demands of work, may explain the use of job enrichment programmes for these workers and SMT in work situations requiring more mentally demanding tasks.

A second explanation centres around the fact that many blue collar work groups are unionized, and union groups have argued forcefully against SMT programmes on the grounds that SMT inappropriately focuses on changing the worker rather than the work environment. This was suggested in a NIOSH-sponsored survey of SMT in blue collar settings (Neale *et al.*, 1982) which revealed distinct, conflicting perspectives of union and management groups on the nature and sources of stress and, accordingly, how best to reduce stress. From a management perspective, stress was defined in personal, biological, and physical terms with few, if any, acknowledgements that the work experience contributed to total stress levels. The emphasis was placed on individual responsibility and coping via lifestyle change. Accordingly, SMT, geared towards reducing the experience of stress by modifying the host, was the preferred approach to stress reduction.

In contrast, Neale *et al.*, (1982) found that labour groups viewed stress as arising from the work experience and mentioned physical conditions of work, lack of individual control over work content and processes, unrealistic task demands, and lack of understanding by management as prevalent stress factors affecting worker health. Unions viewed SMT as a convenient mechanism for organizations to side-step responsibilities for stressor-reduction efforts. From this perspective, the preferred strategy to reduce worker stress was to alter working conditions and processes to create a less stressful environment. To accomplish this, labour groups advocated strong contractual control and legislative restraints on management.

Regarding non-physical work stressors, the preferred union strategy included contractually empowered health and safety committees, which would increase the participation of workers in decisions affecting their work.

The Neale *et al.*, (1982) report highlighted the mutual selective ignoring by both management and union groups of aspects of stress and health relationships enumerated in the scientific literature. In reality, the experience of stress appears to be a function of (1) characteristics of the individual, (2) non-work stressors, *and* (3) aspects of the work experience. The relationship of stressors to health outcomes is equally complex and reflects a synergism of stressors from all life areas. To selectively attend to some stressors and deny the importance (impact) of others is not a constructive strategy for improving worker health and well-being.

Without straying too far afield, some work is underway at NIOSH to merge health promotion and health protection efforts in occupational settings. A plan has been developed to acknowledge the contributions of, and need for, each type of programme and to relate current and future project work to a set of joint goals (Cohen, 1984). The example of the underground coal miner who smokes cigarettes is a case in point, arguing for considering a collaboration of viewpoints.

Research needs

SMT in work settings has been associated with reductions in anxiety, depression, muscle tension levels, and perhaps blood pressure and somatic complaints. While some evidence suggests that the effects erode somewhat over time, long-term reductions have been reported in several studies. On the other hand, SMT appears to have negligible effects on worker perceptions of the work environment and productivity, and small or no effects on absenteeism, worker performance ratings, accidents, or injuries, given the two studies which examined such outcomes.

With the current popularity of worksite SMT, and the likelihood that more studies will be done to evaluate benefits to workers, it is appropriate here to elaborate some specific evaluation needs and knowledge gaps in this young research area.

We need to know a great deal more about the characteristics of non-volunteers for SMT relative to those who self-select into studies and how they might differ on socioeconomic, personality, and work stress measures. Among participants, it would be equally instructive to examine characteristics of workers who (1) do not acquire the training skills, (2) do not show expected changes on self-report and psychophysiological outcome measures, or (3) drop out of programmes. Since all of the SMT studies have employed some type of muscle relaxation exercise, and relaxation-induced anxiety (RIA) has been described for some individuals (Heide and Borkovec, 1984), we also need to be attentive to potential counterproductive effects of SMT, some of which are suggested later.

Too few studies have used more than one SMT technique and assessed their relative merits against a comparison group(s). It would be useful to know if someone who does not do well at biofeedback would benefit from a meditative or cognitive training strategy. The use of more than one training group, or a component analysis of a single technique (e.g. West, Horan, and Ganes, 1984), would permit the isolation of critical elements contributing to observed outcomes. The additional use of a non-volunteer control group would also be useful in identifying effects of self-selection into SMT programmes.

Compliance on the part of workers regarding practice of training skills has been assessed as poor in some studies, while many others did not report measurement of such rates. Factors associated with compliance and determination of the relationship between practice rate and health benefits need to be assessed in all studies. Finding a strong correlation of practice rate with outcome would strengthen the attribution of effects to the training programme relative to other unmeasured factors which undoubtedly change in participants' work, home, and social life.

Over half of the 11 experimental SMT studies reported significant change over time in both trained and comparison groups, although in some cases the magnitude of change was greater in the former. Such results have been obtained on both self-report and psychophysiological measures and for several types of comparison/control groups (e.g. wait-list, stress education, self-relaxation). The operation of non-specific factors hinders the attribution of benefits to the training regime and parallels the situation in many clinical outcome studies (Kazdin and Wilcoxin, 1976). Non-specific factors inherent in SMT programmes include: (1) credibility of training and expectancy for improvement, (2) instructions to participants, (3) participant-trainer relationship, (4) sitting in a comfortable position for 20 to 60 minutes, (5) the intention to relax, (6) use of paid work time to undergo training, (7) motivation due to self-selection into the programme, (8) attitude among employees towards the training programme, and (9) effect of providing educational information on stress and health relationships.

Although only one SMT study was conducted with blue collar workers, health promotion programmes like SMT may be particularly beneficial, given the suggested interactive effects of stress (and lifestyle factors) and exposure to physical and chemical agents (House *et al.*, 1979). Studies in blue collar settings should carefully examine performance effects of SMT in addition to health benefits, as the former may affect safe work behaviour. For example, since all SMT involves a relaxation exercise, does a relaxation break taken at work result in restored vigour and lowered fatigue such that worker performance increases, *or* does such a break create feelings of drowsiness and inattention which could reduce performance, or worse, predispose the worker towards unsafe behaviours? Does relaxation increase or decrease worker vigilance? We might suspect the former in each case, but there is a need to consider competing (though unappealing) hypotheses and determine relative merit.

Other research needs briefly noted here include the generality of SMT effects in settings other than the training environment, potential effects on psychological resources of mastery, self-esteem, and self-denigration, effects on development and selection of coping responses across stressful encounters, and effects on actual worker performance.

CONCLUSIONS

This chapter attempted to review the efficacy of individual-oriented strategies for coping with stress and reducing its health consequences. Coping was defined as anything people do to prevent being harmed by stress (after Pearlin and Scholer, 1978). Two sets of research studies were examined: (1) those attempting to identify coping behaviours and determine the degree to which the use of those behaviours reduce the effects of work stressors on health and (2) those evaluating prescriptive strategies for helping workers manage or control responses to stress. Socially censored coping behaviours (e.g. physical violence, industrial sabotage) and maladaptive coping behaviours (e.g. increased alcohol use), while creating some attendant health problems, have not been examined in the research literature.

Coping behaviours that are problem-focused seem to be valued more highly by researchers than those that are emotion-focused, although the latter appear to be used more frequently in everyday life situations (Dewe, Guest, and Williams, 1979; Folkman and Lazarus, 1980; Fleishman, 1984). The stress management strategies could be classified as emotion-focused coping, but the available literature suggests a more compelling association of SMT with health promotion/disease prevention orientations. This emphasis, however, creates an even greater distance between the sources of stress at work and SMT methods, although such distance may be appropriate.

What can be said of the utility of individual strategies for coping with work stress? Firstly, attempts by individuals to cope with work stressors involve both problem-focused and emotion-focused strategies, each of which seem to be at best ineffective and may generate stress symptoms in themselves. The lack of worker control over organizational attributes and the way work is designed may explain the ineffectiveness of individual coping strategies in this domain relative to other life areas (Pearlin and Schooler, 1978). Secondly, attempts by workers to learn skills aimed at managing the experience of distress via SMT as a health promotion/disease prevention strategy are associated with reductions in felt anxiety, depression, muscle tension levels, and perhaps blood pressure, but these benefits deteriorate somewhat over time. SMT does not seem to produce *impressive* changes in productivity or absenteesim (though studies are sparse) and certainly does not remove or reduce the sources of work stress. SMT seems to have more validity as a health promotion offering and represents, at best, a 'band-aid' approach if employed as a primary stress-reduction strategy when organizational change approaches should be attempted. These findings suggest again that individual change has minimal effects on social structures and that attempts to effect organizational change through individual methods (be it stress management, problem-focused coping, or supervisory training) necessarily invokes the psychological fallacy of assuming that '... since the organization is made up of individuals, we can change the organization by changing its members' (Katz and Kahn, 1978).

Determination of training effects on organizational-focused measures need to acknowledge that SMT programmes are not established in a sociopolitical vacuum nor against a backdrop of stable work and life stress. For example, the reductions in absenteeism and increases in worker productivity observed for *both* trained and control groups by Riley, Friedman, and Winnett (1984) can be explained wholly by the significant organizational changes which occurred concurrently with the training programme. This study signposts the need to overlay upon SMT studies a chronological template of (significant) organizational and individual (where possible) changes (i.e. history) which threaten internal validity (Cook and Campbell, 1976).

REFERENCES

Billings, A. C., and Moos, R. H. (1981). The role of coping responses with social resources in attenuating the stress of life events, *Journal of Behavioral Medicine*, **4**, 139–157.

Burke, R. J. (1971). Are you fed up with work?, *Personal Administration*, **34**, 27–31.

Burke, R. J., and Belcourt, M. L. (1974). Managerial role stress and coping responses, *Journal of Business Administration*, **5**, 55–68.

Burke, R. J., and Weis, T. (1980). Coping with the stress of managerial occupations. In *Current Concerns in Occupational Stress* (Eds. C. L. Cooper and R. Payne), John Wiley and Sons, Chichester, Sussex, pp. 299–335.

Cassel, J. (1976). The contribution of the social environment to host resistance, *American Journal of Epidemiology*, **104**, 107–123.

Caplan, R. D., Naidu, L. K., and Tripathi, R. C. (1984). Coping and defense: constellations and components, *Journal of Health and Social Behavior*, **25**, 303–320.

Cohen, A. (1984). Health promotion/hazard protection at the workplace: a position and planning guide, *Proceedings of Society of Prospective Medicine*, Atlanta, Georgia.

Cohen, F., and Lazarus, R. S. (1973). Active coping processes, coping dispositions, and recovery from surgery, *Psychosomatic Medicine*, **35**, 375–389.

Cohen, F., and Lazarus, R. S. (1979). Coping with the stresses of illness. In *Health Psychology—A Handbook* (Eds. G. C. Stone, F. Cohen, and N. E. Adler), Jossey-Bass, San Francisco, Calif., pp. 217–254.

Cohen, F., (1982).

Cook, T. D., and Campbell, D. T. (1976). The design and conduct of quasi-experiments and true experiments in field settings. In *Handbook of Industrial and Organizational Psychology* (Ed. M. D. Dunnette), Rand McNally College Publishing Company, Chicago, Ill., pp. 223–326.

Cooper, C. L., and Crump, J. (1978). Prevention and coping with occupational stress, *Journal of Occupational Medicine*, **20**, 420–426.

Dewe, P., Guest, D., and Williams, R. (1979). Methods of coping with work-related stress. In *Respnses to Stress: Occupational Aspects* (Eds. C. MacKay and T. Cox), IPC Science and Technology Press, Guildford, Surrey, pp. 69–84.

Dohrenwend, B. S., and Dohrenwend, B. P. (Eds.) (1974). *Stressful Life Events*, John Wiley, New York.

Felton, B. J., Revenson, T. A., and Hinrichsen, G. A. (1984). Stress and coping in the explanation of psychological adjustment among chronically ill adults, *Social Science and Medicine*, **18**, 889–898.

Fielding, J. E., and Breslow, L. (1983). Health promotion programs sponsored by California employees, *American Journal of Public Health*, **73**, 538–542.

Fleishman, J. A. (1984). Personality characteristics and coping patterns, *Journal of Health and Social Behavior*, **25**, 229–244.

Folkman, S., and Lazarus, R. S. (1980). An analysis of coping in a middle-aged community sample, *Journal of Health and Social Behavior*, **21**, 219–239.

Heide, F. J., and Borkovec, T. D. (1984). Relaxation-induced anxiety: mechanisms and theoretical implications, *Behavior Research and Therapy*, **22**, 1–12.

Horowitz, M. J., and Wilver, N. (1980). Life events, stress and coping. In *Aging in the 1980s: Selected Contemporary Issues* (Ed. L. Poom), American Psychological Association, Washington, D.C.

House, J. S., Wells, J. A., Landerman, L. R., McMichael, A. J., and Kaplan, B. H. (1979). Occupational stress and health among factory workers, *Journal of Health and Social Behavior*, **20**, 139–160.

Howard, J. H., Rechnitzer, R. A., and Cunningham, D. A. (1975). Coping with job tension—effective and ineffective methods, *Public Personnel Management*, **4**, 317–326.

Jemmott, J. B., and Locke, S. E. (1984). Psychosocial factors, immunologic mediation, and human susceptibility to infectious diseases: how much do we know?, *Physiological Bulletin*, **95**, 78–108.

Kasl, S. V. (1984). Stress and health, *Annual Review of Public Health*, **5**, 319–341.

Katz, D., and Kahn, R. L. (1978). *The Social Psychology of Organizations*, John Wiley, New York.

Kazdin, A. E., and Wilcoxin, L. A. (1976). Systematic desensitization and non-specific treatment effects: a methodological evaluation, *Psychological Bulletin*, **83**, 729–756.

Krause, N., and Stryker, S. (1984). Stress and well-being: the buffering role of locus of control beliefs, *Social Science and Medicine*, **18**, 783–790.

Lazarus, R. S. (1966). *Psychological Stress and the Coping Process*, McGraw-Hill, New York.

Murphy, L. R. (1984a). Stress management in highway maintenance workers, *Journal of Occupational Medicine*, **26**, 436–442.

Murphy, L. R. (1984b). Occupational stress management: a review and appraisal, *Journal of Occupational Psychology*, **57**, 1–15.

Neale, M. S., Singer, J. A., Schwartz, G. A., and Schwartz, J. (1982). Conflicting perspectives on stress reduction in occupational settings: a systems approach to their resolution, Report to NIOSH on P.O. No. 82-1058, Cincinnati, Ohio, 45226.

Parasuraman, S., and Cleek, M. A. (1984). Coping behaviors and managers' affective reactions to role stressors, *Journal of Vocational Behavior*, **24**, 179–193.

Pearlin, L. I., and Schooler, C. (1978). The structure of coping, *Journal of Health and Social Behavior*, **19**, 2–21.

Pomerleau, D., and Brady, J. P. (1979). *Behavioral Medicine: Theory and Practice*, Williams and Wilkins, Baltimore, Md.

Riley, A. W., Friedman, L. W., and Winett, R. A. (1984). Stress management in the workplace: a time for caution in health promotion, Report to NIOSH on P.O. No. 84-1320, Cincinnati, Ohio 45226.

Selye, H. (1976). *Stress in Health and Disease*, Butterworth Publishers, London.

Syme, S. (1974). Behavioral factors associated with the etiology of physical disease: a social epidemiological approach, *American Journal of Public Health*, **64**, 1043–1045.

Weiner, H. (1977). *Psychobiology and Human Disease*, Elsevier, New York.

West, D. J., Horan, J. J., and Ganes, P. A. (1984). Component analysis of occupational stress inoculation applied to registered nurses in an acute care faciliity, *Journal of Counseling Psychology*, **31**, 209–218.

Index

acute sickness, 2
adaptive and maladaptive coping, 228
adrenaline and cortisol levels, 39
age and shift work, 80
ageing in shift work, 81
aggravation effects, 216
alternative work schedules, 131
ameliorating factors in job stress, 42
anorexia nervosa, 22
anxiety reductions, 232
assembly and production-line work, 100
autonomy, 7

behaviour problems, 105
blood pressure, 235
blue collar women, 13
boredom, 86, 99
buffering model, 212
buffering vs main effects, 214
business provider, 202

causes of occupational diseases, 155
circadian system, 66
classification of paced work, 51
comparable worth as a stress-reliving
    aid, 196
compensation grief, 9
compressed work week, 137
    individual effects, 140
    organizational effects, 139
computer based work, 88
contract change agent, 203
control, 19
    at work, 36
    by avoidance, 25

by irrelevant means, 28
decisions about, 24
decisions model of the perception
    of, 33
domains of, 31, 44
lack of, 2, 58
locus of, 29
loss of, 40
nature of, 22
profile, 32
coping process, 226
coping with shift work, 80
coping with work stress, 227

demand, constraint and support, 90
differential pressures between blue and
    white collar workers, 44
disorders of the digestive system, 105
displacement, 10
division of labour, 87
domestic and social adjustment, 77

effects on health, 98
efficiency of individual-oriented
    strategies, 236
effort and distress model, 39
emerging technology, 149
employee assistance programs, 183
    cost effectiveness of, 190
    essential elements of, 187
    future role of, 191
    growth of, 187
employee counselling, 186
employee populations, 211

employees' personal or emotional
problems, 183
epidemiological findings on the effects
of paced work, 54
epileptic seizures, 79
Eysenck Personality Inventory, 175

fatigue, 141
flextime, 132
individual and family effects, 136
organizational and community
effects, 133
four-factor model of job perceptions, 95

general health factors, 178
genetic screening as a stressor, 197

hazardous environments, 19
health and safety, 8
health consequences of shift work, 79
health cost containment, 199
health promotion, 192
Holmes–Rahe Recent Life Scale, 175
human paced work, 51

ill health and disability, 103
individual coping strategies, 225
industrial psychology as a stressor, 198
industrial revolution, 86
industrial robots, 159
industrial unrest in Japan, 159
influence of work on life and leisure, 37
inspection consistency and
performance, 122
inspection job, 120
inspection task, 115
Internal–External Control Scale, 175
inventory of coping behaviours, 226
interpersonal control, 32
ischaemic heart disease, 1
isolation, 14

Japanese companies, 218
job choice, 151
description, 42
description checklist, 96
design and job pleasantness, 97
dissatisfaction, 57
incongruence and underload, 102
loss, 10, 209
or task analysis, 89
satisfaction, 14
satisfaction and morale, 135

labour vs. NLRB, 199
labour vs. right to work legislation, 199
learned helplessness, 30
legs, 105
leisure activities, 43

machine minding, 20
machine paced work, 51, 52
mass illness in the workplace, 178
mass psychogenic illness, 171
Mini-Mult of the MMPI, 175
monotony, 86, 150
and understimulation, 102
muscle tension, 235

National Institute for Occupational
Safety and Health, 56
nature of stress, 21
negative social exchanges, 215
night shifts, 78
NIOSH study, 92
non-traditional female job holders, 15

organization-centred effects, 232

participative work, 220
perceived helplessness, 35
performance, 73
performance changes, 144
performance rhythm, 74
personality measures, 178
physiological functioning, 141
posture and musculoskeletal problems,
104
predictability and control, 22
pressures on the inspector, 124
private health expenditure, 124
problem-focused coping, 237
production automation, 150
proving oneself, 110
psychological well-being, 38
psychosocial/organizational factors, 177
psychosocial problems, 154

quality circles, 219

reciprocal bargainer, 201
rehabilitation of substance abusers, 192
repetition, 59
repetitive work, 85, 91
rewards, 43
robot-based production, 157
right to know gains, 200

Saab's self-paced work, 164
Saab's sociotechnology, 162
scientific technological revolution, 88
shift rotation speed, 72
shift work, 65, 106
sleep, 76
sleeping performance, 81
sleep/wake cycle, 72
social class, 108
social context to work, 96
social support, 3
   and blue collar workers, 218
   and health, 209
   and other organizational changes, 219
   and stress reduction, 297
sociocultureal variations, 217
sociodemographic factors, 176
sociopolitical control, 32
sources of support, 214
stress and control, 20
stress and mental strain, 153
stress management, 4
stress management strategies, 230
stress management training, 230
stress reduction campaigner, 201
stress reduction and evaluation of EAPs, 190
stress-relieving futuristics, 196
structural factors, 218
suboptimal health, 99
supervisory support, 220
support as a systemic issue, 221
Swedish blue collar unions, 155

task performance, 115

task stress, 117
technomania, 12
ten coping categories, 228
trade union action programmes, 156
transactional approach to occupational stress, 89
trends in the Swedish auto industry, 160

underutilization of skill, 92
unemployed Vietnam veterans, 210
unions as advocates, 195
   as buffers
   as critics, 198
   as initiators, 199
   as provider, 200
unpleasant working environments, 27
upper limbs and neck, 104
usable leisure time, 138

Volvo's biotechnology, 161
Volvo's teamwork, 163

Women's work and women's health, 107
work environment scale, 175
work ethic, 21
worker alienation, 7
worker compensation, 189
workers' views of stress problems, 152
workload and job discretion, 89
workplace authoritarianism, 11
work-pressure, 61
worksite stress management training, 231

zeitgebers, 67